THE BANK
INSIDE THE BANK OF ENGLAND

THE BANK
INSIDE THE BANK OF ENGLAND

DAN CONAGHAN

Biteback Publishing

First published in Great Britain in 2012 by
Biteback Publishing Ltd
Westminster Tower
3 Albert Embankment
London SE1 7SP
Copyright © Daniel Noel Conaghan 2012

ISBN 978-1-84954-287-6

10 9 8 7 6 5 4 3 2 1

A CIP catalogue record for this book is available from the British Library.

Set in Adobe Garamond Pro
Cover design by Namkwan Cho

Printed and bound in Great Britain by
CPI Group (UK) Ltd, Croydon, CR0 4YY

For Florence

CONTENTS

ACKNOWLEDGEMENTS

I am deeply indebted to the many people who have given me assistance with the research and writing of this book, especially those employed at the Bank of England, past and present, and at HM Treasury. Necessarily, most must remain nameless. Many others in Westminster, Whitehall, the City of London and further afield provided valuable insights into the Bank of England's work, also on the condition of anonymity. Other senior figures, including Jean-Claude Trichet and Professor Charles Goodhart, were also generous with their time. A large number of people very kindly effected introductions and helped arrange interviews. The press offices of the Bank of England, HM Treasury, the UK Debt Management Office and the European Central Bank were helpful in answering a large number of questions. I am very grateful to my agent James Wills and to his colleagues Mandy Little and Alison Sutton at Watson, Little for their enthusiasm and hard work; and, in equal measure, to Sam Carter, my editor at Biteback Publishing, and to his colleagues Iain Dale, James Stephens, Namkwan Cho and Emma Young. I would also like to express my gratitude to my cousin Andrew Taylor, who was instrumental in bringing this book to publication, and to the following for their assistance, support and encouragement in divers ways: Antonia Aldous, Charlie Barton, Tim Butcher, Matthew and Johanna

Carse, Gina Coladangelo, Nadia Crandall, David and Penny Cunningham, Nicholas and Nicola Cunningham, Alan and Meg Darby, Alexa de Ferranti, Claudia Downes, Jacqueline Duncan, David Dunsmore, Philine Euler-Rolle-Dumba, Orlando Finzi, Violet Fraser, Natasha Garnett, Allan and Louise Hayward, Hannah Hayward, Shaun and Gabrielle Hullis, Mark Inglefield, Red Johnson, Alastair King, Jonathan King, Robert Kirby, Tom Lywood, Graeme Macdonald, Jack Meaning, Catherine Milner, Rupert and Mary Montagu-Scott, Toby Mott, Jay Patel, Christopher Peacocke, Nick Pedgrift, James Quartermaine, Patrick and Alison Roberts, Tim and Frances Robinson, Jamie Ross, Florence Saumarez, Richard Shepro, Tom and Susanna Stourton, Richard Symington, Heather Taylor, Glafkos Tombolis, Monica Vögele, and Ben Wegg-Prosser.

'First, the only certainty is that there is no certainty. Second, every decision is a matter of weighing probabilities, or the balance of risks, as we say. Third, despite uncertainty we have to decide and act. Fourth, decisions should be judged not only on the results but also on how they were made.'

Sir Mervyn King, quoting Robert Rubin's 'principles for decision-making', the Queen's University, Belfast, May 1999

INTRODUCTION

'Our job is to create a background of stability which enables
other people to do interesting things. They will be interesting;
we will not be and we will be faceless ... But that outcome is
really very important, that we will not be interesting or new or
newsworthy and that will be a sign of our success.'
Mervyn King, Economic Affairs Committee, 27 January 2004

I n the early morning, Chris, the chauffeur of the dark green
Daimler allocated to Sir Mervyn King, the Governor of the
Bank of England, drives him from his flat in Notting Hill
through the City of London to the Bank. As the car slows to
a crawl in Gresham Street, it is possible to glimpse King in the
back, studying his papers under the reading light. A small, well-
upholstered, dark-suited man in late middle age with silver hair
and spectacles, he retains the slightly quizzical air of an academic.
But after twenty-one years of making the daily journey to the
Bank, King has also acquired the frown of a central banker. True
to this peculiar species, he exudes not so much power as influence.

As the Governor's car approaches Lothbury, the Bank itself
looms into view; the gilded-bronze statue of Ariel, perched high
on the cupola above Tivoli Corner, provides the only splash of

colour in the grey façade. Sir John Soane's great Portland stone curtain wall protects the towering citadel, which is King's workplace and that of his 1,850 staff. 'Pinks' – stewards in pink waistcoats, tailcoats and top hats – greet the Governor as he arrives. He pads along halls paved with mosaics, hung with the heavy portraits of his predecessors and lined with eighteenth-century furniture. To left and right are cavernous rooms, filled with flickering computer screens and Bloomberg terminals, which resemble nothing so much as the dealing floors of an investment bank. Everywhere there are reminders of a 300-year history, but also of a very modern role at the heart of Britain's economy and the global capital markets.

In the Parlours, the Bank's inner sanctum, a book-lined anteroom gives way to the palatial Governor's Office, guarded by a double set of doors to prevent eavesdropping. Here, and in the grand committee rooms which flank it, the affairs of the Bank come together. Here, amid the uncertainties, as King might say, probabilities are weighed, risks balanced, decisions made and actions taken.

First and foremost, this is Britain's central bank, banker to the government and manager of the country's official reserves, including its gold bullion. The Bank is both the guardian of the nation's money and, thanks to its monopoly on the issue of banknotes in England and Wales, the very source of much of it. It is banker to Britain's commercial banks and, *in extremis*, their lender of last resort. Soon, after the impending abolition of the 'Tripartite' arrangements between the Bank, the Treasury and the Financial Services Authority (FSA), the Bank will be handed full regulatory authority to oversee the entire banking sector. Inherent in the Bank's considerable powers is its control of monetary policy, with the ability to tighten or loosen it with the levers of interest rates – 'Bank Rate' – and, more recently, with the alchemy of Quantitative Easing.

The decisions taken in its committee rooms affect every citizen in Britain and, in a global economy which is now infinitely interconnected, many elsewhere around the world. And while the Bank's powers are channelled in increasingly sophisticated ways, the famous 'Governor's eyebrows' can still be used to devastating effect in directing a deputy or swatting an MP. The Bank of England remains, as it advises its own staff, 'uniquely influential'.[1]

Influence, as well as power, comes with accountability. The Bank defers to Parliament, although decidedly not to politicians, and to HM Treasury, its sole shareholder; technically, the Bank's capital stock of £14.6m is held by the Treasury Solicitor, Paul Jenkins QC. The Bank's Governor has, on at least one occasion in recent times, had to explain himself to the Queen. But despite these claims on its time, the Bank remains a remarkably autonomous institution, with almost total immunity in its capacity as a monetary authority. It is protected by its Royal Charter, certain subtle exemptions from quotidian legislation and by the Official Secrets Act.

Secrecy, or at least discretion, is the Bank's watchword and its staff are still required to sign a 'Declaration of Secrecy' on joining. A brutish physical presence and an ill-disguised distaste for the Press has made it somewhat paranoid. In its upper echelons, there is an obsessive regard for 'the record', which generates a vast quantity of letters, memoranda, notes and minutes made in triplicate; there are strict rules governing the use of the internet and email and warnings that these 'may be monitored'.[2]

The Bank's public pronouncements are made mostly in the form of carefully honed speeches; indeed, it has pioneered Speechonomics. Hardly a day goes by without King or one of his elite Executive Team making a speech. There has occasionally been a danger of the Bank running out of audiences. As it is, unsuspecting groups of businessmen and women in remote areas of Britain are often regaled with lengthy discourses on the Bank's latest economic theories. (Sir David Lees, chair of the Bank's Court, told the Treasury Committee: 'I am afraid we have so many speeches in the Bank that it is almost impossible to keep up with them all, even the Governor's.'[3]) Many of them are larded with what King himself has referred to as 'tortuous circumlocutions expressed in that special language known as "Bankese"'.[4] The Bank chooses its words with infinite care, however. Accordingly, every utterance is analysed and every nuance weighed: in May 2011, the Governor said the views of the Monetary Policy Committee (MPC) were 'wider than usual', in August there was 'a wide range of views'. Bankers, brokers and journalists have learned that such subtleties move markets. King's impish humour – the stuff of a peculiarly post-war, British upbringing – often breaks through (although it is noticeable that he alone gets to make the jokes at the Bank). In a speech to civic worthies in Newcastle in January 2011 his quotation of a line by Ken Dodd – 'When it comes to measuring success, don't count money, count happiness'[5] – travelled instantly around the world, no doubt baffling central bankers in Frankfurt and bond traders in Tokyo alike.

Besides an idiosyncratic sense of humour, the Bank has a long collective memory. Founded in 1694 as nothing more than a private bank, nationalised in 1946 and finally granted its independence – with strings attached – in 1997, it has weathered more than three centuries of economic ups and downs. Within the Bank, periods of crisis are known as 'war' and relative normality 'peacetime'. In recent times, 'war' has been more common. Under King's stewardship, the Bank has witnessed one of Britain's greatest financial calamities, in which the entire financial system came perilously close to collapse. In October 2008, the chief executives of Britain's leading banks who found themselves in the Bank's secure, underground conference room across a table from a grim-faced Governor were left in no doubt that they were on the edge of an abyss. Catastrophe was avoided only by massive, unprecedented and often reluctant interventions by the Bank. A crisis of credit and confidence, expressed in both the bond and the equity markets, has turned into one of sovereign debt, concentrated in the Eurozone. Its continuing effects have put the Bank back on a 'war' footing in recent months as it grapples with the Doomsday scenarios which may yet unfold.

The Bank has also had to defend itself at home. It has continued to have opprobrium heaped on it by politicians and the media. The Bank's mystique, carefully cultivated by generations of governors, does it no favours. Even after all the travails of the period from 2007 onwards, it was astonishing, for example, that in June 2011 King had to offer the Treasury Committee a one-page summary of what exactly the Court of Directors, the Bank's somnolent governing body, actually does and how it holds the Governor and his staff to account. The Bank's critics are not all strangers to Threadneedle Street, however. A growing number of its MPC alumni have formed a sort of economists' awkward squad, lining up to harangue their former paymaster. Former – indeed, founding – members such as Willem Buiter have been joined by the likes of David Blanchflower, Kate Barker and Sushil Wadhwani to take pot shots at the Bank. Buiter has been the most trenchant of its critics, describing its conduct before the 2007 crisis as 'a night at the improv for about three years'.[6] Even Bank loyalists such as Sir John Gieve, a former deputy governor, acknowledged that when banking supervision was moved out of Threadneedle Street in 1997, the Bank became a 'one-and-a-half-purpose Bank',[7] with an increasingly heavy emphasis on monetary policy; financial stability 'slipped down the agenda'.[8] More recently, Alistair Darling, the former Chancellor of the Exchequer, has laid out the frustrations of dealing with the Bank – and, in particular, with the Governor – in his memoir. The charge sheet is led by the Bank's failure to address stresses in the market which prefaced the credit crunch, its handling of the crisis and its disdain-ful reluctance to conduct any sort of internal inquiry when the dust had finally settled. In time, its rollout of Quantitative Easing, in which £275bn – eventually perhaps as much as £350bn – has been dropped into an unsuspecting gilts market, may also be questioned; it has certainly been the subject of much withering comment from people interviewed for this book.

The Bank's uneasy relationship with the outside world is partly because it is congenitally out of step with it. In many ways, although open-plan offices have long replaced labyrinthine corri-dors and cell-like rooms, it still resembles an academic institu-tion, with Professor King as its unbending principal and an elite corps of economists as his star students. A senior Treasury official discerns this schoolmasterly character in many of the Governor's communications, rolling his eyes as he recalls a recent King memo beginning 'Let us consider…' The Bank may move vast sums of cash, bonds and bullion around the market every day but, in its upper echelons, there is still an air of the senior common room, with its petty rivalries and fractious staff meetings. Not for nothing do the Governor and the deputy governors have private secretaries, respec-tively 'GPS' and 'DGPS'. As one of them puts it: 'we make sure the organisation still works when the governors aren't speaking to each other'. Even when they are speaking to each other, a dysfunctional air often hangs about the Bank's marbled corridors. In his submis-sion to the Treasury Committee during its 2011 inquiry into the accountability of the Bank, Professor Bob Garratt, for one, noted:

> Despite the high status, even grandeur, in which The Bank is held nationally and internationally, I am puzzled that, in the papers I have before me, the mindset of The Bank as an organisa-tion seems to be missing. The papers read more like a fight for national macro-economic power…[9]

The victor in this fight has invariably been King himself, who is universally addressed as 'Mr Governor' within the Bank (and equally universally referred to as 'Merv' by the staff), and has stamped his own strong and often inflexible character on the institution. Intellectually rigorous, he is nevertheless obstinate, particularly about the supremacy of monetary policy, and intractable. Former Chancellor of the Exchequer Alistair Darling has famously described King as 'incredibly stubborn', while Professor Charles Goodhart, who has known King since the mid-1980s, admits he is 'a perfectionist who finds it difficult for things just to be "satisfactory"'. Indeed, once the Governor has made a decision, according to other colleagues, there is no persuading him otherwise. And when his senior team have wanted to promote initiatives which are not directly related to monetary policy they have had to smuggle them past him. Further, King's character has often engendered Machiavellianism among them. Frequently, as the dicta have flowed from the Governor's Office, through the Parlours and into the Bank's many departments there have been exasperation, despair and tears before bedtime. More prosaically, he did not endear himself to his staff when, in December 2007, he is said to have swiped the Bank's Christmas tree, which by long tradition stood in its entrance hall (and had graced its Christmas cards), to have it installed in the Governor's Office.

More worryingly, it is widely acknowledged within the Bank's upper echelons and elsewhere that the relationship between King and Paul Tucker, his deputy governor and a veteran of some thirty years at the Bank, has deteriorated over the past few years. One very senior figure at the Bank describes it as being, at times, 'a battleground', where the battles over policy, direction and structure are common. Another senior official at the Treasury concedes that they 'do not get on, to put it mildly'. Both men, arguably two of the most powerful in Britain, are complex characters – King at the pinnacle of his career with a deep sense of his own legacy, Tucker expert at playing the long game but hugely ambitious and facing a momentous last push to reach the summit. It is an explosive mix, bound up in personality, intellect and their respective visions for Britain's central bank, what responsibilities it should bear and how it should conduct itself. Indeed, throughout the Bank, there has long been deep division over whether the Bank should be led by economic theory or pragmatic central banking as the champion of the City.

For his part, King is not a man to wear his emotions on his sleeve and has only ever made one comment about the psychological consolations of his job: in a somewhat valedictory interview with the *Daily Telegraph* in March 2011, Charles Moore, former editor of that newspaper, posed the question 'does he enjoy it all?' King replied: 'Enjoyment is the wrong word, because of the pressure.'[10] Some of his most senior colleagues go further, openly questioning whether the pressure, combined with an autocratic style – government by 'fiat' in the words of one – has not become too much for the Governor. They note, too, that he is ill at ease in a large staff of young men and women, many of whom are accustomed to a less formal working environment. King's internal critics say his social interactions at the Bank are invariably 'scripted and endlessly rehearsed' and that 'he simply can't deal with a lot of people around, in an unstructured environment'.

Fatally, perhaps, King has never been – or wanted to be – a City insider. Despite the Bank's historic role as 'the bankers' bank', he has little time for schmoozing with chief executives. When the head of one of the world's top three investment banks visited London recently and asked for an audience with King, he was offered a junior instead. Such snubs hurt and are remembered long afterwards. Although King understands more about risk, let alone quantitative economics, than most of his peers at the large commercial and investment banks, he regards such institutions – particularly the latter – as irredeemably short-termist, not to say downright greedy and irresponsible. The notion of 'too big to fail' – or 'too important to fail', as King prefers – has received short shrift from the Governor: let them fail and let them fear failure has been his mantra. Rather, it is the honest and hardworking manufacturing companies of the Midlands or the North East which the Governor is drawn to and which he regards as infinitely more deserving of the Bank's attention. Equally, King has become shackled to a code which has at its core the dangers of 'moral hazard', in which risks are taken in the knowledge that they will be mitigated by another party. It has been his constant refrain in the Bank's dealings with the banking sector.

Soon, much of this will change. The culture of an idiosyncratic personality which King has unwittingly imposed on the Bank will be challenged in 2013, when a new Governor takes over and Hector Sants, the current chief executive of the FSA, arrives at Threadneedle Street with his Prudential Regulatory Authority battalions. But it will be a difficult transition, particularly as there are still many at the Bank who have bought into the supremacy of Monetary Analysis – King's single-minded 'MA Way' – and who thought they had seen the back of banking supervision when that division was banished to Canary Wharf in 1997.

As they look ahead into 2012 and beyond, the Bank of England's staff, who retain a quiet, collective pride in their work, speak of a rather defeated atmosphere in Threadneedle Street and not simply because of the combined effects of a two-year pay freeze and, as they know all too well, inflation at double the 2 per cent target. Rather, their despondency derives from cynicism that the Conservative government's early decision to hand back powers to the Bank was rather more of a political move than many originally suspected; having promised the Bank the tools for the job, there is a growing suspicion that the government will bind its hands.

The Governor, for his part, must prepare for the handover as best he can. His successor will likely be named in the autumn of 2012 and will, perhaps, throw into relief King's own character as 'the Last Governor' in the scholar-economist mould. None of the likely candidates to follow him in that office have King's brilliant, analytical mind; nor do they have the worldliness to invoke Ken Dodd and Leo Tolstoy in the same speech, or quite the same insistent way of reminding the here-today-gone-tomorrow MPs on the Treasury Committee of their Parliamentary responsibilities. It is difficult to imagine Paul Tucker or Sir John Vickers, let alone Lord Sassoon, indefatigably gladhanding the great and the good of Merthyr Tydfil, Wakefield and Portsmouth, swapping statistics of long-forgotten cricket matches with Henry Blofeld on *Test Match Special* or finding time to indulge – indeed, seeking out – the editors of the *Hebden Bridge Times* and the *Bolton Evening News*, as King has done. He will leave a peculiarly Mervyn King-shaped hole at the Bank.

At the time of writing, in early 2012, however, the Governor is still at the crease, despite many appeals from his critics to sundry umpires. He has plenty on his desk and in his diary to keep him busy between now and the end of his term. The MPC must meet each month to try to direct monetary policy to meet the inflation target; the Bank's prodigious stock of gilts, sitting existentially on the Asset Purchase Facility's balance sheet, must be tended to; and the banking and financial services industries, so vital to the wider British economy, must be nurtured back to health. For King, it has been a long journey to create what he has described as the 'modern' Bank from a 'fractured system'[11] and, while that process has definitely begun, it is not over yet.

PART I

INDEPENDENCE

'There should be no delicacy about altering the constitution of
the Bank of England.'
Walter Bagehot, Economic Essays

Something was afoot in the Parlours of the Bank of England.
In the spring of 1997, an air of intrigue hung about the
Bank's inner sanctum, which comprises the offices of the
Governor, his deputies and his most senior advisers. Although it
was firmly out of bounds to the rest of the Bank's staff, many
sensed that Eddie George was up to something. The Governor, a
neat, stocky man rarely parted from a cigarette, spent long hours
closeted with Howard Davies, his deputy governor, Mervyn King,
then the Bank's chief economist, and Paul Tucker, one of its rising
stars. They were noticed leaving the Bank for meetings which went
unrecorded in their private secretaries' diaries. The secrecy which
pervaded the Bank's gloomy corridors ratcheted up a notch.

On Monday 17 March, when the incumbent Prime Minister,
John Major, announced he was calling a general election for 1
May, some at the Bank realised that this was the moment that

George and his colleagues had been secretly preparing for. It was widely acknowledged that a change in government might have implications for the Bank. The Labour Party's election manifesto, published a few months earlier to showcase a raft of 'New Labour' policies, had included the following paragraph:

> We will reform the Bank of England to ensure that decision-making on monetary policy is more effective, open, accountable and free from short-term political manipulation.[12]

This had struck a chord at the Bank. After all, the phrase 'short-term political manipulation' reverberated down its 300-year history. Ever since its founding in 1694 to raise money for an impoverished William IV, the Bank had been at the mercy of the government of the day. The Old Lady of Threadneedle Street, a nickname coined by James Gillray in *Political Ravishment*, a cartoon depicting the Bank being stripped of its gold by William Pitt the Younger, had suffered many indignities at the hands of self-serving politicians. In modern times, she had been subordinated to the Treasury, nationalised by a post-war government and seen her officials subjugated to Prime Ministers, Chancellors and permanent secretaries. As long as the government continued to direct Britain's monetary policy – in particular, the setting of interest rates – the Bank was its servant and *consigliere*, giving it advice and guidance, but no more.

Now, at last, there was a chance to change things. The secret meetings between George, Davies, King and Tucker – and their equally clandestine ones with senior Labour politicians well away from Threadneedle Street – were to plan for this eventuality under a Labour government. At the same time, the four men worked on the confidential draft of a paper laying out the Bank's position and its case for a degree of autonomy. At the heart of their deliberations was the question: how far would Labour go? Not, surely, as far as full independence for the Bank, but further than the incumbent Conservative administration, which still regarded the Bank as its underling.

Kenneth Clarke, the Chancellor of the Exchequer, had already granted the Bank some small freedoms, inviting George, Davies and King along with their counterparts from the Treasury to monthly meetings at which interest rate decisions were taken. The minutes of these meetings were published, after a decent interval, to allow the public to see the decision-making process. This had the side-effect of making George, in Clarke's words, 'a public figure':

> Suddenly his views were known when you read the minutes. This was most useful because, apart from anything else, heaven forbid that any political pressures were put upon me in order to adjust interest rates against the governor's advice.[13]

Outwardly, at least, Clarke and George got along famously. Indeed, the 'Ken and Eddie show' seemed to embody the optimism of recovery after the recession of the early 1990s. In fact, the term had been coined by Clarke in a moment of irony; in reality, the government and the Bank often disagreed. Although Clarke recalled later that, on interest rates, 'Eddie and I never got more than twenty-five basis points [0.25 per cent] apart',[14] King and Davies were sometimes 'great outliers'. Clarke took a particularly dim view of the complex econometric models which King, the quintessential technocrat, brandished under his nose.

This access to Clarke's meetings merely tantalised and frustrated George and his colleagues. They wanted a bigger role for the Bank and to escape the day-to-day interference of politicians. The Tories had promised much to the Bank and delivered little. Successive Chancellors had talked of full independence for the

Bank since the late 1980s. In 1988, Nigel Lawson raised the question with Margaret Thatcher, sending her a long memo drafted by Michael Scholar, a senior Treasury official. She demurred, fearing that the public would conclude that the government was abnegating responsibility for its monetary policy. Four years later, in the autumn of 1992, Norman Lamont broached the idea of independence for the Bank to John Major. Major was sceptical. 'I disliked this idea on democratic grounds,' he wrote later, 'believing that the person responsible for monetary policy should be answerable for it in the House of Commons. I also feared that the culture of an independent bank would ensure that interest rates went up rapidly but fell only slowly.'[15] Lamont did not pursue the idea, but, according to Major, 'it simmered on, unloved by me, unsupported by Terry Burns at the Treasury, but not surprisingly, it received enthusiastic backing from the Bank itself.'[16]

As time went by, the Bank's leadership lost patience with the Tories and began to look elsewhere for support. In Labour they observed a new corps emerging from the traditional, hidebound party and one which had its own strong views about the direction of the country's economic affairs. While Tony Blair was outlining New Labour's vision, Gordon Brown, his putative Chancellor, has assembled a precocious team to take charge of the economy. A garrulous young economist called Ed Balls, formerly a leader writer at the *Financial Times*, and an even younger one called Ed Miliband, fresh from Harriet Harman's office, joined Brown's team. Balls was already known as the author of a pamphlet published by the Fabian Society entitled *Euro-Monetarism: Why Britain Was Ensnared and How It Should Escape* in December 1992. It was a robust analysis of what Balls saw as twenty years of economic failure, and argued for a redefined approach to Britain's role in Europe. It also argued for an independent central bank. By the time of the approaching election, Brown and his team had also looked further afield for comparisons. In February 1997, they were in Washington to meet Alan Greenspan, chairman of the Federal Reserve, to canvass his opinion on what a restructured Bank of England might look like.

In London, the initial contacts between the Bank and Brown's team were limited to informal and *ad hoc* conversations. Surprisingly, these had been sanctioned by Kenneth Clarke as early as 1995, when George had asked whether he might be allowed to have meetings with opposition politicians. For the next two years, George met Brown, Balls and, occasionally, Tony Blair. 'It was important in two respects,' George said in a later interview.[17] 'In the structure and in giving me the opportunity to gain confidence in Gordon. I knew I wouldn't gossip with the other side. I didn't press irrelevant questions like "when will you do it?"' While George was gaining confidence – misplaced, as it turned out – in Brown, King was getting to know Ed Balls. They were unlikely partners in such skullduggery, but King would slip out of his office for discreet discussions with Balls on the detail of a possible way forward to a more independent Bank of England.

That was the rub. The 'it' George referred to was still a great unknown, but as the general election neared, the conversations between the central bankers and the politicians became more urgent. The Bank's ambitions were still modest. George, Davies and King envisaged an arrangement whereby the Bank formed an 'advisory committee'[18] to advise Chancellor Brown on monetary policy; if this was seen to be doing well, the reasoning went, the new government might look favourably, in time, on the idea of handing the Bank the ultimate prize: independence to direct monetary policy altogether, including the setting of interest rates. As it was, Brown asked George and his colleagues to work up a proposal for the advisory committee. Sitting in the Governor's Office, George, Davies and King gathered their thoughts, sensing history in the making. This was, at the very least, a first step to independence. As they discussed the possible structure, constitution and *modus operandi* of a group to lead, influence, perhaps even direct, monetary policy, they asked their young colleague Paul Tucker to draft the paper. It was Tucker, then head of the Bank's Monetary Assessment & Strategy Division but with his gaze firmly fixed on much greater things, who, as he put it later, 'held the pen'.[19]

The Bank's inner circle watched and waited as the general election campaign unfolded over six scrappy and bad-tempered weeks. The Conservatives were a spent force and increasingly riven by internal squabbles over Europe and whether Britain should join the single currency. The party was unable to shake off the accusations of 'sleaze', some entirely justified, which had dogged it for years. In his autobiography, Major noted drily that 'team spirit was absent' during the campaign. He spent most of the period trying to stop his Cabinet fighting each other and his junior MPs succumbing to the attentions of the tabloid press. Sir James Goldsmith's Referendum Party, which ultimately proved a damp squib, was another distraction and was seized on by the media as another sign of the Tories' imminent demise. Labour, for its part, was busy reinventing itself as 'New Labour' and successfully positioned its leader, Tony Blair, as a youthful and energetic visionary. On the economy, which singularly failed to climb the agenda during the campaign, the electorate was reluctant to give credit to the Conservatives for the recovery from the recession of the early 1990s. Brown was seen as a credible putative Chancellor and a suitably dour alternative to the freewheeling Clarke. The campaign became increasingly rancorous. Outwardly at least, the Bank of England played no part in these blood sports. At its citadel in Threadneedle Street, it maintained a dignified silence, punctuated by occasional announcements concerning the issuance of Treasury bills.

George waited anxiously for Brown's thoughts on the paper outlining the role of a possible advisory committee. While he studied it, Brown's mind turned to more Machiavellian matters. Should he keep George at the Bank at all? Several others were considered for the Governor's job: the most favoured candidate was Gavyn Davies, a close friend and adviser of Brown's and one of Goldman Sachs's most senior economists. Other City figures, including Martin Taylor, then chief executive of Barclays, and Sir David Scholey, former chairman of SBC Warburg, were also suggested. In the final analysis, Brown bridled at the idea of forcing George to resign, a move which would have risked seeming peremptory. Brown decided that the Governor could stay, at least for the time being. His first five-year term of office was, in any case, due to end in June 1998, giving Brown time to see how well the Governor performed and to scout for a replacement if necessary.

£££

As the 1 May election day – a Thursday – dawned, George and his three colleagues reflected that the Bank was once more at a critical moment in its history. In 1997, it was still weighed down by that history and desperately in need of reform and realignment. Although it had shrunk considerably from the hugely bloated bureaucracy it had become in the 1970s, when it employed nearly 10,000 staff, it was still a shambling beast. Some 3,000 people were spread across five sites, including the sprawling headquarters at Threadneedle Street, and many beavered away in anonymous departments run on Dickensian lines. For better or worse, the Bank retained an air of Victorian paternalism: a job for life, generous salaries, index-linked pensions and innumerable perks. Away from Threadneedle Street, the Bank's staff could enjoy the expansive green acres and much-discussed cricket fixtures of the Bank of England Sports Club, join the Bank's Operatic and Dramatic Society or enter a ballot to secure its box at the Royal Albert Hall.

While the Court acted as the Bank's board, meeting around a doughnut-shaped mahogany table in the ravishing eighteenth-century surroundings of the Court Room, the Governor was expected to be its paterfamilias. Stocky, dapper and with a famously gruff voice, Eddie George played the role perfectly. 'Steady Eddie', as he was known to the Press, was one of the Bank's many 'lifers'. He had joined the Bank as a 'Third Class Clerk on Probation (Special Entrant)' back in 1962, when the Earl of Cromer was Governor. George's lowly title, with its echoes of an antediluvian bureaucracy, belied a strong academic record – a county scholarship to Dulwich College and an economics degree from Emmanuel College, Cambridge – and a gimlet eye. His superiors at the Bank had quickly recognised his talents:

> In conversation he radiates intelligence and shows an exception-
> ally attractive balance of confidence and modesty. His interest
> is considerable. He appears to be a man who should be trained
> immediately for a position of trust where a sense of responsibil-
> ity, hard work, vision and a high level of intelligence are required.
> It is clear that he wishes to live by high ideals and is probing for
> sure foundations from which they can rise.[20]

By 1980, George he had become head of the Bank's Gilt-Edged Division and was senior enough to be grilled by Margaret Thatcher. In the following decade, he became the acknowledged authority on the money and foreign exchange markets, being described by Nigel Lawson as 'the Bank's real monetary expert'. In 1990, he was appointed Deputy Governor, serving under Robin Leigh-Pemberton, a patrician former lawyer and banker. Two years later, it was announced that George would succeed him as Governor. His appointment did not meet with universal approval. Peter Hain, then the young backbench Labour MP for Neath, tabled an Early Day Motion in January 1993, which robustly declared:

> That this House has no confidence in the newly appointed Governor of the Bank of England, Mr Eddie George, who has been part of the Bank's anachronistic and inefficient culture since 1962, was a senior official while the Bank failed abjectly to discharge its supervisory and regulatory responsibilities, leading to a series of banking scandals such as Johnson Matthey, Blue Arrow and, above all, BCCI ... and further believes that Parliament should be invited to endorse a fresh appointment of Governor who will ensure that the Bank discharges its supervisory responsibilities in an honest and effective way to protect both the reputation of British finance and the interests of ordinary citizens.[21]

Hain was in a minority, but the references to Johnson Matthey, Blue Arrow and BCCI were fair comment. They were scars on George's back. The Bank had been forced to rescue Johnson Matthey, a much overextended bank, in 1984. Three years later, in 1987, Blue Arrow, a large recruitment company, became embroiled in a financial scandal with its advisers County NatWest; and the fall of BCCI (Bank of Credit and Commerce International) was a major regulatory imbroglio which would continue to occupy George – and subsequently Mervyn King – until the middle of the next decade. Besides these brawls, there was a similarly bruising experience when Britain exited from the Exchange Rate Mechanism in September 1992.

Although he still had to fight its corner, George had largely protected the Bank's reputation. He moved easily in the company of City grandees, but maintained a self-deprecating sense of humour: he delighted in relating the occasion on which a journalist had overhead him confiding to a lunch companion in Cornwall that 'we are going into the euro'; when the national newspapers got hold of this sensational story and asked him whether it was true, George had to disappoint them: he had actually said that he was intending to go 'into Truro'.

In March 1995, George had the unedifying task of presiding over the Bank's first sex scandal, which attached itself to his deputy governor, Rupert Pennant-Rea. Pennant-Rea had his first stint at the Bank in the 1970s, left to edit *The Economist* newspaper and returned to Threadneedle Street in 1993. His ignominious fall is well recorded. In a spectacular lapse of judgement, this unlikely lothario had allowed his mistress, the Irish-American journalist Mary Ellen Synon, to visit him at the Bank. On one of these occasions, he had allegedly made love to her on the carpet of the Governor's dressing room. (The Governor, it was said, later had the carpet cut up.) Unsurprisingly, after this Hogarthian liaison was revealed in the Press ('*The Bonk of England*' was the tabloids' gleeful refrain), resignation was the only option. George was diplomatic about the debacle, Synon less so. 'If you are going to dump,' she told the newspapers, 'don't dump a financial journalist if you are the deputy governor of the Bank of England. That's dumb.'

The Governor and the Chancellor of the Exchequer played safe with Pennant-Rea's replacement, appointing Howard Davies as the new deputy governor. Davies was an outsider but a safe pair of hands. He had come to the Bank via the Foreign Office, the Treasury, McKinsey & Co., the Audit Commission and, finally, from 1992 to 1995, a stint as director of the Confederation of British Industry. He had been warned that the Bank was a somewhat different proposition to his previous employers:

The Treasury invited me in for a briefing, which amounted to a lengthy catalogue of complaints about the Bank's obsessive secrecy and its constipated working methods, whereby all issues of any substance had to be elevated to the governor's office before a view could be expressed.[22]

When Davies arrived in April 1995, he found Mervyn King, the Bank's chief economist, hovering at the Governor's elbow. King, then forty-seven with a slightly intimidating professorial air, had been at the Bank for five years (a mere warm-up for many of his colleagues) after a successful career as an academic, latterly at the London School of Economics. After a brief period as a non-executive director at the Bank, King became chief economist in 1991, a role which he originally viewed as 'an interesting secondment' from the LSE. At the Bank, he had quickly won Eddie George's confidence. Indeed, George was later to say that one of the first things he had done on his appointment as Governor in 1993 was to persuade King, technically on secondment from the LSE, to stay on at the Bank; George held King in sufficiently high regard to maintain that he might have been a contender for a Nobel Prize for Economics.

Paul Tucker, the man who had drafted the paper about the 'advisory committee', had also been admitted into the Governor's inner circle. In 1997, Tucker had already been at the Bank seventeen years. Having taking a degree in maths and philosophy from Trinity College, Cambridge, he had cut his teeth at the Bank in the Banking Supervision Division, overseeing 'small banks and problem banks'. Tucker made his mark as someone who saw the Bank in the wider context of the City, of which he had some first-hand experience. In 1985–1986, he spent the best part of two years on secondment to Baring Brothers & Co., joining the famously blue-blooded bank's corporate finance department. In 1985, ten years before the bank was brought to its knees by Nick Leeson, one of its securities arm's star traders, Barings was busy with mandates such as the government's privatisation of British Leyland. Tucker's detailed, typewritten account of his secondment provides a fascinating glimpse of the gulf between the antiquated Bank and the go-getting City firm. While Barings ostensibly practised so-called 'gentlemanly capitalism', it was still bloodthirsty work – 'I am conscious that this is a delicate area,' Tucker wrote – and he found himself struggling to make sense of it:

> My initiation into the mysteries of corporate finance proved far from easy. I knew even less than I had expected and it was clearly the case that, with four years of Bank experience under my belt, junior and middle management (at least) expected me to make a contribution from arrival. Thus, on my first day, I was asked by a manager to prepare [a] briefing on Company B and on whether B would be a suitable target for Company A, a client, including an assessment of commercial fit and whether A's shareholders would suffer earnings dilution etc for a range of offer terms. My only guidance was a precedent note and a deadline of the next morning. With the help of a rapidly purchased primer and an old friend in the department, I missed the deadline, completing the work in three days.[23]

Tucker went on grimly: 'The learning curve was therefore steep and the consequent feeling of giddiness persisted for around a month.'[24]

Besides being thrown such carnivorous tasks, Tucker also had to grapple with Barings' new-fangled information technology, which was rapidly changing the face of modern investment banking in the City of London. In his report, Tucker admits that systems such as Topic, Textline, Datastream and even Lotus Notes, which was widely used in the financial community, were 'all completely foreign'. Despite these travails, Tucker stuck it out and returned to the safety of the Bank of England at the end of 1986. His report, delivered on 30 January 1987, concluded (somewhat prophetically, given Barings' spectacular collapse eight years later):

> I hope that the secondment helped me to develop. If it did, it would be largely due to having to make judgements, take decisions and assume responsibility for issues and people, and having to cope with a series of near emergency situations. To some extent, corporate finance is continual crisis-management.[25]

Tucker's report was widely circulated among his superiors at the Bank; the late Rodney Galpin scribbled on it: 'Very interesting and clearly a worthwhile secondment. Have you handed a copy to Sir John Baring?' Tucker's stint at Barings stood him in good stead. By the 1990s, he was also rather more at ease with his City counterparts. He became particularly devoted to the Bank's market intelligence function, sallying forth from the Bank to do the rounds of City firms and gathering their views on the market. Like his colleagues, Tucker realised the significance of the move to an independent Bank and noted the shift in power it represented. Looking back in 2007, he recalled: 'It really was a novelty – in a way, a constitutional departure, foreshadowed perhaps only by the judiciary – to give such a politically sensitive lever to a body of unelected technicians.'[26]

£££

The 'unelected technicians' in Threadneedle Street held their collective breath as power rumbled and rolled around Whitehall in the last few days of April 1997. The election ballot on Thursday

1 May delivered a landslide victory for New Labour, with 419 seats compared to the Conservatives' paltry 165. A clutch of leading Tories – Rifkind, Portillo, Lang, Forsyth and Lamont – lost their seats and the remainder were left to lick their wounds. Tony Blair became, at forty-three, the youngest Prime Minister of the century, his youthful exuberance exemplified by the party's raucous victory celebrations, held at the Royal Festival Hall to the accompaniment of D:Ream's 'Things Can Only Get Better'.

As the Friday morning dawned, Gordon Brown, the new Chancellor of the Exchequer, was already at the Treasury, brandishing detailed plans for the Bank's future. Sensationally, Brown had decided that the Bank should be given its independence. The idea of an 'advisory committee' had been swept aside in favour of a full Monetary Policy Committee (MPC), chaired by the Bank's Governor, which would direct monetary policy and set interest rates without, as it were, fear or favour.

At the Treasury, it fell to Tom Scholar – the son of Michael Scholar, who had drafted Nigel Lawson's paper on Bank independence for Margaret Thatcher – to work over the Bank Holiday weekend as preparations for a formal announcement were made. It soon became clear that in granting independence, Brown had other designs on the Bank, including stripping it of its responsibilities for both banking supervision and the management of the government's debt (its 'Gilt-Edged Division'). The Permanent Secretary, Sir Terence Burns, believed this was too much, too soon. Brown was persuaded to stagger the process and confine his initial announcement to the main event. On the Sunday, Brown and his team finalised two letters for George, the first – addressed to the Bank in 'EC1' rather than the correct 'EC2' – was headed 'The New Monetary Policy Framework' and contained a detailed outline of the administration's plans for the Bank, including the establishment of the MPC and the removal of the Bank's Gilt-Edged division. The second letter offered a much briefer proposal – and no more than that – for a review of banking supervision.

At 8 a.m. on Bank Holiday Monday, 5 May, Mervyn King was on his way home after an early-morning game of tennis when, he later recalled, he took the call from George: 'It's Eddie. Can you meet me in the Bank as soon as possible?' When King arrived at the Governor's Office, George broke the momentous news that the Bank would finally get its independence the very next day. For King, who had been unsure as to whether his career really lay in Threadneedle Street, the matter was decided. George looked at him and said: 'So, you can't leave now, can you?'[27] King later recalled:

> That was the last I saw of the sun for some time. We sat in his office with a sense of excitement that now we really did have a chance to show what the Bank of England and price stability could do for this country. Eddie charged me with the task of preparing ideas on how the new committee – the Monetary Policy Committee – would decide and set the level of interest rates.[28]

Besides the enormous satisfaction and sense of history in the making afforded by securing independence for one of the world's leading central banks, it was also a moment when the balance of power shifted. Even King found that intoxicating. Looking back ten years later, in May 2007, he reflected:

> When Eddie George and I sat in the Governor's Office on that sunny Bank Holiday morning in 1997, we knew we had been given an opportunity to change monetary policy for the better. We had to grab it with both hands.[29]

The next morning, Tuesday 6 May, Brown met George to agree a base rate rise of twenty-five basis points, to 6.25 per cent. It was a historic first – and, as it turned out, final – formal meeting between the two men as Prime Minister and Governor, which otherwise would have continued its regular monthly pattern. From this meeting, Brown went immediately to a press conference, at which, to the astonishment of the assembled journalists, he announced the decisions to give the Bank its independence and to form a Monetary Policy Committee.

Those expansive gestures hid a careful control of the detail. Brown and Balls wanted an independent Bank, but on their terms. To this end, crucially, the Chancellor retained the authority to set the inflation target – 2.5 per cent or less – and to appoint external members of the new MPC for three-year terms, no less. Another important aspect of the machinery was that the target was to be a 'symmetrical' one. The Governor would be required to write an open letter to the Chancellor should inflation deviate by 1 per cent above or below the target. In other words, the 2.5 per cent was not to be regarded as a ceiling and the committee would have to grapple with the problem of being above the target as much as being below it, which would mitigate the risks of deflation as much as of inflation. The politicians also determined that the index measure of inflation to be used was RPIX, the Retail Prices Index excluding – the 'X' – mortgage interest payments. Finally, Brown and Balls dictated how the committee would operate, with monthly meetings, after which decisions on interest rates would be released immediately with minutes following in due course.

The announcement was a great coup for Brown, made all the more remarkable by the fact that, although it had the Prime Minister's blessing, it was the creature of Brown's own very distinct office, which began to operate almost as a rival to No. 10. It was accompanied by suitably high-flown rhetoric. Brown declared he wanted 'British economic success to be built on the solid rock of prudent and consistent economic management, not the shifting sands of boom and bust', and went on:

> This is the time to take the tough decisions we need for the long-term interests and prosperity of the country. I will not shrink from the tough decisions needed to deliver stability for long-term growth. I have therefore decided to give the Bank of England operational responsibility for setting interest rates, with immediate effect.[30]

The MPC was inaugurated with nine members, five Bank people and four external members chosen by the Chancellor. He was at pains that the latter should breathe new life into the Bank and hold its Governor and his lieutenants to account. Various suggestions were made as to how such 'externals' might be found, including one – 'the worst',[31] according to Sir Samuel Brittan, the economic commentator – that they might be drawn from various representative groups – 'women, manufacturing industry, the north, the south'.[32] This notion was swiftly squashed in favour of having economic expertise. Ultimately, therefore, the Bank fielded the Governor, Davies and King (deputy and deputy-elect) and two executive directors, while the 'externals' were named as Professor Charles Goodhart, DeAnne Julius, Sir Alan Budd and Willem Buiter. Goodhart was an academic with a considerable reputation at the London School of Economics and had a long-standing association with the Bank, having acted as its monetary adviser for nearly two decades. He was well liked in Threadneedle Street, as Anthony Hotson, a former Bank economist, recalled:

> Charles Goodhart was no typical Bank salaryman. Whereas other senior officials operated in an introverted world and under a cloak of secrecy, Charles served as a Samuel Johnson (or perhaps

a Boris Johnson) of monetary policy, maintaining a semi-open dialogue with academics and market practitioners. When the BIS and other international organizations wanted to discuss the new-fangled monetary targets, it was Charles who was invited in preference to the usual representative from ID [International Division] armed with a briefing note.[33]

Budd, newly knighted in 1997, came to the MPC from the Treasury, where he had been chief economic adviser since 1991, and had a solid economics background. Julius was a rather more exotic proposition, as an American who had taken her own economics degree to the CIA, where she worked briefly as an intelligence analyst before heading to the World Bank in Washington. She later crossed the Atlantic to become chief economist of Shell and then of British Airways, a post which she held until 1997. The quartet was completed by Buiter, a Dutch economist who had risen steadily through the academic hierarchies of Yale, Cambridge, Bristol and the London School of Economics, before becoming Professor of International Macroeconomics at Cambridge in 1994.

The four external members had a series of meetings in Downing Street before being formally introduced to Eddie George. Buiter, who had been interviewed by Budd and Ed Balls on Friday 30 May, had reason to believe his name was mud at the Bank, having disagreed in print with George's views on European monetary union, rubbishing his opinion that 'real economic convergence' was a prerequisite for successful union. Despite this, Buiter was summoned to Threadneedle Street on Monday 2 June:

[At] 14.30, I met with the Governor in his palatial office at the Bank ... The Governor was most gracious. I had decided to wear an Emmanuel College tie to mollify him ... Eddie immediately remind me not only of the article, but also of a lecture I had given (forgotten by me) in which I had said that he knew less economics than Winston Churchill (the statement referred to Churchill's decision to put the UK back on the gold standard in 1925). Eddie chuckled and said he only mentioned it so that we could get it out of the way and get on with business. I replied that it could hardly be considered insulting to be compared to Winston Churchill.[34]

Buiter's appointment was duly confirmed and he found himself caught up in the final preparations for the first MPC meeting, scheduled for Thursday 5 and Friday 6 June. As King recalled, it had been a scramble to get everything ready before 'the show opened'.[35] Arrangements were made for pre-MPC briefings, whereby the Bank's economists were to brief the committee's members on recent economic data, and decisions were made as to the format of the actual voting process. The preparations culminated in a series of dry runs in which Bank staff played the roles of committee members. As King recalled:

> So short was the time available that some of the dress rehearsals came after the first night of other parts of the policy process. Such was the adrenalin flow that at one rehearsal a row broke out about how a decision would be reached if the Committee split three ways in equal numbers.[36]

The interim Monetary Policy Committee had its first two-day meeting, still without its full complement of members, in the octagonal Committee Room on the first floor of the Bank. Seven men took their places around the table: Eddie George, Howard Davies, Mervyn King and Ian Plenderleith represented the Bank, while Willem Buiter and Charles Goodhart were there as external members; finally, Alan Budd was in attendance as Treasury representative. They sat under the watchful gaze of Augustus John's portrait of Montagu Norman, legendary Governor of the Bank from 1920 to 1944, and began their deliberations as to the direction of Britain's monetary policy.

Among the issues discussed during the MPC's inaugural meeting was whether 'activism' or 'gradualism' was appropriate in the committee's decision-making. King was later to recall that this 'lively debate'[37] centred around the question of 'how active should we be?'. In other words, how often should the MPC actually change rates and would it be better to do so gradually or in a staccato manner? In practice, King recalled, the question fell away: '[The committee] has never deliberately set out to do things slowly. It's actually set up to change rates.'[38] But the main issue before the committee was a proposal to raise the 'official dealing rate', always known in Threadneedle Street as Bank Rate, by 0.25 per cent to 6.50 per cent. On the Friday morning, the committee had a final three hours to reach its decision and shortly before noon they cast their votes. The motion was carried unanimously and the Bank's administrative wheels began to turn, an occasion which has now become a solemn tradition: the committee's decision was committed to paper, checked and double-checked, before being sealed in an envelope marked 'SECRET' in red letters and hurried down to the Bank's Dealing Room, the hub of its market operations. From there, the Bank's most senior dealer keyed the historic nugget of data onto his screen and pressed a button, transmitting it to the wider world.

£££

The Bank's honeymoon with Labour did not last long. Within two weeks of the handing over of the garland of independence came a further call from Gordon Brown's office. George was summoned to 11 Downing Street and reminded of the contents of the second letter he had received. While George was under the impression it simply heralded a period of consultation about banking supervision, Brown told him that there would be an announcement in Parliament the next day. The new administration had decided to fold banking supervision – long the preserve of the Bank of England – and the regulation of investment services into the existing Securities and Investments Board (SIB). A new entity was conjured up, codenamed NewRO (New Regulatory Organisation), or, as the media preferred, 'SuperSIB'. It was eventually christened the Financial Services Authority (FSA). The SIB had been set up in 1985 and had gradually gobbled up the old Financial Intermediaries, Managers and Brokers Regulatory Association (FIMBRA) and the Personal Investment Authority (PIA). It was a shambling beast and badly needed reform. The FSA, which eventually came into being in October 1997, combined the regulatory functions of no less than nine bodies, including those of the Bank of England. It was to be a showpiece of the new Labour administration.

While news of the new agency formed from this avalanche of acronyms was received with widespread indifference by the public, it caused consternation at the Bank. George was furious. He had been assured that he would be fully consulted about any further changes the Labour administration might make to the Bank and had reassured his colleagues to this effect. George sought out senior civil servants in the Cabinet Office and demanded that what appeared to be an arbitrary decision be reversed. He threatened to tender his resignation. When news of this threat reached Tony Blair, all of two weeks into his premiership, he was, according to Lord Mandelson, 'alarmed'.[39] Blair telephoned George and 'talked him back from the brink'.[40]

George returned sulkily to the Bank and prepared to break

the bad news to his staff. The Supervision and Surveillance Department – universally known as 'S&S' – was the Bank's largest division and employed 500 people, of whom 450 now faced the prospect of being decoupled from the great paternalistic structure of the Bank and translated to a mongrel super-agency based in Canary Wharf, in London's Docklands. In 1997, Canary Wharf was still, in large part, a dusty building site, littered with roadworks and served by a light railway which was prone to sudden and inexplicable stoppages. Compared to the clubby grandeur of Threadneedle Street, it was Outer Siberia. The announcement to the Bank's staff at a hastily convened meeting shocked no one more than Michael Foot, an executive director and something of a legendary figure. He had been at the Bank since 1969 and had worked his way up through its hierarchy, becoming variously head of the Foreign Exchange, European and Banking Supervision divisions. Foot's long-held ambition to accede to the Governorship was dashed by the announcement, as he realised with horror that his future now lay at the FSA. The moment passed into Bank folklore as 'The Day Michael Foot Cried'.

The blow was doubly cruel as it seemed to have been partly delivered from within. Brown and his colleagues had bypassed George and canvassed his deputy governor Howard Davies's views on their plans for the new regulatory authority. Davies, who got on well with George but was, according to colleagues, increasingly frustrated by the Bank's petty bureaucracies, had previously turned down the chairmanship of the SIB. But when Labour's plans coalesced around a single super-agency, his interest was piqued. Brown offered Davies the chairmanship and, after a long conversation with George, he accepted. By this time, George had recovered enough of his good humour to take a long view of the loss of banking supervision. He presented Davies with a dollar bill, inscribed with the words: 'One buck: to Howard, you will have my strongest possible support and my best wishes, Eddie.' The buck duly passed, Davies cleared his desk and prepared to lead the exodus to Canary Wharf. While the Governor reflected on the high price of independence, for his colleague Mervyn King it was a different story. The prospect of a Bank unencumbered by having to keep an eye on recalcitrant banks and insurers delighted him; moreover, Davies's departure created an obvious vacancy. According to one former colleague: 'You could almost hear him cheering in the background.'

The birth of the FSA occasioned the drawing up of a Memorandum of Understanding (MoU), outlining the Tripartite Relationship, which was to define the way in which the Treasury, the Bank of England and the new regulator would work together. Davies, who helped draft the MoU, described the tensions between the Bank and the Treasury in this great carve-up:

> In 1997, internal controversy centred on the extent to which the Bank of England could be allowed discretion to perform support operations without reference back to the Treasury. The first version [of the MoU] provided that the Treasury could prevent the Bank of England from extending liquidity support, but not that it could require it so to do. That drafting reflected the ancestry of the relationship between the Treasury and the Bank. The Treasury suspected the Bank of England of having extended support to institutions (such as Johnson Matthey) which were not systemic, in order to preserve banks with which it had a close relationship, or indeed to cover up failings in its supervision.[41]

While the MoU was heralded by the Bank as 'a practical framework for cooperation between the Bank and the FSA, and for coordination between the Bank, FSA and the Treasury in the event of a financial crisis', it was, in fact, nothing of the sort. Observers in the legal profession, such as Farrer & Co., were later to declare:

> [The MoU] was characterised by its almost calculated brevity and vagueness especially concerning relevant emergency responses. The drafting read as if the deliberate intention had been to be as unspecific as possible to allow maximum operational flexibility.[42]

The horse-trading was put even more bluntly some years later, by Peter Viggers MP, in a hearing of the Treasury Select Committee:

> What really happened, surely, is that the Labour Government came in with a landslide majority in 1997 and in came a great clunking fist with one big idea and, as a result of that, making the Bank of England independent, we had this Memorandum of Understanding in 1997. Paragraph two: 'The Bank's responsibilities. The Bank will be responsible for the overall stability of the financial system as a whole.' The Treasury then fought back, 'My God, what have we done?'[43]

The MoU had, in effect, forced the Bank and the Treasury to admit that hitherto they had enjoyed their own discrete turf and had got used to it. Even by 2009, the Treasury was not above reiterating the fact that it was the Bank's failings which prompted the new Tripartite: as Sir Nick Macpherson, Permanent Secretary to the Treasury, put it, there was 'the view that the Bank of England had been found wanting as a banking supervisor' and there was 'the risk of a conflict of interest between the Bank's new role as the independent monetary policy authority and its old responsibilities for banking supervision.'[44]

Unsurprisingly, the MoU, which was not even legally binding, did not stand up to practical use and was thoroughly revised in 2006, although arguably it still proved ineffectual when precisely the sort of 'financial crisis' it had been designed to cope with arrived in the summer of 2007. Back in 1997, however, the MoU's weasel words managed to capture the essence of the new Tripartite Relationship, which was an arrangement to cooperate between parties who very rapidly reached the conclusion that they would much rather not talk to each other.

Despite this, Davies was determined that the FSA would be a showpiece. Above all, he was adamant it should not duplicate the Bank's stuffy hierarchies and he set about creating a thoroughly modern working environment in the new agency's glass and steel headquarters, complete with open-plan offices which were a far cry from the warren of small rooms in Threadneedle Street. Working with McKinsey, the management consultancy firm, he formulated a flat management structure with himself as executive chairman but with no chief executive. Instead, he installed three managing directors – Michael Foot from the Bank, Richard Farrant, head of the old Securities and Futures Authority (also a former Bank man), and Philip Thorpe, head of IMRO. The working culture could not have been more different to that at the Bank and, although the two institutions were bound together in the Tripartite MoU, in reality they were soon living very separate lives.

Having bade farewell to banking supervision, the Bank was also preparing to do without another limb of its operations: the management of government debt. To remove what Labour regarded as a potential conflict of interest (the Bank setting interest rates while also issuing government debt securities or 'gilts') a new agency, which was to report directly to the Treasury, appeared. This was christened the UK Debt Management Office (DMO). If anything, this was a bigger blow to the Bank's prestige than the loss of banking supervision. The Bank's Gilt-Edged Division, which had hitherto dealt with 'gilts', issued by the government to finance its budgets, effectively lost its largest customer. The Gilt-Edged Division had considerable cachet at the Bank and was the favoured billet for many of its brightest recruits. No longer. Its loss was a heavy blow to the Old Lady's pride. The DMO was duly incorporated and opened its doors on 1 April 1998, with Mike Williams, then a deputy director at the Treasury's finance regulation and industry division, as its first chief executive. Williams assembled a somewhat mongrel staff, some on loan from the Treasury, others on secondment from the Bank, and moved into modest offices in Cheapside.

Eddie George described the grant of independence for the Bank as 'the final piece of the jigsaw', but as he and his lieutenants surveyed the aftermath of the Labour's electoral victory, it was clear that one or two pieces had subsequently gone missing. Nevertheless, for Mervyn King and his team of economists it was a price well worth paying. A young journalist called Robert Chote, whose hour would come in 2010, when he was appointed chairman of the Office for Budget Responsibility, captured the *Zeitgeist* in a newspaper article:

> The winners in the Bank's revolution are the monetary analysis divisions. No longer will their 160 staff be condemned to provide advice for a chancellor who habitually ignored it. Instead, they serve an in-house monetary policy committee that takes decisions on base rate itself. It is great for the Bank's economists – their lives have suddenly become more meaningful, argues one former Bank official. They are working their socks off, not least because they are worried about getting it wrong.[45]

The Brown–Balls–Miliband team had quickly found its feet at 11 Downing Street. In October 1997, Ed Balls delivered a self-assured lecture – 'Open Macroeconomics in an Open Economy' – to the

Scottish Economic Society in Edinburgh, under Chatham House rules. A revised version was later published in the society's journal and Mervyn King was among the 'colleagues' Balls thanked warmly for their comments on the draft text. (King's characteristically beady eye had alighted on Balls's description of the Bank maintaining 'stability through discretion' and suggested he change it to 'stability through constrained discretion' – the 'constraint' being the all-powerful inflation target). With characteristic bravado, Balls reiterated the underlying philosophy of the government's changes, that by hiving off regulation to the new FSA and the management of government debt to the DMO, 'there is now no risk of mixed motives or reputational contagion between supervision and monetary policy-making while the Bank is responsible for "financial stability". As lender of last resort, responsibility for avoiding problems in the first place is [the FSA's] and the risk of moral hazard is gone.'[46]

Balls continued to be a key point of contact for George and King and the latter found the young politician speaking the same language of economics. By 1999, Balls had been elevated to the role of Treasury chief economic adviser, effectively the conduit between the Treasury and the Chancellor. His influence and his fondness for economic jargon rapidly became apparent in Brown's speeches; Michael Heseltine famously described one speech which made reference to 'neo-classical endogenous growth theory' as 'It's not Brown's, it's Balls'!'

The actual meat of the Labour government's reforms was contained in the Bank of England Act, which came into force in June 1998, a full year after the election victory and the dramatic announcement of independence for the Bank. The new Act overhauled the previous Act, of 1946, making it into something resembling a constitution for a modern central bank by strengthening its internal governance, as well as setting out its new remit in monetary policy. The objectives of the Bank were spelt out: '(a) to maintain price stability, and (b) subject to that, to support the economic policy of Her Majesty's Government, including its objectives for growth and employment.'

The new legislation also shone a light into the Bank's Court of Directors, which had long been a dusty graveyard for time-serving bureaucrats. Certain functions of the Court, it was decided, would be delegated to a sub-committee of non-executive Directors, known as NedCo. NedCo duly sprang into life with a large posse recruited from the City and public life. There were some familiar names on the list, such as Sir Colin Southgate, Sir Chips Keswick and Sir David Cooksey, and some much less so: Roy Bailie was a veteran of the printing industry, Graham Hawker the chief executive of a large water company and Sheila McKechnie the director of the Consumers' Association. They were joined by the likes of Bill Morris, general secretary of the Transport & General Workers' Union, and Jim Stretton, a chief executive of the Standard Life Assurance Company. To some, it seemed like a convocation of 'all the talents', while others were bemused at what they saw as a ragbag of City grandees, salarymen, a couple of do-gooders and a union boss. The hiring spree for both the Court and NedCo resulted in a body of some nineteen people, which immediately looked unwieldy. (In 2009, the Court was slimmed down to twelve, including Mervyn King, Charlie Bean and Paul Tucker. At the time of writing, in early 2012, there is still a union boss, however, in the burly form of Brendan Barber, general secretary of the TUC.)

Along with this flurry of appointments came confirmation of Eddie George's second five-year term, from 1 July 1998, and of Mervyn King's appointment as deputy governor (Monetary Stability) alongside David Clementi, who had been appointed to replace Howard Davies. King's appointment was significant, in that it created a clear role for a monetary policy head, quite separate from that of the day-to-day administrative role carried out by the other deputy governor. Hitherto, the Bank had regarded its Governor as effectively its chairman and his deputy as its chief executive. The arrival of a second deputy split the Bank in two. There soon appeared a King 'camp', populated largely by economists who were dedicated wholly to the formulation and dissemination of monetary policy. It began to dominate the Bank entirely, as Sushil Wadhwani, who was appointed to the MPC in June 1999, recalled:

> In my time at the MPC at the Bank, I was surprised by the lack of interest in issues relating to financial markets. Indeed there seemed to be a deliberate policy to run down resource in the Financial Stability wing.[47]

Indeed, King's focus became almost entirely fixed on the smooth running of the MPC. It was not without its teething problems, some of them no doubt caused by having a large number of economists in the same room. At one of the MPC's earliest meetings, one external member suggested that the committee adopt a rule whereby it changed interest rates at every meeting, even if it was only by a couple of basis points, the idea being that constant change would remove the undue weight attached to change or no change. At another early meeting, Willem Buiter abandoned the convention of increments of 0.25 per cent and voted for a 0.4 per cent change to Bank Rate; it was decided that no one could really distinguish between such small differences. Occasionally, the externals' suggestions would float up from the committee to the Parlours, where they found little favour: Wadhwani's proposal for a modest amendment to the Bank's main macroeconomic model caused a scene reminiscent of an H. M. Bateman cartoon.

Eighteen months into the MPC's life, the apparently innocent question of whether the four external members (Wadhwani, Charles Goodhart, Willem Buiter and DeAnne Julius) might receive some form of independent research assistance (such as a PhD student) to assist them with analysing data between the committee's monthly meetings erupted into a full-scale row. Buiter, writing in the *Financial Times*, later recalled:

> Eddie George considered our request for independent, dedicated resources for the external MPC members a vote of no confidence in himself and the institution. He felt the external members were accusing him of not being in good faith as regards access to the Bank's resources. And he felt strongly we were dividing and even balkanising his Bank. Eddie George had a short fuse and a perceived attack on the integrity of his Bank was more than enough to light that fuse. I received a spectacular one-on-one dressing down from him on the issue. Voices were raised and tempers lost.[48]

The argument raged on, in spectacular fashion, with 'similar unpleasant one-on-one shouting matches on the issue with both David Clementi and with Mervyn King', according to Buiter. In the absence of any resolution, Buiter and his colleagues took the dramatic step of taking the matter to the Bank's Court. Shortly afterwards, the furore leaked into the Press, the external members got their way. Each was allocated a Masters-degree-level and a PhD-level researcher to assist them in their preparation for the committee; a department called the External MPC Unit was set up at the Bank to accommodate the new research team.

Despite this ugly episode – admirably summed up by Michael Fallon MP as essentially being about 'whether the day boys should use the library'[49] – the MPC's actual decision-making process was a relatively smooth one. Two years after its inauguration, it was something for King to be proud of. In a speech at the Queen's University, in Belfast, in May 1999, he found a parallel for its *modus operandi* in the four principles for decision-making espoused by Robert Rubin, the former US Treasury Secretary:

> They encapsulate exactly the philosophy of the MPC. First, the only certainty is that there is no certainty. Second, every decision is a matter of weighing probabilities, or the balance of risks, as we say. Third, despite uncertainty we have to decide and act. Fourth, decisions should be judged not only on the results but also on how they were made. The first three principles guide every meeting of the MPC. And the fourth is one I commend to all those who wish to make their own judgement about the MPC two years on.[50]

To be sure, 1997 had been a break with the past. Before then, monetary policy had been a cloak and dagger affair, hatched in murky political quarters and then slavishly implemented by the Bank. Worse, previous governments' approach had, as Mervyn King observed, been along the lines of 'make it up as you go along'.[51] Now it was free to be applied with a new objectivity and, if not in the full view of the public eye (the MPC's minutes are still small masterpieces of concision), then at least subject to its regular scrutiny. All this strengthened Mervyn King's position at the Bank. By the end of 1998, George was still firmly at the helm, but King, as a new deputy governor, was in the ascendant.

PAPER AGAINST GOLD

'The Treasury and we at the Bank were never under any illusion that
this would be a popular decision with gold producers or investors.'
David Clementi, FT World Gold Conference, London, 14 June 1999

In Ian Fleming's *Goldfinger*, it is the redoubtable, pipe-
smoking Colonel Smithers of the Bank of England who tells
James Bond that it is his department's job 'to watch for any
leakage of gold out of England' and when any fugitive gold is
found to 'try and get it back in our vaults, plug the leak and arrest
the people responsible'. Bond is suitably impressed by Smithers's
eloquent defence of the sanctity of the Bank's gold reserves (less
so by Smithers's secretary, who 'looked as if she had once taken a
double first').

Smithers would have been outraged by the next project visited
on the Bank by the new Labour government – to divest it of its
proverbially safest assets. In the course of their plotting about
the Bank's future, Brown, Balls and Miliband had scrutinised a
document called the Exchange Equalisation Account (EEA), an
exemplary piece of anonymous Whitehall paperwork which is
put together each year by one of the Treasury's accounting officers. Essentially, the EEA keeps track of the UK's foreign currency

reserves and of its gold – together referred to as the country's 'reserve holdings', which are administered by the Bank.

As the EEA noted, the gold bars and coin in the reserves '[are] stored physically at the Bank's premises'. Besides fulfilling their role as reserve holdings, the gold is endowed with a totemic importance by the general public and its reassuring presence allows Britain to sleep soundly at night. The bullion has remained stacked on pallets in the Bank's gargantuan underground vaults, lined in concrete and behind massive doors, for centuries. It is, after the Federal Reserve's vaults in New York, the world's largest depository of gold. The Bank's vaults have changed very little since 1901, when Arthur Beavan recorded a visit in his book *Imperial London*:

> A courtyard, just within the fine Lothbury entrance, led to the bullion vaults, inaccessible to visitors except by special order, and even then a director or other Government official had to accompany them. In this courtyard could often be seen vans laden with uninteresting-looking ingots of silver, or with bars of gold that individually measure 8 x 3 x 1 inches, worth about £800 each; too heavy, however, to be walked off with. A lock – to open which required several keys, each one being in the possession of different individuals – gave access, through heavy iron doors, to the dimly-lighted, heavy-vaulted, white-washed cellar containing untold wealth; bars of gold, in trucks to facilitate removal, and gold coin in bags piled against the wall in lavish carelessness, 35 to 40 million sterling being not infrequently stored here. Every sovereign or half-sovereign sent into the Bank was weighed with unfailing accuracy by means of wonderful little automatic machines, some of which had been in use ever since the Great Exhibition of 1851, when they were first shown to the public.[52]

In modern times, the secrecy remains much the same but the security has been updated. John Footman, the Bank's Executive Director of Central Services, has startlingly recalled that the bullion vault is 'deep underground and if you disappear down a corridor then you will encounter all sorts of metal grilles, video cameras and chaps with machine guns'.[53]

The Bank does not just gloat idly over its gold stocks; rather, it actively manages them. For its commercial gold customers, it provides an 'account management service' on what is called an 'allocated' basis. This means that clients have title to specific bars of gold, rather than on the Bank itself ('unallocated'). Besides this reassuring title to their gold, clients are able to mobilise their holdings by making or receiving so-called 'electronic book entry transfers' between their account at the Bank and accounts elsewhere. The physical gold stays put, but the title to it may be transferred. In other words, the Bank – uniquely – facilitates a basic form of gold-trading, for which it charges fees. Further revenues accrue from gold-lending, usually back to gold producers who wish to hedge their future output.

Given the synthetic nature of so many of the financial transactions overseen by the Bank, its stocks of gold – bars and coins – remain reassuring, if a little quaint. The bars are named London Good Delivery, an old-fashioned but solid descriptor for the benchmark of the bullion industry and a standard measure of quality accepted worldwide. Besides being of superior quality – at least 995 parts per 1,000 pure gold – each LGD bar must bear a serial number, or 'chop', of a refiner approved by the London Good Delivery List of 'acceptable smelters and assayers'. The Bank sits, literally, on the bulk of the UK's gold reserves, and those of other depositors, including the central banks of other countries. Indeed, the storage, administration and even lending of the gold contribute substantially to the Bank's revenues.

Historically, as the Labour team noticed in 1998, Britain had held large quantities of gold. In 1948, it had some 1,432 tonnes, a stock which grew to between 2,000 and 2,500 tonnes between 1958 and 1965. In the period 1966 to 1972, a hefty 1,356 tonnes were sold. Reserves grew again in the late 1970s and had remained stable at around 715 tonnes. This was the situation when Labour came to power. The 715 tonnes comprised some twenty-three million fine troy ounces of gold with a then market value of approximately $6.5bn, accounting for around one sixth of the UK's total reserve holdings of $37bn.

The questions posed by the bright young economists in the Brown camp were these: what did gold have to do with the exercise of monetary policy? Why not cash it in? Why not buy something which generates a return rather than sits around doing nothing? In fact, these same questions had been posed by Kenneth Clarke, as Chancellor of the Exchequer in the previous administration. He recalled some 'entertaining' meetings at the Bank when some of its officials had been brought out to persuade him that its gold was sacrosanct. Clarke was not convinced: 'I remember the one that they all used to fall back on was, "Chancellor, if we ever have a third world war it might be the only means of exchange upon which we could fall back". I thought that if we had a third world war, there would be bigger problems than that.'[54]

By the time Labour's bruisers arrived, the Bank was, therefore, somewhat resigned to the gold issue being raised again. On 10 August 1998, Tom Scholar, who had been appointed Brown's principal private secretary, requested that his colleagues at the Treasury begin work with the Bank on a 'programme for gold sales'. Two weeks later, the two sides met and Ian Plenderleith, then responsible for the Bank's financial markets operations, was asked to assist in drawing up a paper outlining options for the process. Correspondence between the two sides was copied to Ed Balls and Ed Miliband.

The results of these discussions were presented to Brown in late November, but appeared not to have the backing of the Bank, which viewed the project with distaste. It seemed like an assault on its integrity and one which previous administrations had never countenanced. Naturally, the Bank maintained close links with London bullion traders – both at the major investment banks and at longstanding independent firms – and suspected they would be appalled at the idea of the Bank dumping some of its stocks into a weak and stagnant market.

Brown's office observed the Bank's reluctance coolly. On 23 December, one of the Chancellor's aides sent an email to the Treasury officials:

> The Chancellor is keen that officials at the Treasury and the Bank work together to produce a joint proposal. As I understand it the latest proposal is not a joint one. The Chancellor needs to know the status of the proposal, what the difficulties are in drawing up a joint proposal, how you think we can move forward in achieving a joint proposal.

This joint proposal proved elusive, as the Bank dug its heels in. In early January 1999, Brown and Eddie George met for lunch to discuss the prospective gold sales. The file note which was made of their meeting was preserved, but when the document was finally released in 2010, the sections recording George's comments on the matter were blacked out. Whatever passed between them evidently did not dissuade Brown. His team pressed on. A few months later, the London market's leading gold traders were called to a meeting in a committee room at the Bank, where Plenderleith told them that the government would shortly announce its series of gold sales. The traders raised a series of objections, the principal one being that if specific timings and lot sizes were disclosed in advance, it would cause the gold price to plummet. Plenderleith and his colleagues acknowledged the traders' concerns but intimated that Bank was powerless to stop the process: Brown's mind was made up.

The Treasury's announcement finally came on 7 May, a slow Friday in the House of Commons, in response to a question by Ivor Caplin, a Labour MP, about the 'government's investments'.[55] Patricia Hewitt, then a junior Treasury minister, described the gold sales as 'a restructuring of the UK's reserve holdings to achieve a better balance in the portfolio by increasing the proportion held in currency'.[56] She added that the Treasury intended to sell 125 tonnes of gold – or '3 per cent of the total reserves' – in a series of five auctions beginning in July and ending in mid-2000. The 3 per cent figure was entirely disingenuous, because it referred to a percentage of 'total reserves', which included vast amounts of foreign currency holdings. Nor did Hewitt disclose the full extent of the proposed gold sales. Only later was it revealed that the government intended to dispose of no less than 395 tonnes, 55 per cent of the UK's gold reserves, leaving the Bank with 320 tonnes.

While Hewitt was on her feet in the Commons, the Bank and the Treasury were putting the finishing touches to an information memorandum which outlined the gold auction process. The bullion auctions were conducted on a single, or uniform, price basis, whereby a competitive bidding process would result in gold bars being allotted to the highest bidders, but all successful bidders would pay a single price equal to the lowest accepted bid. Eligible bidders, paying in dollars, would only be drawn from the members of the London Bullion Market Association, central banks and monetary institutions holding gold accounts at the Bank. While the Bank's preference was to credit allotted bars to the existing gold accounts of successful bidders, there was no prohibition on cash-and-carry: the memorandum noted that 'physical collection from the Bank of England in London will also be possible', although a standard charge of '£3.35 per bar' would apply.

A matter of days after the publication of the information memorandum, on 11 June, the Bank dispatched David Clementi, its deputy governor, to the FT World Gold Conference, at the Intercontinental Hotel, in London's Mayfair, to smooth the market's ruffled feathers:

> Of course, the Treasury and we at the Bank were never under any illusion that that this would be a popular decision with gold producers or investors. But I can assure you that the whole process has been designed to provide maximum transparency, and full information about the scale and timing of supply ... Our whole approach is designed to minimise uncertainty about our intentions in the market; and as far as the gold price is concerned we obviously have as much interest as anyone (except those who are short!) in seeing some recovery from current levels.[57]

Many of those in the audience were indeed 'short'. As Hewitt's announcement reverberated around the market, traders had quickly begun taking out short positions, in the expectation that the price of gold would fall heavily. Unsurprisingly, it did, eventually reaching a twenty-year low, a level which became unaffectionately known as the 'Brown Bottom'.

The World Gold Council took a particularly dim view of what, it had no doubt, was 'a political decision by the Treasury' and which had little to do with the prudent restructuring which the Treasury had claimed. A few days after the announcement, the council noted that the result had been 'an immediately damaging effect' on the gold price, which fell by nearly $7.50 to $281.50. The council railed that the 'damaging reverberations of such a symbolically-charged action by the Treasury will be felt for many months to come'. The council smelt a conspiracy: it spelt out its view that a cynical motive lay behind the gold sales, namely that it was a precursor to the UK joining the European Monetary Union and the European Central Bank: 'If Britain becomes part of the ECB its gold or foreign currency reserves will effectively be frozen as, under ECB guidelines, any gold sales by individual central banks will be subject to control by the ECB. Thus in some sense this move appears to be pre-empting the promised referendum for UK citizens about whether or not they wish to join the Euro.'

Although becoming part of the ECB was a distant and unlikely prospect, it was true that the Bank had edged closer to it, particularly *vis à vis* its gold holdings. In September 1999, the Bank was a signatory to a joint statement with fourteen other central banks, including the ECB, which committed them to a promise that they would 'not enter the market as sellers, with the exception of already decided sales'.[58] The communique also included the provision that 'the gold sales already decided will be achieved through a concerted programme of sales over the next five years. Annual sales will not exceed approximately 400 tons and total sales over this period will not exceed 2,000 tons.'[59] Given that Britain eventually disposed of a total of 395 tonnes, its proportion of this limit was very considerable. Another of the WGC's accusations was probably closer to the mark: that there were other central bank sales afoot and the Treasury wanted to 'get in early'. The Swiss National Bank was attempting to offload more than a third – some 1,300 tonnes – of its gold reserves, while the International Monetary Fund was also discussing whether to sell 300 tonnes.

Despite criticism from the WGC and others, the Bank's sales went ahead as planned. A total of seventeen auctions, beginning on 6 July 1999 and ending in 2002, raised the sum of £1.9bn. As Hewitt had intimated, the proceeds were used by the Bank to acquire dollar, euro and yen 'interest-bearing assets' for the Treasury – in all likelihood, corporate and government bonds. In the event, Britain's gold went very cheap. The seventeen auctions achieved prices of between $256 and $296 an ounce, with an average of $275 an ounce. Although few people could have predicted gold's extraordinary rise since that 1999–2000 period, the fact remains that in mid-2011 the metal was trading as high as $1,800 an ounce, latterly driven inexorably upwards by the fear induced by sovereign debt crises engulfing the Eurozone. Correspondingly, the Bank's remaining stocks have benefited considerably from the boom. According to the EEA's recent balance sheets, the gold was worth some £4.68bn in March 2008 and rose to £6.37bn in March 2009, £7.34bn in March 2010 and – the most recent figure – £8.95bn in March 2011, with the price of gold having risen from £735 to £898 an ounce, an increase of 22 per cent in these last twelve months alone.

£££

By the spring of 2000, the Monetary Policy Committee was three years old and it had, by and large, resolved the adolescent squabbles between the Bank and external members so graphically described by Willem Buiter. It continued to recruit its external members, largely from academe. One such was Professor Stephen Nickell, an economist at the LSE, who became the first external member to serve two three-year terms. He recalled the process of recruitment, which began for him in early 2000 with a telephone call out of the blue from Gus O'Donnell, then Permanent Secretary at the Treasury, followed by a meeting with O'Donnell and Ed Balls at the Treasury. The offer of a seat on the MPC duly made and accepted, there was a 'chat' with Eddie George and then the gruesome prospect of an 'appointment hearing' before the Treasury Committee and the Press. First, however, Nickell had to complete a lengthy 'exam paper on various aspects of monetary policy-making',[60] which was set by Charlie Bean, the then adviser to the Treasury Committee and subsequently recruited to the Bank itself.

Nickell was inducted into the formalities of the committee's proceedings, which includes the decision itself, taken by strict majority vote:

> On the Thursday morning, the governor invites each member to present their vote on rates along with their reasons, each member being expected to talk for about ten minutes. The deputy governor in charge of monetary analysis is always invited to go first, the next seven members are then asked in apparently random order and the governor always goes last.[61]

Nickell observed that the voting system worked well:

> There is no block voting, and within both internal and external groups, there are often divisions with deputy governors voting against the governor, for example. Indeed the committee is not concerned with consensus, split votes are common and the governor has twice been on the losing side. Note that since governors always vote last, they can choose whether to join the winning or losing side except in the unusual circumstance when they have the casting vote, with the previous eight members' votes tied at four-four.[62]

The sheer scale of the MPC machine also impressed its external members. At this early stage in its life, some 120 economists already laboured on its behalf in the Monetary Analysis Division. Aside from their duties inside the Bank, the

MPC's early members were sent on a gruelling programme of regional visits:

> So about ten times a year, I would set off for some distant part of the UK both to listen and to explain. These visits usually lasted two days and involved a great deal of eating. The basic format was to meet large groups of business people, trade unionists, academics and so on, over, successively, lunch, dinner, breakfast, lunch.[63]

While these local audiences flocked to meet the MPC's peripatetic members, they were usually more interested in talking about official regulation or the decline in manufacturing – 'monetary policy rarely seemed a cause for concern'. Nevertheless, there was, as Nickell recalled, often a warm welcome for the Bank, particularly in Northern Ireland:

> The Omagh Chamber of Commerce annual dinner was particularly memorable: arriving at 7 p.m. for pre-dinner drinks, sitting down to dinner at 9.30 p.m., standing up to speak on monetary policy at around midnight, and finally taking my leave of an event still in full cry well after 3 a.m.[64]

While Nickell and his MPC colleagues accustomed themselves to these rituals, the Bank also extended an invitation to Don Kohn, a veteran of the Federal Reserve who was then director of the Fed's Division of Monetary Affairs, to cast an eye over the committee. He was asked to ascertain how it was performing and how it interacted with the rest of the Bank. Cast in the role of school inspector, Kohn installed himself in an office in the Bank for seven weeks and set about interviewing the entire committee, as well as the legions of Bank staff whose work fed into its deliberations.

Many of them made their feelings plain. The Kohn report was delivered in October 2000 and provided something of an end-of-term report which made disquieting reading for the Bank's Court.

Above all, Kohn's report highlighted the subjugation of large swathes of the Bank to the MPC's service and its remit of meeting the government's inflation target. The instigation of the MPC, with its nine data- and research-hungry members, had clearly come as something of a shock to the system in the wider Bank. Firstly, Kohn noted that the MPC was, by general agreement and 'universal recommendation', meeting too often. He wrote that one 'nearly universal recommendation was to change the legislation to allow fewer meetings each year. The monthly frequency was seen as not justified by the amount of new information becoming available between meetings, and in that context, as imposing considerable and unnecessary demands on policymakers and staff.'[65]

Indeed, Kohn found that the basic construction of the committee, with its nine individually accountable members, 'greatly complicates transparency'. His report also shed light on a hitherto little-known part of the process, the 'pre-MPC' briefings, in which members of the committee spent half a day chewing over 'incoming information' about the economy, including reports from the Bank's regional agents. Despite the general usefulness of these briefings, Kohn noted that 'staff emphasised the considerable burden imposed on a relatively small number of people by having to do the pre-MPC briefings each month'.[66]

Turning his attention to the Bank's quarterly *Inflation Report*, Kohn identified the problematic nature of the inflation forecast – traditionally described as the 'best collective judgement' of the committee – and how it was constructed. Kohn noted that the 'tight framework' of the MPC's research agenda meant that some young economists at the Bank felt constrained and often left as a result:

Both staff and MPC perceived staff turnover to be high and costly in terms of meeting the objectives of MA [Monetary Analysis] and the MPC. In particular, the staff was relatively young, and although quite talented, turnover had meant that its overall level of experience was low, and so the build-up in the type of judgement that comes with experience had been impeded.[67]

He also detected some animosity between the Bank's staffers and the MPC:

A more difficult issue related to the general tone of the relationships with the MPC. While MPC members often stated that they desired more analytical presentations from the staff, many staff perceived that this would not really be welcome. In their view, the MPC tended to see the staff more as suppliers of data than as expert analysts whose opinions were sought and respected.[68]

The Bank took the unusual step of publishing the Kohn report, as well as its own polite response, acknowledging that it must try harder. It reported that it had implemented several of Kohn's suggestions. Kohn, who went on to become vice chairman of the Federal Reserve during the Bush administration, remained a trusted ally of the Bank. (In February 2011, he was welcomed back as a member of its new Financial Policy Committee, set up to keep an eye on the UK's financial system and act as a report into the Bank's financial stability function. Thankfully, from Kohn's point of view, it was decided it should meet only four times a year.)

For his part, King remained justifiably proud of his achievement in helping to create the MPC. By his measures, it was to prove remarkably successful. In its first few years, the MPC managed to keep inflation within its RPIX 2.5 per cent target band and mostly to within 0.5 per cent of the central target, helped along by a mostly benign macroeconomic climate. While not without its teething problems, the committee had established itself as a cornerstone of the Bank. It developed, too, something of a sense of superiority over other public bodies, partly because of the grave nature of its work and partly because of the innate self-confidence of the Bank itself. It was noticed by the House of Lords Economics Affairs Committee, for example, that when a new external member of the MPC was appointed, it did not trouble itself with strictures such as the Nolan rules, which governed public appointments. Lord Peston put it thus:

> We, as a Committee, have never understood what there is special about the MPC where someone picks up the phone and says, 'Fancy being a member of the MPC?' 'Yes.' 'Okay.' We have been told in evidence that that is how it works.[69]

But these quibbles were batted away by the Governor and his inner circle. Overall, the MPC was deemed a great success. And for the deputy governor, it was also a success to build upon.

THE GOVERNOR

'A permanent Governor would be one of the greatest men in England. He would be a 'little monarch' in the City ... He would be the personal embodiment of the Bank of England; he would be constantly clothed with an infinite prestige.'
Walter Bagehot, Lombard Street, *1873*

In early 2002, as the fifth anniversary of the Bank's independence hove into view, the question of a successor to Eddie George began to play upon minds both at the Bank and in Whitehall. George would turn sixty-five in the coming September and it was widely acknowledged this would be his last year in office. At the Bank, there was a sense of the Governor preparing to take his leave for a retirement which would eventually be cushioned by a peerage as Lord George, of St Tudy in the County of Cornwall. It was equally noticeable that King, one of his two deputies, was the heir not only apparent but also expectant. Indeed, it was King rather than George who rose to his feet on 22 May in front of the Society of Business Economists, gathered at the Royal College of Pathologists in Carlton House Terrace, to deliver a speech entitled 'The Monetary Policy Committee: Five Years On'. King was on good form, leavening his cricket scorer's analysis of the MPC role

('Of the fifty-four meetings since January 1998, four dissenting votes have been cast on six occasions...') with historical anecdote and gentle self-deprecation.

He reflected on whether there were any historical anteced-ents for the nine-strong MPC and suggested one might be the nine 'warriors' depicted in a plasterwork frieze in Aston Hall, a Jacobean house in Birmingham:

> These are known as the 'nine worthies', described as 'high relief figures in their own niches separated by scrolling', a pretty good description of the MPC. The Nine Worthies of Chivalry, as they are known, comprise three groups: three honest heathens, three Old Testament heroes and three champions of Christendom ... But, wait a moment, there are two additional figures in the frieze. One is Perseus – presumably the minute taker. The other is described as a 'so-far unidentified figure, certainly a later pastiche'. This must be the Treasury representative.[70]

King's speech was something of a classic, displaying the slightly *soi-disant* confidence which allowed him a dig at the Treasury, and which was to become a hallmark of his public persona. An element of playing to the gallery would certainly do him no harm as the issue of George's succession came to the fore. Some still perceived King as an academic – and many still do – and he was at pains to present a more human side, which could translate into something approaching the paternalism which George had so skilfully cultivated at the Bank.

In November 2002, Gordon Brown, the Chancellor of the Exchequer, received a lengthy memo from the Treasury enti-tled 'Bank Appointments' which addressed the issue of the Governorship and deputy governorship. The memo described the two roles as 'highly market sensitive'. The memo outlined the 'key qualities' required for the post of Governor of the Bank of England:

- Sound judgement and the resolution to back that judgement in difficult circumstances;
- An established reputation, with credibility with domestic and international financial markets;
- Exceptional communication skills;
- Good chairmanship skills;
- Technical competence in monetary policy;
- Ability to manage the Bank of England.[71]

With these in mind, the memo noted that 'there are few potential candidates for the post of Governor. We have identified six who broadly meet the requirements above.' Although the names of the six candidates have never been released, King was certainly joined by Andrew Crockett and Howard Davies. Many felt the contest was really between King and Crockett. They were fellow Cambridge economists and longstanding colleagues, but very different men.

Crockett, a genial Scot, was the choice of many in the Bank itself, despite the fact that he had not worked there for nearly ten years. At the time of the succession question he was general manager of the Bank for International Settlements and based at its headquarters in Basel, Switzerland. Five years King's senior, he had joined the Bank of England in 1966, but moved to the International Monetary Fund in 1972 for a lengthy stint, before returning to Threadneedle Street in 1989 as an executive director. Four years later, he had been spirited away to the BIS. Even today, there are many who maintain that had Crockett been picked, the Bank would have become a more enlightened institution with a place at the table in Europe. He was in favour of joining the euro, which automatically put him at odds with the UK government's policy and, indeed, Mervyn King's own Eurosceptic views.

Notwithstanding the powerful lobby which wanted to see Crockett return to the Bank as Governor, there is little doubt that King was top of the list and firmly intent on staying there. The Treasury memo also noted that there had been much speculation about his elevation. It concluded: 'There is every sign that the appointment will be both unsurprising and well-received. This augurs well for maintaining a smooth transition to the new regime.' Crockett's name faded from the ring. As it was he went on to serve a further year at the BIS, before taking a job as president of J. P. Morgan Chase International, the investment bank.

The announcement of King's appointment came on 27 November 2002, brought forward, by the Treasury, according to one observer, to offset less auspicious news about higher borrowing and a gloomy economic outlook. Tradition dictates that Governors of the Bank of England are appointed by the Crown and the Queen duly issued a warrant which confirmed 'our Trusty and Well-beloved Professor Mervyn Allister King to be the Governor, to hold the said office', which he would take up on 1 July 2003.

The official announcement was accompanied by a briefing note for Treasury press officers, entitled 'New Governor – Points to Watch'. It included a potential bear-trap: King was an interest rate hawk. His elevation had to mean that interest rates would be going up/not coming down, to which the official answer was to be: '[It is] wrong to conclude that Mr King's appointment has any message for short term interest rate decisions. He has unrivalled Monetary Policy decision making experience, and will continue to bring that to bear at the MPC.'[72]

£££

On his appointment as Governor, King had been at the Bank for eleven years and had acted as deputy governor for four. He could look back with pride at what he had achieved in his fifty-three years: a carefully calibrated progression through a series of venerable academic institutions, high-profile think tanks and the Bank's own idiosyncratic hierarchy. But who was the new Governor?

King's personal history is one of self-determination, academic industry and hard work. He was born in Amersham, Buckinghamshire, on 30 March 1948, the son of Eric King and Kathleen (*née* Passingham), who had married five years previously. Eric King was a railway worker who, at the advent of the Second World War, joined the Royal Engineers and was involved in the planning for the D-Day landings in Normandy in June 1944. When he was demobbed in 1945, King joined an army training programme to become a teacher, apparently choosing geography as his subject. In the mid-1950s, his new profession took King and his family to Calderdale, in Yorkshire. King had secured a teaching post at Calder High School, in the town of Mytholmroyd, which had opened in May 1952 and was Yorkshire's first comprehensive school (and the first anywhere to send a child with a comprehensive school education to Oxbridge).

It was here in Calderdale that the young, short-trousered Mervyn spent his first years. In the 1950s, the Calder Valley industrial towns and moorland villages were bastions of Methodism, and King's father was a Methodist preacher at some of the austere stone chapels which dotted the area. Mervyn was enrolled at Old Town Primary School, a foursquare Victorian building complete with separate 'Boys' and 'Girls' entrances, set on a windswept moor above Hebden Bridge and looking out over the Hebden valley towards Heptonstall. The school gave King a solid elementary education and a thorough introduction to cricket, a game which remains a major preoccupation in the area. In June 1957, as a nine-year-old schoolboy, King would doubtless have been marched out to welcome Lord Trefgarne, head of the National Playing Fields Association, when he arrived to open Old Town Cricket Club's new three-acre Boston Hill ground – one of the highest in Yorkshire – following spirited local fundraising and earth-moving efforts. The grand opening day saw the club's members, immaculate in cricket whites and sports jackets, and their families gathered for a celebratory tea in the modest wooden pavilion. The new cricket ground was a source of immense local pride and in its first season its supporters were able to cheer Old Town to victory in the play-off final in the Hebden Bridge League. A year later, in the rain-sodden summer of 1958, King was taken by his father to Leeds to watch his first Test match, England versus New Zealand at Headingley, a match which inspired him:

> It rained all day on both Thursday and Friday, and, when play started in mid-afternoon on Saturday, on a drying wicket New Zealand were bowled out by [Jim] Laker and [Tony] Lock for 67. So I became a slow bowler. I was taught to bowl – slow left arm – at Old Town primary school by the headmaster, Alfred Stephenson. During the morning break he would mark the wickets in chalk in the playground, and draw a small circle exactly on a length. If we could pitch the ball within that circle he would give us a farthing. As we improved, and the payout of farthings increased, the morning break became shorter and shorter – my first lesson in economic incentives or what is known in the trade as 'moral hazard'.

The perils of 'moral hazard' – whereby risks are taken because of the knowledge that another party will bear any loss – aside, King clearly enjoyed his time at the Old Town school. In 2006, the Governor – described by the *Hebden Bridge Times* as a 'former high-flying pupil' – sent a farewell message to the school's retiring headteacher, describing it as 'very special. Children, parents and even the alumni are very much in your debt.'[73]

While Yorkshire had provided an early grounding in cricket and even the rudiments of economic theory, it was not to remain the family home. After the upland fastness of the West Riding, came the comparative metropolis of Wolverhampton, in Staffordshire. Eric King had successfully applied for the job of headmaster of Redhall Secondary Modern school in Lower Gornal, Dudley. In early 1958, the family moved to Wolverhampton, setting up home in a modest, semi-detached house in tree-lined Canterbury Road, in the Penn suburb of the town. The quiet neighbourhood was enlivened by the arrival of Bobby Thomson and Nigel Sims, Wolverhampton Wanderers footballers who lived in club-owned houses near the Kings. Both Thomson and Sims left Wolves for Aston Villa, the great rival team in the area, but continued to live in Canterbury Road. For the young King, the presence of these two local celebrities – Thomson became Villa's top goal scorer, while the burly Sims was one of the best goalkeepers of his generation – was a source of great excitement. It was only enhanced by visits to the footballers' houses by Villa's manager, Joe Mercer (himself a former Arsenal player), who dropped in periodically to check on the so-called 'Mercer Minors'. Naturally, King became a passionate Aston Villa fan and even today recalls the first match he attended at Villa Park, in the centre of Birmingham, in October 1960. When he was not keeping an eye on the comings and goings at the Thomson and Sims residences, it was a short walk for King from the family home to Warstones Junior School, a low-built brick affair which retained its World War Two air raid shelters. Here he sat the all-important Eleven Plus exam, which was the prerequisite for admittance to grammar school.

In King's case, a pass secured a prized place at Wolverhampton

Grammar School, which had a long history, a fine academic reputation and close links with the Merchant Taylors, the City livery company. Its main building, a solid lump of Victorian brick surmounted by a crenelated tower on Wolverhampton's Compton Road, must have seemed a forbidding place to King and the other new boys arriving there in the last years of the 1950s. WGS, as it was universally known, had high standards across its curriculum. King recalled later that on his first day there he was required to take, of all things, a singing test:

> All the new entrants to the school were asked on the first morning to sing up and down a scale, on their own, in turn. We all lined up, I made my attempt and I failed. And I was told that the sheep and the goats meant that I was a goat. I wasn't in the school choir, I wasn't allowed to have lunch in the first sitting, I had to have lunch on the second sitting every day for the rest of my school career, and I was told that I was 'not musical'. We were divided into two groups – those who were musical and those who weren't.[74]

This early blight on King's school career was mitigated by his success in other subjects. He excelled at mathematics and physics; economics in those days was largely an undergraduate discipline and not taught in schools. WGS gave its boys an unapologetically traditional education, preparing them for university and the professions, but the outside world was kept largely at arm's length. One of King's near contemporaries dared to suggest in an essay that Chairman Mao's Cultural Revolution, then unfolding in China, might allow it eventually to industrialise and become a global superpower; he found himself having to explain his Communist sympathies to the unimpressed headmaster. Like many schools of its time and traditions, the rigid curriculum

taught in WGS's classrooms was offset by an unbridled enthusiasm for sport – the winter terms meant rugby, while the summer
was devoted to cricket. Cricket remained King's real forte and he
successfully captained one of the school's teams. To this day, he
remains intensely proud of a particular match against Shrewsbury
School in the summer of 1965, when he took seven wickets before
lunch. Out of school, he would often take the Midland Red bus
to Worcestershire County Cricket Club (of which he is now
patron), in nearby Worcester. There, he could watch his heroes
Tom Graveney, a superb batsman and useful wrist spinner, and
Basil D'Oliveira, an all-rounder who found himself at the centre
of controversy over his inclusion in the England team's 1968 tour
of his native South Africa. In September 1963, King and his father
made a rare trip to London to watch the final of the Gillette
Cup, a hard-fought county cricket tournament, at Lord's Cricket
Ground. His beloved Worcestershire took on Sussex and although
Sussex won, by fourteen runs, Norman Gifford, another of King's
favourite players, was named Player of the Match. King had the
schoolboy's knack for remembering cricket statistics and was still
able to rattle off details of the old Worcestershire team forty years
later, when Henry Blofeld invited him into the BBC's *Test Match
Special* commentary box.

Wolverhampton in the 1960s still retained the air of a prosperous market town, its citizens' fortunes built upon the industry of
companies such as Goodyear, Sunbeam and Norton-Villiers. The
monstrous Mander and Wulfrun shopping centres, which would
largely obliterate its old centre, were still on the city planners'
drawing boards and countless small shops such as Craddocks,
Arthur Dodd & Co. and Tweedies ('Sports and Camping
Equipment, Scout and Guide Depot') lined the streets. Trolley
buses in green and cream livery completed a Betjemanesque
scene of a respectable, hardworking and plain-speaking corner

of England. It bred what King has called 'a sense of independence and self-reliance'.[75] The dramatic industrial landscape made a strong impression on King: 'As a boy, I remember the short train trip from Wolverhampton to Birmingham, through the heart of the Black Country, as a journey through manufacturing history. The flames from the blast furnaces lit up the grey sky on winter afternoons.'[76]

Politically, Wolverhampton was very much the domain of Enoch Powell, the firebrand Conservative MP for Wolverhampton South West, a seat he won in the 1950 general election and which he was to hold until 1974. King would have been nine years old in January 1958 when Powell sensationally resigned his post as Financial Secretary to the Treasury – deputy to the Chancellor of the Exchequer – along with the Chancellor himself, Peter Thorneycroft, in protest at the Macmillan government's increased public spending plans. Powell was re-elected at the October 1959 general election and remained a force to be reckoned with in Edward Heath's Conservative Shadow Cabinet until 1964. Powell's views on the economy – essentially monetarist (before that term was coined) and advocating disinflation and the freedom of the market – gathered momentum over the following years. As King grew up in Wolverhampton, he would have seen the headlines generated by Powell's electioneering and observed the debate around his enthusiasm for the free market and his prescient call for the privatisation of the Post Office and the telephone network.

In his final year at WGS, the teenage King considered his choices for further education and, indeed, a career. By this time, he had developed a strong interest in cosmology, but undergraduate courses in celestial matters were few and far between. Instead, he chose a more traditional route, applying successfully to King's College, Cambridge, to read mathematics. He matriculated there in October 1966 and joined his fellow freshmen in their first meetings with tutors, as well as attending the customary Freshers' Fair and social events such as the 'college squashes'. Notwithstanding the 'Coming-up Dance' in the city's Victoria Ballroom, it was still an almost entirely male world: the first female fellow of King's was not elected until 1970 and female students did not arrive until two years after that. Despite the all-male population and the heavy traditions of formal dinners in Hall, at which undergraduates were required to wear their black gowns, the atmosphere at King's was enlightened. It was meritocratic, with an unusually high number of students from selective state schools, and even iconoclastic. According to the late Professor Tony Judt, who was Mervyn King's exact contemporary at the college, 'King's [College] prided itself on the enthusiasm with which it embraced change and radical disruption.'[77] Perhaps sensing there was more to life here than the mathematics tripos, King embraced change himself and sought out the college fellows to request a switch to economics. It was a subject which the college, as the *alma mater* of John Maynard Keynes, took particular pride in. It was suitably selective about its undergraduates. Permission was granted, however, and King embarked on his new economics course; it was an academic discipline he immediately took to.

There was no shortage of inspiration. While Keynes himself had died in 1946, the great man's students and collaborators were still much in evidence at King's. Among them was Professor Richard Kahn, the economist who devised the concept of the 'multiplier' – the measure of the change in one variable caused by the change in another – which became a founding principle of macroeconomics. Kahn's lectures – and the 'secret seminar' held each Monday in his rooms for the most talented economists – were well attended; King later recalled that one of his 'vivid recollections as a student in Cambridge … was listening to the late Lord Kahn … trying to alert us to the dangers of "creeping inflation"'.[78] Alongside Kahn were younger men such as Professor Brian Reddaway, who had been taught by both Kahn and Keynes and who was now director of the Department of Applied Economics, where King was eventually to find a postgraduate perch. Reddaway had worked briefly at the Bank of England and travelled widely in Russia and Australia before applying himself to academic life. At Cambridge, Reddaway found a talented but relaxed department (one contemporary recalled that '[he] used to say ironically that we academics needed to stick up for the 40-hour year'[79]). He encouraged his research team to focus on the effects of foreign investment on the British economy and, with the appointment of Nicholas Kaldor as Professor of Economics at King's College in 1966, on taxation. Kaldor, a Hungarian by birth, came with the dust of Downing Street on his boots, having been economics adviser to Harold Wilson's Labour government. The effects of Kaldor's so-called selective employment tax – a tax on the employment of those in the service industries – were to occupy so much of Reddaway's time from 1966 onwards that, according to a friend, 'he doubted his remaining working life would be long enough'.[80] In the event, the tax was abolished by Edward Heath's incoming Conservative government in 1970 (and replaced with VAT). While the relationship between academe and public policy was never an easy one, there was no doubting the influence of this generation of Cambridge economists. Kahn, Reddaway, Kaldor and the legendary Richard 'Dick' Stone, a professor of finance and accounting and a future Nobel laureate, took both Keynes's legacy and their own innovations forward at breakneck speed, securing Cambridge's position at the forefront of new economic thinking.

This cosmopolitan and intellectually stimulating environment suited King perfectly. He was, by all accounts, a model student. Tony Judt recalled that as his undergraduate career developed King would come to be regarded as 'the most promising economist of our generation'.[81] There were few diversions from King's lectures and economics books, but there was the odd foray into the wider university world. He was active in student politics, joining the Cambridge University Liberal Club and becoming its junior treasurer for the Lent and Easter terms in 1968. The club, known as CULC, had been founded in 1886, with William Gladstone as its external president, and counted Keynes and Bertrand Russell among its early members. In King's day, it continued to be a serious forum for political debate with a strong following in the university and there was considerable competition for its offices: the undergraduate presidency lasted only a single term. In his role as junior treasurer, King's responsibility was to manage the club's day-to-day accounts, which would then be consolidated for the senior treasurer – John Derry, a history don at Downing College – to check and sign off.

Then as now, political societies at Cambridge attracted a steady stream of MPs and government ministers to their speaker meetings. King would have had a hand in organising such visits, from the likes of Michael Winstanley, Liberal MP for Cheadle and a GP who complemented his political career with numerous appearances as a television and radio doctor in the 1960s. There were also numerous club discussions with suitably solemn agendas: in November 1967, for example, a CULC policy meeting discussed 'a range of topics, including: aviation; civil service reform; David Steel; drugs; Europe; House of Lords reform; immigration; population; Rhodesia; wasteful expenditure'.

While the majority of undergraduate politics was a civilised affair, allowing the students to make useful contacts and secure postgraduate work, Cambridge was not immune to growing restlessness among the student population. In March 1968, when Denis Healey, then Defence Minister, came to Cambridge to give a speech, there was a large protest against the Vietnam War and scuffles between left- and right-wing students. Two years later, in February 1970, shortly after King had graduated, there was the notorious Garden House Hotel Riot, in which undergraduates stormed a Cambridge hotel where an exiled Greek politician was to speak. There were ugly scenes, a dozen arrests and a full-blown trial before Mr Justice Melford Stevenson (a noted disciplinarian whose country home rejoiced in the name 'Truncheons'). Six students were sentenced to terms of imprisonment, which were upheld despite an appeal.

King took no part in such riotous assemblies, focusing instead on his academic work, which his college took for granted would be of the highest standard. He graduated in June 1969 with First Class honours. Cambridge clearly suited him and by the time of his graduation he had already secured a postgraduate position as a junior research officer at the university's Department of Applied Economics. His work there was largely focused on the Cambridge Growth Project (CGP), one of its most prestigious programmes. The CGP had been founded in 1960 by Richard Stone and Alan Brown, a fellow Cambridge economist. Their ambition, simply put, was to build a model of the British economy which would allow the relationships between its production and expenditure to be calculated using different scenarios and forecasts. This endeavour was to continue until the late 1980s and the model became both huge – with no less than 5,686 variables – and hugely influential. It was also practical, allowing economists to assess how the economy might look in, say, ten years' time based on growth rates of the past ten. Stone had been given a fellowship at King's College along with his professorship and it was here that Mervyn King first encountered him. King seized the opportunity to work with Stone on the CGP, which had, by 1969, grown into a group comprising a dozen economists. Brown had by then left the CGP to take up a professorship in Bristol, but Stone continued to run the project with great vigour. King was one of five new recruits to bolster the CGP's research effort and he found himself working in a team of talented young economists, particularly those concerned with econometrics who were taking the first steps in developing computer-based economic models. Among his colleagues were Angus Deaton and David Livesey, who went on to become distinguished academics, and Lucy Slater, one of the university's most formidable mathematicians. Deaton later recalled the highly charged atmosphere of the department's tea room, which became the forum for impassioned debate among giants, such as Kaldor, and postgraduates alike:

> Although much of the discussion flew over my head, I picked up a lot, including just how much there was to know. One notable lesson was the breadth of economics; many different positions were held in that room, often well-thought through and eloquently defended in what could be a cacophonous and even bitter debate ... Kaldor's intelligence, wit, eloquence, and deep knowledge of economics shone brilliantly in a group where none of those qualities were in short supply. He was the best debater I have ever heard, but his dismissals and arguments could wound, no less so for their wittincss and the merriment that they provoked. The tea-room atmosphere did not favour those with a limited taste for this sort of thing.[82]

Besides his argumentative colleagues at the CGP, King mixed with a steady flow of visitors to the Cambridge Economics Faculty. One formative encounter was with a young Frenchman called Jean-Claude Trichet, a recent graduate of the elite Ecole Nationale d'Administration and an Inspecteur adjoint des Finances in France's Ministry of Finance. Trichet was on a fact-finding trip to Britain to study its taxation methods (including capital gains tax, which President Georges Pompidou was bent on introducing in France). During his visit to Cambridge to interview Professor Nicholas Kaldor, Trichet met King amid the splendours of St John's College. The two young economists struck up a friendship which has endured throughout their careers. (Forty years on, shortly after stepping down as president of the European Central Bank, Trichet retains vivid memories of the 'intellectual excellence'[83] of St John's, as well as King's hospitality and the college's superior claret and port.)

King's association with the CGP continued to a greater or lesser degree until 1977, but it also allowed him the flexibility to pursue other interests. In 1971, he applied for and won a place at Harvard University as a Kennedy Scholar, which involved spending a year at the university to pursue further research. The Kennedy Scholarship programme had been initiated in 1964 as a continuing memorial to the assassinated American President and involved the dispatch to Harvard and to the Massachusetts Institute of Technology (MIT) of around ten scholars each year. King's cohort for the 1971–1972 academic year included Peter Hennessy, who had spent his undergraduate years at St John's College, Cambridge, and who was to become one of King's closest friends and confidants. The gaggle of young graduates congregated in a hotel in Euston, in central London, before the flight to Boston, excited not only by, in most cases, their first trip to the United States, but also that they had a relatively free rein and a very generous allowance for the year ahead.

Although as older graduates on a visiting programme, King and his fellow Kennedy Scholars were out of the mainstream of Harvard's student population, they witnessed the venerable university at its most radical and liberated. Doubtless King's mind was on higher things, but he cannot have failed to notice some of the activities vividly described by one American contemporary from the Class of '72, Kenneth E. Reeves (who went on to become mayor of Cambridge, Massachusetts), interviewed in the *Harvard Crimson* in June 1997:

> It was the proverbial best and worst of times. The best included the freedom that being a Harvard undergraduate offered – reasonable housing, relatively accessible professors and tutors, all within close range of greater Boston and its attractions. Harvard Square transformed its staid self into a virtual carnival of hippies, druggies, politicos, panhandlers and townies curious to watch it all … American society actually experienced a sea change while we were undergraduates. Music exploded from Motown to the Beatles and Laura Nyro to Sly. Recreational pot, hashish, uppers, downers and hallucinogens were part of campus reality. Not everyone drugged but most drank something and cigarette smoking was an acceptable social activity. Adult-like sex was now quite available as well and there was much discussion about 'free love', communal living [and] black separatist states.

Perhaps anxious to leave this extraordinary bacchanal behind for a few weeks, King set off to travel further into America with Christopher Peacocke, a friend and one of his fellow Kennedy Scholars, in the summer of 1972. Arriving in Las Vegas, they spent a happy few days and nights sampling its seedy delights. Although Peacocke did not gamble, King's mathematical talents were suitably tested on the slot machines and the blackjack and roulette tables. The pair decided against taking in a concert by Elvis Presley, then at the height of his fame and packing in the crowds at the Las Vegas Hilton with 'An American Trilogy' and 'Burning Love'; sadly, there was to be no meeting between King and The King. Instead, the two students hired a beige Oldsmobile and sped off on a two-week road trip across the Nevada desert and

into Arizona, taking in the vast, scorched landscapes and precipi-
tous canyons of the national parks. With King at the wheel, they
covered many hundreds of miles of open road and had time to
talk. Peacocke, who was also deeply interested in economics,
recalls a spirited but serious-minded King who was unapologetically ambitious, particularly to get his work published (he had
already had seen articles appear in the *Review of Economic Studies*
and contributed a memorandum to a House of Commons' Select
Committee). He was upset on a rare occasion when the editor of a
periodical declined to publish an article he had submitted. King's
background and very British education had made their mark on
his character and, although he was delighted by America – he later
said he found the experience 'intellectually liberating and exhila-
rating'[84] – he was adamant that his future lay in Britain and that
it was there he would build an academic career. As yet, however,
there was no desire to seek public office: Peacocke was left in no
doubt that King's ambitions lay in economic theory, rather than
its practical application in central banking, let alone in the new
financial services industries which were beginning to take shape.

When King returned to Cambridge in the autumn, he was
able to resume his association with the Department of Applied
Economics as a 'research officer' (one up from 'junior research
officer'). He was also elected to a fellowship at St John's College,
strengthening his relationship with that college and giving him a
base from which to teach and to seek new opportunities. Although
his financial situation would have been eased by a modest fellow's
stipend as well as a brace of scholarships – the hard-won Wrenbury
Scholarship and a senior scholarship from King's – there were few
luxuries in his digs. He later recalled having a 'tiny record player'
on which he would play a disc of Edith Piaf singing 'Non, je
ne regrette rien'. Piaf's throaty rendition made a deep impression
on King:

There was something haunting about the way she sings it. In many ways it's her life story ... The self-confidence, the self-confidence that she does, is willing to follow her own choices. She doesn't regret anything. She will carry on. She believes in herself, even if the world has not believed in her for very long.[85]

King's own future depended entirely on his own academic achievements and his continued appetite for hard work. Luck also played a part. Shortly after his return from the United States, he heard about the launch of a new think tank, in the form of the Institute for Fiscal Studies (IFS), which was to supplement his work at St John's College. While he continued to anchor himself at the university, the IFS provided King with a springboard into a much more cosmopolitan world, peopled by London financiers and businessmen, as well as a refreshing antidote to the left-wing politics of the Cambridge Economics Faculty, which, according to his friends, King had begun to find deeply frustrating.

The IFS was the brainchild of four businessmen – Nils Taube, Will Hopper, Bob Buist and John Chown – who were united in vehement opposition to the 1965 Finance Act and to its passage onto the statute book. The Act had its genesis in a speech by James Callaghan, the then Chancellor of the Exchequer, in which he described sweeping changes to the tax system, including the intro-duction of capital gains and corporation taxes. Taube, a young stockbroker at Kitcat & Aitken who went on to forge a legendary reputation as a fund manager, asked Chown, a Cambridge econo-mist and tax specialist, to review the Callaghan speech. Chown reported that 'the same half-baked proposals were rehashed in the Budget Speech, and the Finance Bill, when published, read as if the draftsman had simply been given the Callaghan speech and been told to turn it into legislation.'

Taube and his colleagues toyed with formalising their *ad hoc* activities. In 1967, they convened at the Bell, a hotel in the bucolic Buckinghamshire village of Aston Clinton, to discuss a more formal collaboration. Some months later, in July 1968, they met again, at the Stella Alpina restaurant in North Audley Street, in London's Mayfair, where they made the final decision to found an economics research institute. The IFS was incorporated in May 1969 and Taube suggested that Dick (now Lord) Taverne QC, who had been Financial Secretary to the Treasury in the Chancellorship of Roy Jenkins, should be its first director. Taverne was enthusiastic:

> The idea of this institute appealed to me immensely. [As Financial Secretary under Jenkins] I had become acutely aware of the lack of tax expertise outside the Inland Revenue, as it then was. The Revenue seemed to have a virtual monopoly of specialist knowledge and could demonstrate beyond argument that any major reform of the system suggested by outsiders was impossible on technical or administrative grounds. What was clearly needed was a kind of 'shadow' Inland Revenue and Treasury.[86]

From the beginning, the IFS had ambitious plans, not only to publish research and hold the Inland Revenue and the Treasury to account, but to change the UK's fiscal strategy. Above all, it sought to rationalise what it saw as a chaotic and ramshackle tax system, patched together by politicians and bureaucrats. Funding came relatively easily. Its four founders canvassed sympathetic solicitors and accountants and companies such as Marks and Spencer to provide financial support.

The IFS spent its first couple of years laying the foundations of a council, led by Sir Richard Powell, recruiting staff and forging links with potential supporters. In 1974, it came up with what Taverne referred to as 'our big idea' – a committee to look at the

UK's entire tax system. Partly inspired by the Carter Commission, which had conducted similar enquiries in Canada, the committee provided a focus for the IFS's energies and promised to put it on the map. In 1975, therefore, it commissioned James Meade, Emeritus Professor of Political Economy at Cambridge, to 'take a fundamental look at the UK tax structure'. Taverne recalled the genesis of the project:

> In retrospect we were almost recklessly ambitious. Soon after the committee was set up, James Meade, that wonderful man who was an inspirational chairman and who wrote most of the report himself, said to me 'Now that I have thought about what I have undertaken, I am appalled and overwhelmed by the enormity of the task you have given me. I am over seventy, you know.'[87]

The committee assembled by Meade required a staff of suitably qualified researchers and assistants. Taverne recalled:

> Another factor [in the success of the committee] was our prescience in our choice of members, especially the three young economic advisers, later made full members of the committee. The original two were John Flemming (later chief economist at the Bank of England) and a very young Mervyn King, whom I knew well and for whom I had a very high regard. Mervyn recommended another very young economist, an Oxford don, John Kay, who looked about sixteen years old.[88]

Both King and Kay were, in fact, twenty-seven. King's recommendation of Kay cemented a friendship which was also to become a longstanding professional association. Kay was something of a *Wunderkind*, having been appointed to a permanent teaching post at Oxford University and a concomitant fellowship at St John's

College at the tender age of twenty-one. He had spent his six years at Oxford busily building an academic career and working on his first book, *Concentration in Modern Industry*. King's introduction to the IFS was fortuitous, as Kay eventually became the institute's director.

In October 1975, Meade appointed King, Kay, Flemming and Graeme Macdonald, a lecturer in tax law at the University of Kent, as his 'research secretaries'[89] and mapped out the project, which would occupy them for the best part of two years. Meade referred to the group as his 'Young Turks' and encouraged them to think and debate among themselves. King found it fascinating, reflecting later that the project 'proved to be one of the formative experiences of my professional career'.[90] As he began his work with the group, King could also take pride in the publication of his first book, *Indexing for Inflation*, a collection of essays about indexation (the process whereby an index is applied to payments to protect them from inflation) which he co-edited with Thelma Liesner, the IFS's research director, and which was published by Heinemann.

By summer of 1977, with the Meade report's committee reaching its final conclusions, King was able to look around him. By now he had been elevated to a lecturership at the Economics Faculty in Cambridge, a stepping stone to a long-term academic career at the university. King's reputation was bolstered by the publication of *Public Policy and the Corporation*, a book he completed in 1976 and which was published by Chapman and Hall in January 1977. He was also in demand by the Press and wrote articles for a catholic array of newspapers, from the *Financial Times* to *The Guardian*. There was time, too, to participate in the CLARE Group, an influential society of middle-of-the-road economists formed by Professor Robin Matthews, master of Clare College, Cambridge (the group's name, it was said, was also an acronym for 'Cambridge, London and the Rest of England').

Despite his coveted position at St John's and the steady stream of invitations from the Cambridge economics elite, King was restless for a wider platform and perhaps a more progressive environment. An opportunity presented itself in 1977, when he received an offer from Birmingham University to hold its Esmée Fairbairn Chair of Investment, a position which would make King, at twenty-nine, the youngest person ever to hold a professorial chair in Britain. Making a decision which, according to his colleagues, was accompanied by much soul-searching, he decided to return to the West Midlands. He said his farewells in Cambridge – St John's College did not forget him, awarding him an honorary fellowship twenty years later – and took up his new position in October 1977.

A few months after his arrival at Birmingham, in early 1978, the newly anointed Professor King had the pleasure of seeing the Meade report – technically, *The Structure and Reform of Direct Taxation* – in published form. His name appeared on the list of the final membership of the committee. The report was a *succès d'estime*. Taverne later noted that its publication 'was met with all the respect and deference due to a major Royal Commission. In fact, it was often thought to be a Royal Commission. The *Financial Times* devoted page after page to its analysis.' Further plaudits flowed, not least to Meade, who was shortly to receive the Nobel Prize for Economics – a signal honour which was, in fact, awarded for his work on trade, although American President Jimmy Carter sent him a congratulatory telegram saying that the prize was richly deserved 'for your work on tax'.

None of this did Meade's team, including King, any harm at all. As the Meade report was heaped with praise, the young professor must have been something of a celebrity in the corridors of the Economics Department at Birmingham. Taverne was clear, however, that it had been King's friend John Kay who had made the 'most important academic contribution after James Meade'. Taverne recalled that there were a series of public seminars following the report's publication, at which 'James Meade consistently answered difficult questions by saying "I think John Kay should answer this one."'

If there was any professional rivalry between King and Kay, it did not prevent their next collaboration. Kay secured a contract with Oxford University Press, which published *The British Tax System* in 1978, with both their names on the cover. The book, a lucid exposition of the intricacies of tax aimed principally at a student readership, was a productive way for the two young men to build on the work they had done with Meade, and for King in particular to further his reputation as a tax specialist.

At Birmingham, King applied himself to academic life, which in the late 1970s was still very much measured out in terms of getting published in the appropriate journals, building a reputation in the lecture rooms and delivering carefully crafted papers to conferences of fellow academics. King's focus remained on taxation and he made the subject his own over the next few years, lecturing and publishing widely. He also brought his American contacts to bear on the department. In early 1979, King was contacted by Martin Feldstein, a distinguished economist and president of the National Bureau of Economic Research, who suggested that King's book *Public Policy and the Corporation* might provide an approach to compare tax systems in several different countries. The idea eventually found expression in *The Taxation of Income from Capital*, which King co-edited with Don Fullerton, an economics professor at Princeton University. The book, which took five years to complete, compared the taxation of income from capital in the United States, the United Kingdom, Sweden and West Germany. It brought together leading economists from those countries, as well as John Flemming, King's youthful colleague at the IFS, who was now installed at the Bank of England. The well-funded project also allowed King to travel, occasionally exchanging Birmingham for Cambridge, Massachusetts, Stockholm and Munich to discuss the progress of the book with his contributors. In 1982, he was back at Harvard University, where a new generation of clean-living students was busy preparing for careers on Wall Street, as a visiting professor of economics. The following year King continued this role in a return to the Massachusetts Institute of Technology. It was here that he met Ben Bernanke, then an assistant professor. The two young economists formed a friendship which has continued throughout their careers, as King progressed through the Bank of England and Bernanke climbed the ladder to the top of the Federal Reserve.

King's *Taxation of Income from Capital* was finally published in April 1984, sealing his reputation both at Birmingham and further afield. By the autumn of that year, he was being courted by the London School of Economics, which beckoned him to London to discuss taking up the post of Professor of Economics. It was too prestigious a role to refuse and one he was eventually to hold for a full decade. King said his farewells to his colleagues at Birmingham, packed up his books and headed back to the capital.

In 1984, the LSE was mourning the death of Lord (Lionel) Robbins, one of its founding fathers who died that year, but his name would have largely been lost on the students whom King encountered there. More fresh in their minds was Ralph Dahrendorf, the charismatic outgoing director, who stepped down in 1984, and its new one, Indraprasad Gordhanbhai Patel, universally known as I. G. Patel. Dr Patel arrived in London from a term as Governor of the Reserve Bank of India and was to enhance hugely the LSE's reach and reputation in Asia.

Arriving at the LSE's Holborn campus, King found a kindred spirit in a new colleague, Charles Goodhart. Goodhart was an urbane Old Etonian, who had taken a first in economics at Cambridge and made his career at the LSE, where he was a lecturer in monetary economics. He had also formed a close association with the Bank of England, which had begun in 1969 and which was to burgeon in the 1980s and 1990s, when he became chief adviser to the Bank and, with King's blessing, an external member of its nascent Monetary Policy Committee from 1997 to 2000.

In the first years of King's tenure at the LSE, he and Goodhart formed something of a professional partnership, manifested as the Financial Markets Group (FMG). Its formation was partly driven by the seismic changes taking place in the City of London. October 1986 witnessed the City's 'Big Bang', when many of its anachronistic practices were swept aside, making way for modern stockbroking, investment banking and a new breed of financial entrepreneur. Big Bang did away with the distinction between jobbers and brokers (market-makers and traders) and allowed foreign ownership of stockbroking houses, notably without the formal consent of the Bank of England. It also ended the monopoly enjoyed by so-called discount houses over the issuance of government securities. Alongside these changes, the traditional floor-based share-trading on the London Stock Exchange was replaced by a screen-based system. The coda to these upheavals was that, within ten years, barely any of the British merchant banks or securities houses remained in British hands. Americans, largely, sounded the death knell for what had been known as 'gentlemanly capitalism' and laid the foundations for London's role as an international financial centre.

King and Goodhart's Financial Markets Group at the LSE, was, therefore, a creature very much of its time. The body, conceived in 1986 and run under the chairmanship of David Walker, a former Treasury mandarin and at this point a director of the Bank of

England, was designed to help close the yawning gap between the LSE and the City, which was charging headlong at the global market. The group's mandate was to produce 'real-world' research and analysis. Goodhart took the revolutionary step of installing a Reuters terminal so that the group's students could study the market in real time. They sat hunched over the flickering green screen, watching the fluctuations of the markets, even noticing how they subsided when traders in Japan departed for lunch. One FMG alumnus recalled the stern admonition not to use the terminal's 'TRADE' button, in case anyone was tempted to do so. Gradually, King and Goodhart built up a team of data-hungry students, who spent long hours crunching numbers to produce ever more expansive models. Many were later recruited by City investment banks as their first wave of quantitative analysts – so-called 'quants' – who were much in demand for their mathematical and modelling skills and who, ironically, were the architects of many of the exotic derivative instruments which so ensnared the financial world in years to come. Economic data, rather than theory, were very much in the ascendant and King brought his statistician's mind to bear on them with great effect. Richard Shepro, a contemporary at the LSE, remembers King being in his element. He was, according to Shepro, 'a brilliant young man with an astonishing amount of energy; always on the move'.

King clearly enjoyed the interaction with his colleagues and students at the LSE and found the atmosphere intellectually stimulating. On one occasion, his students were surprised to see him sitting in on a lecture by Roger Guesnerie, a visiting French academic, on the economic characteristics and 'equilibria' of sunspots. The LSE also provided King with a public profile, particularly at Budget time, when his meticulously prepared analysis would be disseminated to the City and the media at short notice.

Few of King's peers – and even fewer of his students – at the LSE expected him to leave academe, but the FMG became a stepping stone to the outside world. The Bank of England was an obvious possible destination and King had already heard a great deal about its inner workings from Goodhart and from his old IFS friend John Flemming. Flemming had enjoyed a rapid rise at the Bank, becoming chief economic adviser in 1980 and, after eight years' service, an executive director. He may well have had a hand in encouraging Robin Leigh-Pemberton, the Bank's then Governor, to extend an invitation to King to join the Bank. This duly occurred in March 1990, when King was appointed a non-executive director, a part-time role which would allow him to get to know the institution – and *vice versa*. It did not take long. In the early spring of 1991, Flemming was recruited to be the founding chief economist for European Bank for Reconstruction and Development, which had recently set up shop in London, leaving a large gap at the Bank. King was an obvious choice to fill it.

The opportunity had perhaps come sooner than King had anticipated. He seems to have hesitated, seeking out his old friend and Las Vegas road trip companion Christopher Peacocke to discuss whether to join the Bank full time. They sat for over an hour in a café in Holborn as King laid out the pros and cons. He was forty-two and at a critical point in his academic career, with perhaps a return to Cambridge and a professorship there within his sights. In the final analysis, however, the prestigious role at the Bank seemed too good an opportunity to let go. King negotiated an extended sabbatical with the LSE (which subsequently regarded him as technically 'on leave' from 1991 to 1995) and accepted the Bank's offer.

King still had misgivings about abandoning academe, saying that he regarded his role at the Bank as an 'interesting secondment' from the LSE rather than a permanent break. Little did he realise when he reported for duty in Threadneedle Street as the Bank's new chief economist on the morning of 1 March 1991, that he was beginning a career there which would span more than twenty years.

On his arrival at the Bank that March morning King found a rather hangdog economics team in its far-flung Economics Division, known as 'ED'. The department was lost in the labyrinthine corridors of the Bank, in rooms described by one of its historians, Anthony Hotson, as 'a route march away from the Bank's leadership on the ground floor and only one lift stop away from Premises Division in its fifth floor garret'.[91] Squirrelled away as it was, the Economics Division was largely ignored by the government officials it was supposed to advise in advance of the monthly meetings between the Governor and the Chancellor. Nevertheless, there were talented staff there, including Lionel Price, head of the division. Price, who had joined the Bank in 1967 armed with the obligatory economics degree from Cambridge, got on well with King and the two men formed a good working relationship, which was partly directed towards recruiting a new corps of highly qualified young economists. Together, they laid the first foundations of King's 'modern bank', which started to emerge in the early 1990s and to gather pace in the later years of the decade as independence for the Bank became a reality. Price decided to leave the Bank at the crucial moment, in 1997, after thirty years in Threadneedle Street, to join Fitch Ratings as its chief economist, but he was instrumental in the crusade, as a former colleague puts it, 'to make economics the language of the Bank'. While this doctrine had its supporters, others questioned what they saw as a retreat into academic isolation, with the Bank populated by theoretical economists who were, in Walter Bagehot's phrase, 'like astronomers who have never seen the stars'.

King had chosen an interesting moment to start at the Bank. In 1991, Robin Leigh-Pemberton, the Bank's patrician Governor of eight years' standing, was grappling with what became known as 'the small banks crisis'. Britain's small and medium-sized banks faced mounting pressures from the effects of recession, as borrowers struggled to service their debts, and from dwindling wholesale deposits. The announcement on 5 July that the Bank of England was closing the Bank of Credit and Commerce International (BCCI) for suspected fraud – an imbroglio which lasted for many years – did nothing to shore up confidence in the sector. At one time, the Bank had forty small banks under close surveillance, helping some secure long-term funding but also assisting with winding down those which were failing. The gravity of the situation was reflected in the decision, in mid-1991, to embark upon a programme of emergency liquidity support. This was made by the Bank with the government's knowledge but without a government guarantee. As an anonymous author of a Bank report noted later: 'The operation was not without risk to the Bank. It had to make provisions in respect of the indemnities it gave in relation to the small number of banks that received support. These reached a maximum of £115 million in 1993.'[92] Overall, in the early 1990s, some twenty-five small banks failed; one, the National Mortgage Bank, became insolvent and was ultimately acquired by the Bank for one pound. It was a banking crisis which, in retrospect, was all the more striking for its parallels with events which were to unfold in 2007 and 2008.

King would have had little involvement in the minutiae of the rescue package for these small banks. But he took a more central role a year later, during the late summer of 1992, when Britain's participation in the Exchange Rate Mechanism (ERM) began to unravel. Britain had joined the ERM in October 1990, but not before much wrangling and bitterness in the Conservative government's ranks. Nigel Lawson had resigned as Chancellor over the matter a year earlier, leaving John Major to carry out the project, which was predicated on sterling tracking other European currencies – above all, the mighty Deutschmark – within a 6 per cent band, effectively harnessing Britain's monetary policy to those of its European fellows. Britain entered the ERM at DM2.95 to the pound, but was soon being squeezed by the effects of high interest rates in Germany and a falling US dollar. Political events compounded economic pressures. In the spring of 1992, when Denmark rejected the Maastricht Treaty in a referendum, foreign exchange traders smelt blood and descended on the weak currencies. The prospect of another vote – this time by the French in the coming September – caused further disquiet in the currency markets. Before July, sterling was reasonably secure within its wide ERM band, but by August the Bank of England was 'seriously alarmed'[93] by its steepening decline. It saw the makings of a crisis:

> Given the present market sentiment towards both dollar and sterling, it must be questionable whether we can carry on even until 20 September [the French vote on Maastricht] with our current operational stance, without getting sufficiently close to limit down against the D[eutsch]M[ark] for official determination to defend the parity to be put completely on the line.[94]

Further, it noted that it faced, effectively, a game of 'chicken' with the currency markets:

> If we failed to devote considerable efforts to the defence of the [DM 2.80 level, the markets] would conclude that we were content for the DM/£ rate to move to the point of obligatory intervention, and might well decide that we were inviting them to test the extent of our determination to support at that

point. Were that battle to be joined, the potential offerings of sterling could substantially exceed our present gross exchange reserves.[95]

The Bank found this dangerous prospect acutely distasteful. It proposed stepping up the rate of its 'covert'[96] interventions – buying sterling to prop up the currency – before moving to 'overt'[97] interventions and, if necessary, a programme of foreign currency borrowing. The other heavy weapon in the government's arsenal was to raise interest rates and Major and Norman Lamont, the Chancellor of the Exchequer, duly lifted them to 10 per cent. They also authorised the Bank of England to purchase billions of pounds worth of sterling. In the second half of August, the Bank conducted more than $1bn worth of its covert support operation (which it managed to smuggle past most market participants and the media) and on 26 August, it moved to an overt programme, buying about £1bn of sterling, backing up a statement by Lamont that Britain would not devalue or leave the ERM.

By the beginning of the week of 14 September, however, none of these measures had managed to stem sterling's apparently inexorable decline. At the Bank, King played his own part in the drama of that week. That Monday morning he was in Frankfurt to interview the Bundesbank. He arrived at its monolithic headquarters in the middle of a suitably Wagnerian thunderstorm, complete with flashes of lightning, and was admitted into the presence of Otmar Issing, one of the German central bank's most senior figures (and a man with whom King would eventually become great friends). Against the background of a rapidly depreciating pound, King laid out the Bank's arguments as to why an exchange rate of DM2.95 – the core and original target – was appropriate and why the link between the Deutschmark and the pound should be maintained: 'I presented my arguments to Otmar with the aid of many coloured charts. He listened carefully but, at the end, he looked at me and said "Mr King, a good answer, pity it's the wrong question."[98]

King admitted defeat. Later he was to reflect that the question should have been 'dictated by the theory', in other words whether the level of short-term interest rates appropriate to Germany at that time was similarly appropriate to the United Kingdom. A despondent King returned to London, to brief the Governor and his other senior colleagues. There was worse to come in the ERM saga, however. During the evening of Tuesday 15 September, the news wires carried early reports of an interview with Helmut Schlesinger, the president of the Bundesbank, conducted by *Handelsblatt*, the German financial newspaper:

> Schlesinger does not rule out the possibility that, even after the realignment and the cut in German interest rates, one or two currencies could come under pressure before the referendum in France. He conceded in an interview that the problems are of course not solved completely by the measures taken.

In the interview, Professor Schlesinger was said to cast doubt over whether the ERM could hold together. The implication that sterling might follow the Italian lira, which had recently suffered the ignominious fate of a forced devaluation, was clear. Fearing a cataclysm when the markets opened the next morning, the Bank of England telephoned the Bundesbank to request a retraction. The Bundesbank's hastily issued statement said: 'The text was not authorised. [Schlesinger] did not say that, and it was not what he intended to say.'

The markets were unconvinced. The next morning, Wednesday 16 – thereafter, 'Black Wednesday' – the Bank felt the full force of their opprobrium. One Bank official told a British newspaper:

'This generation at the Bank had never seen anything like it. It was as if an avalanche was coming at us.'[99] That day, it made further 'huge'[100] interventions in sterling's defence, with its net reserves (which had stood at $26.6bn in early August) falling by a massive $27.71bn, to a negative position of -$15.34bn. For its part, the government raised interest rates from 10 to 12 per cent in a last-ditch attempt to persuade investors to buy sterling. Even the prospect of a further rate rise, to a dizzying 15 per cent, failed to stop the currency's slide and by 7 p.m., after a series of emergency meetings, Norman Lamont announced that Britain would exit the ERM altogether. (The pound duly plummeted from the bottom of its band at DM2.78 to DM2.50 by the end of September). King's excursion to Frankfurt was lost in the maelstrom, although he was later to reflect that it led 'many commentators to describe the trip as the least successful diplomatic mission in history'.[101]

Besides the bruised egos and shattered political reputations, there was a financial price to pay for the ERM debacle. The Bank lost some £800m on its reserves operations in August and September 1992 and put the 'opportunity cost' of its interventions in the currency markets on sterling's behalf at £2.4bn. In the subsequent weeks, the Bank scrambled to rebuild its reserves and to readjust the 'large currency composition imbalances'[102] which had occurred.

The Bank struggled back to its feet. For King, the drama of Britain's exit from the ERM had been a salutary introduction to the harsh realities of central banking and, outside the Bank's own walls, the pack instinct which prevailed in increasingly global markets. He would doubtless have taken note of the Bank's strategy in dealing with the crisis, notably its use of covert operations, which came to the fore again in 2008.

There were less frenetic moments for the Bank's new chief economist. One of the first of King's initiatives to bear fruit was the wider dissemination of the Bank's quarterly *Inflation Report*, which had first appeared in February 1993. It was timely: since Britain's dramatic exit from the ERM the previous September, the Conservative government had directed its monetary policy towards achieving an explicit inflation target, initially in the range of 1–4 per cent and then of 2.5 per cent or less. With the advent of the new inflation-targeting regime, the Bank's *Inflation Report* had two objectives: first, to assess inflation in the UK – in King's phrase, 'everything you wanted to know about inflation but were afraid to ask'; second, to stimulate debate and build the Bank's reputation as an authority on the subject. King described it as 'a *commentary* on the consequences of decisions taken by Government',[103] later to become, in his carefully weighed words, 'an *explanation* of decisions taken by the Monetary Policy Committee'. In its early years, there was something of a buzz about the report, not least because it did seem rather to hold the government to account. Its first public edition, hot off the press at 5.30 p.m., was rushed to bookshops around Britain and put on sale at £4 a copy (today, ironically, it is just £3). Perhaps unsurprisingly, the public's initial enthusiasm for such forensic analysis of inflation metrics waned and they stopped queuing for it. Before long the *Inflation Report* was relegated to the Bank's website. Nevertheless, it gave a certain profile to King – now editor of the school magazine, as it were – and his fellow economists at the Bank. It has also proved long lived and continues to be published, pored over by City analysts, if not by the general public.

£££

King's work at the Bank kept him there for long hours and there were few distractions from the outside world. He did, however, stay in touch with the Kennedy Memorial Trust, which administers the Kennedy Scholarships, and where he had been a trustee since 1990. In the mid-1990s, while he was busily occupied as the Bank's chief economist, King was prevailed upon to lend the trust his financial expertise. On 22 June 1995, King became a director of J.F.K. Investments Limited, which had first been incorporated at Clifford's Inn back in 1967. The management of the company, which existed, according to the trust, 'to underwrite securities', was entrusted to Barings Bank but it had a board drawn from the trustees.

Generally the Bank frowns on such extra-curricular business activities; indeed, the staff handbook states that 'permission will not normally be granted for a member of staff to become a director of a trading company, which can give rise to a range of financial, legal and reputational risks.'[104] Technically, J.F.K. Investments had become dormant in 1994, a year before King's appointment, and, as such, was not 'trading'.

Nevertheless, there were comings and goings on J.F.K.'s board. King's fellow directors included Simon Webley, who had taken the directorship of J.F.K. himself three years earlier, in June 1992. Webley had read economics at Trinity College, Dublin, in the 1950s, before joining Reed International, the paper and publishing company. His stint at Reed instilled an interest in business ethics, which became his passion. In 1971, he instigated Britain's first survey of businessmen's professional and moral conduct, the results of which were published as *An Enquiry into Some Aspects of British Businessmen's Behaviour*. Since those heady days, Webley has forged a career out of business ethics, taking in a decade-long fellowship at the City (now Cass) Business School, and is today research director of the Institute of Business Ethics, in London. In October 1995, Webley and King were joined on the Board by Peter Hennessy, King's old friend from Cambridge, who had carved a successful career as a journalist, historian and academic (and who was raised to the peerage as Baron Hennessy of Nympsfield in 2010). Hennessy had become close to King and the Governor's speeches are littered with compliments to Hennessy's many books and newspaper articles on Whitehall and the dark arts of government.

Sadly, J.F.K.'s principal documents – abbreviated accounts and a mournful record of the company's eventual dissolution in July 1997 – are silent on this triumvirate's activities and there is no indication of whether it was successful on behalf of the Kennedy Memorial Trust. The only other party to the enterprise was its company secretary, Anna Mason. When she was not taking the minutes of J.F.K. Investments' board meetings, Mrs Mason was the wife of the then vicar of All Saints, Maldon, in Essex, and is recorded as being resident at All Saints' Vicarage, in Church Walk. For King, it was a modest and solitary foray into the commercial world, something he was clearly not tempted to pursue further. He has, however, continued his long association with the Kennedy Memorial Trust, where he now acts as patron.

£££

While King's time as the Bank's chief economist had its moments, it was not until the mid-1990s that it seemed he might have a long-term future there, possibly even as its Governor. The next five years were to be formative, as he developed a working relationship with Eddie George in the Bank. King's meticulous attention to detail and academic rigour complemented George's more statesmanlike, top-down and smoke-wreathed view of the world. King perhaps also saw an opportunity to exploit the gradual thawing in the Bank's relations with the outside world. In October 1996, King made a particularly finely honed speech, given for the Economic and Social Research Council's Annual Lecture, in

London. It reaffirmed his position as the Bank's chief economist, but also communicated that he was, at forty-eight, at the top of his game. The speech – 'Monetary Stability: Rhyme or Reason' – was a defence of price stability as the *sine qua non* of a successful stewardship of Britain's economy. Wide-ranging and worldly, it was something of a personal best for King. After five and half years in Threadneedle Street, he had become the consummate central banker and thoroughly at ease with the ebb and flow of monetary policy:

> Suppose that we were to stroll the few yards from this room down to the Embankment and to imagine that the price level was represented by the height of water in the River Thames. Variations in wind and weather lead to changes in the height of the water. In 1800 the Thames was approximately eight feet deep. Between then and 1914, the prevailing economic weather led to movements in the height of the inflationary river. For most of the time the water depth was between five and seven feet, and was never less than four feet and never more than ten feet. Even under the stormy conditions of two world wars and the inflation and subsequent deflation of the inter-war period, the water depth never moved outside of a range of six to thirteen feet, and by 1945 was ten feet, only a little above the level in 1800. But from 1945 we have been out of our depth. The flood tide of price rises has led to the latest wave registering a depth of well over 200 feet, enough to swamp any craft that did not anticipate the impending inflation.[105]

King's speech, reproduced in the Bank's subsequent *Quarterly Bulletin*, marked a further rung on the ladder to the top. By the time King took up his appointment as the Bank's second deputy governor in 1998, it began to seem a distinct possibility that he might succeed George as Governor.

Few other candidates emerged in these years. David Clementi, the Bank's other deputy governor, posed little threat. An accountant and investment banker, Clementi had risen through the ranks of Arthur Andersen and Kleinwort Benson, where he had advised Margaret Thatcher's government on privatisations including that of British Telecom. He had joined the Bank in 1997 after Howard Davies's departure for the FSA and acted as a steadying influence as it set out on its independent course. Clementi served the Bank diligently, if quietly. He made the required number of speeches, often in self-deprecating tones – 'Having arrived at the Bank over three years ago, I am often asked what I actually do there'[106] – and maintained gentlemanly links with the City in his role as overseer of financial stability. But his work at the Bank preparing for Britain's possible entry into the single currency came to nothing. His one moment in the limelight occurred in 2002, when he warned the Treasury Select Committee that he expected a dramatic fall in house prices, given that house price inflation – which was running at over 18 per cent – was unsustainable. He told the committee: 'It is a moment for considerable caution for both those borrowing and those doing the lending.' He was, of course, proved correct. Clementi bowed out in August 2002, at the end of his five-year term, and headed back to the private sector. If he had ever harboured ambitions to become Governor, he had not displayed them; in the end, by all accounts, he found the Bank a frustrating and bureaucratic place. He was replaced by Sir Andrew Large, who was cut from the same cloth and suffered more or less the same fate. A banker and regulator by profession, he joined the Bank from Barclays, where he had been deputy chairman. Ultimately, he did not serve a full term, announcing his resignation and, again, a swift return to the private sector, after just three and a half years.

Both Clementi and Large were, to some extent, casualties of the dramatic shift in the Bank's centre of gravity since 1997. With banking supervision dispatched to the FSA, the Bank's interest in any form of regulation had dissipated and the role of those who remained with responsibility for financial stability was much diminished. The supremacy of monetary policy and the MPC was complete. Clementi observed the arrival of King's cohorts of economists rather like a Christian noting the increasing number of lions in a Roman amphitheatre: 'We have needed to increase the analytical capacity of the Bank, in part by additional recruitment of economists. Indeed we are among the largest employers of professional economists in the country.'[107]

This was, of course, Mervyn King's domain, and an increasingly powerful one. His colleagues observed King's ascendancy with interest. As he grew into his role of deputy governor, there were some bruising encounters, particularly with those who were used to the mostly affable rule of Eddie George. 'Eddie liked a good argument and he didn't mind losing; you could go back and argue with him again,' recalls one former colleague of both men. 'With Mervyn, absolutely not. He was always absolutely convinced of his position. If you argued against him, you were cast out as a naughty boy.' Equally, King had little time for subjects which he did not feel were relevant. A colleague recalls how a young analyst making a presentation on the Spanish banking sector, for example, was asked impatiently 'how is this relevant?' King would leave the distinct impression that he was wasting his time: 'He could make someone feel pretty stupid.'

£££

In the summer of 2003, as King's accession drew closer, there were valedictions to be said for Eddie George. He had been at the Bank for forty-one years, seen it change out of all recognition and was leaving it in relatively good shape, basking in the reflected glory of a thirty-year low in inflation. It had been a long and bumpy road to get there, however. In an interview with *The Observer*, George was diplomatic about his relations with his Chancellors, but acknowledged that Britain's ejection from the ERM had been a low point – 'a pretty grim moment'[108] – and he still shuddered at memories of the collapse of BCCI and Barings. But equally he derived great satisfaction at having contributed to Britain's economic 'stability', his great watchword. In retirement, George was to become chairman of the board of governors of Dulwich College, his *alma mater*, but in the tradition of the Bank's previous governors, he withdrew from the public eye: 'I have no intention of spending my retirement as a politician ... It is not for an appointed central banker to pontificate on retirement.'[109]

On 18 June 2003, George attended his last Lord Mayor's Banquet, at the Mansion House, as Governor. Gordon Brown, the Chancellor of the Exchequer, paid a warm tribute to his tenure of the Bank. The blistering telephone calls and threats of resignation in May 1997 were forgotten as Brown recalled 'from my own personal experience that Eddie not only enthusiastically promoted and welcomed the independence of the Bank of England after 1997, but he supervised the creation of the monetary policy committee [and] chaired its proceedings with great distinction'.[110] George had both influenced and presided over one of greatest moments in the history of the Bank, although the bargain struck with New Labour had also cost it dearly. Nevertheless, George left Threadneedle Street with his reputation for, as Brown put it, 'steadfastness at all times' and 'unshakeable integrity' intact. In his own farewell speech, George was characteristically modest, noting that his retirement was simply 'the transition from *Who's Who* to *Who's He?*'.[111] He concluded by wishing his successor Mervyn King well. George would be a hard, not to mention steady, act to follow.

PART II

THE 'MA WAY'

'There is almost always some hesitation when a Governor begins to reign. He is Prime Minister of the Bank Cabinet; and when so important a functionary changes, naturally much else changes, too.'
Walter Bagehot, Lombard Street, *1873*

Mervyn King took possession of the Governor's Office early on the morning of Tuesday 1 July 2003. Colleagues who had bade him goodnight the previous evening as 'Mervyn' or 'Mr King' were now required to call him 'Mr Governor'. King showed no inclination to end the tradition. His new quarters were suitably grand, retaining a large, square writing desk and a set of chairs designed by Sir John Soane, and with such lofty ceilings that King had its acoustic specially altered to reduce the echo. A heavy eighteenth-century oil by William Marlow – *View of Ludgate Street from Ludgate Hill* – hangs on one wall. French windows open onto the Garden Court, which has at its centre a bronze statue of St Christopher, by Reginald Goulden, unveiled in 1921 as a memorial to the Great War. This plot, once the graveyard of the church of St Christopher-le-Stocks, is very much the Governor's garden – other staff are admitted only on special occasions. In the summer, under the shade of a quartet of mulberry trees (the origins of paper money), he can talk privately to his guests. Altogether, the setting is magnificent, sombre and designed to reflect a complex hierarchy, with the Governor very much at the centre of things. As Anthony Hotson, a former Bank economist, recalled:

> Whereas the upper echelons of most organizations commandeer the higher floors of buildings, the offices of the Bank seem to have been modelled on a Renaissance palace. The offices of the Governors are at ground level and can be seen across the garden courtyard as you enter the front of the building. Directors and valued advisers are granted offices on either side of the Governors' with views over the courtyard, an inner sanctum known as the Parlours. The traditional operating arms of the Bank – Chief Cashier's office, Banking Department and Issue Office – were housed close to the Parlours and at ground level, providing easy access for market practitioners. The second floor, more accurately the piano nobile, was taken up with the Court room, other key meeting rooms and the Governors' dining room. Thereafter status traditionally declined with distance from the Parlours.[112]

Amid these calm and rarefied surroundings, King set about his work, creating his vision of a modern Bank of England. It was designed to maintain, even enhance, the Bank's status but to bring it into the twenty-first century as the very model of a modern central bank. It was, however, a very personal and, as it turned out, idiosyncratic vision. While there was a generous dollop of McKinsey-style 'change management', organisation charts and best practice, King's own character was also stamped heavily on the plans. The Bank's old guard of 'lifers' would soon be replaced by bright young economists, traders and risk managers from far-flung universities and business schools. In the Governor's Office, there was still 1950s West Midlands grit in the air. Many of his colleagues quickly recognised that his style of government would be authoritarian – one has described it as being 'by fiat' – and couched in plain-speaking terms.

While he prepared to roll out his grand design for the Bank, the new Governor allowed himself time for reflection on the singular achievement of the boy from the Black Country – the place, in his poignant words, 'where it all began'.[113] There was something of a victory tour: King's first official visits as Governor were not to Washington to visit the Federal Reserve or to Frankfurt to call on the European Central Bank, but to Wolverhampton and Wakefield. In July, a month after his first day in his new role, he was in the West Midlands visiting Beatties, the department store operator, Worcestershire Cricket Ground and Wolverhampton and Dudley Breweries. Six weeks later, he was in West Yorkshire meeting a Wakefield shirt manufacturer and Timothy Taylor, another brewer. There was time, too, for a nostalgic trip to Old Town Primary School, perched on its windswept moor and last seen forty-five years before. King presented the schoolchildren with three copies of Kenneth Grahame's *The Wind in the Willows* (Grahame was, famously, an alumnus of the Bank of England, where he had a somewhat chequered career) and answered their questions about whether what remained of the gold in the Bank's underground vaults was indeed real.

King also made time to keep up with his passion for cricket and football. That same summer, he was invited onto BBC Radio's *Test Match Special*, a programme dear to his heart. In relaxed mood, King patiently explained the intricacies of his new job to Henry Blofeld (a fellow undergraduate, if not graduate, of King's College, Cambridge) and elaborated a little on his interests outside the Bank. The Governor was asked whom he would pick as his perfect dinner party guests. He chose Zhou Enlai – the first

Premier of the People's Republic of China – Che Guevara and
Catherine Deneuve, the French film star:

> Zhou Enlai – he led China and China is now turning into a
> market economy. What does he think of it? Che Guevara – did
> you know he was a central bank governor? I would [like] to know
> what he thought about his time as a central bank governor. Then,
> probably to lighten it and to get onto more artistic and intellec-
> tual topics, Catherine Deneuve is someone I have always wanted
> to meet. She would be splendid.[114]

This was all good public relations – and perhaps the first time any
Governor of the Bank of England has admitted to a weakness for a
sultry French film actress – and allowed King to present a human
face to his 'new' Bank of England. King also maintained his close
links with Aston Villa, the club he has supported since childhood.
In high office, his devotion to the club led to enduring friend-
ships with Doug Ellis, its former chairman, and with some of its
leading players. One such was Thomas Hitzlsperger, a talented
German midfielder who played for the club from 2002 to 2005,
subsequently joining VfB Stuttgart and then West Ham. Shortly
after leaving Aston Villa, Hitzlsperger told a Sunday newspaper
about his long conversations with the Governor:

> We talked a little about football because that is his passion and
> I would ask him questions about his business. I would question
> him when the Bank published its quarterly inflation reports or
> its monthly interest rates. He is very busy so I went down to the
> Bank of England to see him a few times or would meet up with
> him after games at Villa Park. I didn't try to give him any advice.
> After all, he didn't try and tell me how to play football.[115]

Back in Threadneedle Street, apart from the odd visit from Hitzlsperger, the Governor's diary was full of meetings to push forward a restructuring of the institution bequeathed him by Eddie George. King started his reforms at the very top. First, he 'suggested'[116] that there should be separation between chairing the Bank's board and running the day-to-day business. From now on, matters which would previously have been directed to the Court, the Bank's governing body, would stop first at NedCo – the committee of non-executive directors – with the Court's executive members and other officials present by invitation. Having made this 'small but significant'[117] change in the Bank's governance, King embarked on what he described as 'a fundamental review of the Bank's Strategy and Objectives'.[118] While he reaffirmed the Bank's commitment to its first two core purposes – monetary policy and financial stability – he declared time on its third: maintaining the efficiency and effectiveness of the financial system: 'while the Bank may from time to time wish to support particular initiatives in the financial sector, we have concluded that the possibility of doing so should not in itself be a core purpose.'[119]

With the Bank's core tasks pruned back, nobody at the Bank was left in any doubt as to the supremacy of monetary policy. This was to be its *raison d'être*, tacitly agreed by the Treasury, which had tasked the new Governor to mould a 'small' Bank out of the old-fashioned behemoth with a tight focus on monetary policy rather than financial regulation. With this principle firmly established, King took a scythe to the Bank's management structure, removing senior committees and layers of what David Clementi referred to as its 'formidable hierarchy'.[120] The Governor then gathered his most loyal cohorts around him, in the form of a new Executive Team – soon, simply 'ET', which gave rise to the inevitable filmic jokes. It rapidly took on the character of a praetorian guard.

King's own promotion to Governor had created a vacancy for a deputy governor to oversee monetary policy; this plum job, albeit one very much in King's shadow, went to Rachel Lomax, a civil servant whose curriculum vitae was filled with stints at several government departments, including the Treasury. She was the Bank's first ever female deputy governor, which immediately presented her colleagues with the problem of how she should be addressed. Should she be 'Mrs Deputy Governor', following the convention accorded to her male predecessors? After much solemn discussion, much to her own amusement, it was decided she would be simply 'Mrs Lomax'. Alongside Lomax sat Sir Andrew Large, who continued blamelessly in his role as deputy governor responsible for financial stability. The two deputies were joined by six others to form the Executive Team: Charlie Bean (head of the Monetary Policy Division), Nigel Jenkinson (his counterpart in Financial Stability) Paul Tucker (Markets), Andrew Bailey (Banking Services), John Footman (Central Services) and, finally, Alastair Clark, King's most trusted ally who enjoyed the title 'adviser to the Governor'.

This inner circle had a satellite of three further advisers to the Governor: Professor Charles Goodhart, King's former colleague from the London School of Economics; Michael Glover, a lawyer who headed the Bank's legal unit; finally, Professor Mario Blejer, a former head of Argentina's central bank and a man for whom, in central banking terms, there were few surprises.

The new configuration at the top of the Bank was observed with interest and a sense of foreboding down in the ranks. It was exacerbated by an overhaul of the Bank's staff handbook – a sure sign of trouble ahead. In his foreword, the Governor advised his colleagues that 'this is a challenging environment, but one which offers many opportunities. I hope it is also great fun.' He encouraged them to read the Bank's newly minted mission statement, no doubt courtesy of McKinsey, which outlined its 'Values'. They were listed as 'Commitment to public service', 'Trust and integrity', 'Pursuit of excellence' and 'Co-operation and teamwork'.

Despite these high ideals, the next few years were to be difficult ones and the Bank's metamorphosis came at a price. Departments were unceremoniously closed or reshuffled and scores of staff faced redundancy. In December 2004, the Bank's Registrar's Department, which had been part of the institution since its foundation in 1694, was closed and its functions 'successfully moved to a new service provider'. Another notable casualty of King's strategy review was the Co-ordination Division for Europe, which was responsible for the Bank's relations with the European System of Central Banks (ESCB), the European Commission and other EU institutions. Ostensibly, the reason the axe fell on this division was that Britain's entry into the euro was deemed increasingly unlikely and its role in preparing for such an eventuality had become obsolete. Nevertheless, all its other activities, principally building bridges between the Bank and its European counterparts, which might have proved useful in, say, 2011, were swept away in the process. News of the redundancies was doled out unceremoniously to employees in the Bank's canteen. Staff members recalled the surreal experience of having to wade through their tearful colleagues, surrounded by boxes of paper handkerchiefs, in order to get their lunch. Scenes such as these were unheard of – and undreamt of – at the Bank. For generations, it had fostered a paternalistic and familial spirit which had in turn engendered the idea of 'a job for life', including the ability to move between departments and retrain into another role, virtually on request. An overhaul was no doubt long overdue, but the Bank's staff were ill prepared for its scale, let alone the sight of 'family men being reduced to tears', as one employee put it.

There was a raft of other changes to the Bank's *modus operandi*, which extended even to its physical appearance. Wherever possible, open-plan offices were constructed out of the old-fashioned warrens which had hidden the Bank's inner workings. There was a flurry of building work, a great tearing down of walls, and with it a dismantling of small but jealously guarded empires. Once these improvements had been carried out and modern lighting installed, much of the antique furniture looked out of place. In the autumn of 2003, a man from Christie's, the auctioneer, was summoned to cast an eye over the heavy mahogany partners' desks, leather-upholstered dining chairs, secretaire bookcases and coatstands. Each bore a Bank inventory number and the patina of years of Bank history. Nearly 300 lots appeared in the subsequent sale at Christie's, in July 2004, raising a modest £266,000. The Bank used the money to put towards the upkeep of its better antiques, which were spared the purge and allowed to remain *in situ*. The changes wrought at the Bank's headquarters were mirrored by those at one of its most venerable outposts. Its printing works in Debden, Essex, which employed 250 people, had its fate sealed when the contract to print a billion sterling notes each year was awarded to De La Rue, the banknote printing company, which subsequently acquired the Bank's entire operation for £10m. Even the Bank's three-man design team which produced the intricate designs under the famous promise 'to pay the bearer on demand' eventually departed.

There were more technical reforms to be accomplished, in the interests of the Bank's key customers, those banks which held reserve accounts, used to handle payment transactions which might amount to billions of pounds each day. On the day he took office in July 2003, King spoke to Paul Tucker about a much-needed overhaul of the Bank's sterling money market operations, which would make it, in King's words, 'very much simpler and [have] much less volatility in the overnight rate'.[121]

In essence, the system King had inherited was causing glitches in the Bank's daily open-market operations – known as 'OMOs'. The Bank regularly made OMO loans to the dozen or so sterling settlement banks in the City of London which were required to hold positive overnight balances with the Bank; if they became overdrawn they incurred a penalty rate. But often these loans, which allowed the Bank to 'square' its system, ended up carrying a different rate from the MPC's Bank Rate – hence the reference to undesirable 'volatility'. King and Tucker formulated a new, simpler system – the 'reserves averaging scheme' – in which the Bank's bank customers agreed to hold positive balances with it on an average basis, the average being calculated over the period from one monthly MPC meeting to the next. In addition, for the first time in its history, the Bank would pay a modest amount of interest on these banks' so-called 'voluntary reserves'. These and associated changes to the Bank's Sterling Monetary Framework Operations were to take a full three years, being finally completed in May 2006.

King did not get everything his own way during his first years as Governor, however. On 10 December 2003, the Bank implemented Gordon Brown's diktat that henceforth the Bank's inflation target should be 2.0 per cent and be based on the Consumer Prices Index (CPI), rather than the historic target of 2.5 per cent based on the Retail Prices Index (RPIX). CPI, which had been hastily renamed that same month from the rather less snappy Harmonised Index of Consumer Prices (HICP), differed from the RPIX measure largely in that it excluded the costs of council tax and of owner-occupied housing (RPIX included these but excluded mortgage interest payments). While the index and the target changed, the requirement for the Governor to write an open letter to the Chancellor if inflation reached 1 per cent either side of the target remained in place. Brown had, in fact, intended to make the change from RPIX to CPI at the same time as ceding the power to set interest rates to the Bank in May 1997, but declined to do so then, fearing it might 'disrupt the new system'[122] and create uncertainty. When the change was finally visited upon the Bank nearly five years later, the Governor did little to conceal his distaste for new measure, the implied meddling by No. 11 and the enormous communications task it had presented the Bank with. The potential 'presentational difficulties'[123] noted by King derived from the fact that, historically, the old RPIX had been above the Bank's 2.5 per cent target and was expected to remain so for the coming two years – the MPC's preferred forecasting window. The new measure of CPI, on the other hand, showed a gap on the downside: the CPI measure was 1.3 per cent in November 2003. So a vote anytime soon by the MPC to raise interest rates in such an apparently low-inflation environment might look decidedly odd. The Bank put a brave face on the conundrum, wearily reminding the markets and the publicly of the need to focus on a two-year horizon in which the effect of the MPC's decisions should be weighed. As for the new CPI measure, King's later comment that 'we weren't terribly enthusiastic about it'[124] was as close as he came to publicly criticising the change, but it contributed to the gradual decline in his relationship with Brown, who was still only halfway through his marathon ten-year stretch as Chancellor.

£££

While King completed his initial pruning of the Bank's straggling tendrils, one matter sat obstinately in his in-tray, refusing to go away. This was the continuing saga of litigation between the Bank and the creditors of BCCI, the bank which had collapsed in 1991 and whose demise had dogged the Bank, its regulator, ever since. There was more than a whiff of *Jarndyce and Jarndyce* about the case, in its complexity, longevity and the fact that, for the Bank, at least, it had become a monumental bore. There were a few moments of high drama, but many more of great tedium. The brief history was that the Bank of Credit and Commerce International had been founded in 1972 by Agha Hasan Abedi, an Indian who carved a career in banking in Pakistan (and who was unkindly described by one Bank official as 'the living personification of Uriah Heep'). BCCI grew rapidly to become one of the world's largest private banks. In 1980, it received a banking licence from the Bank of England and set about opening dozens of branches in Britain. Over the next decade, it attracted many wealthy depositors but also aroused the suspicions of regulators in numerous jurisdictions. By 1991, its operations in Britain concerned the Bank of England enough for Robin Leigh-Pemberton, the then Governor, to commission the so-called 'Sandstorm report' from Price Waterhouse, the accountancy firm. Among other discoveries, some of which found their way into the newspapers, Price Waterhouse found that the bank had links with the Abu Nidal terrorist network.

In July 1991, regulators successfully applied for a court order in Luxembourg to put BCCI into liquidation. Accordingly, the bank's offices in five countries were shut down, leaving over a million depositors stranded. Amid the wreckage, it seemed that the bank had been running rings around its regulators, including the Bank of England. In 1992, the then Chancellor of the Exchequer, John Major, announced the Bingham inquiry into the Bank of England's supervision of BCCI; the inquiry duly reported later that year. It fell to Paul Tucker to head the Bank's Bingham inquiry Unit, which fed into Bingham's work. Sensationally, the inquiry prompted Deloitte & Touche, BCCI's liquidators, to launch a 'misfeasance' case, against the Bank of England, alleging wilful misconduct. The proceedings, brought on behalf of around 6,500 of BCCI's British creditors, claimed that twenty-two named officials of the Bank had neglected their duty of supervision. The creditors sought £850m in damages. Although this claim was struck out in 1997 and Deloitte's appeal dismissed the following year, the BCCI affair refused to go away. In 2001, the House of Lords ruled that the issue of 'misfeasance in public office' must be heard at trial.

The Bank of England was not accustomed to being sued; indeed, it was unprecedented in its 300-year history. Worse, the BCCI creditors' action challenged its statutory immunity. It was a heavy blow for the Bank, which vehemently denied any wrongdoing, and a huge distraction for its new Governor. It was all the more galling for King as it rehashed all the tribulations of the Bank's banking supervision operations at a time when they were becoming a happily distant memory.

In January 2004, when the trial came before Mr Justice Tomlinson sitting in the High Court, it exposed the Bank to the full glare of publicity. Billed as a 'mega-trial', it involved no fewer than three QCs for each side, with Gordon Pollock QC leading for Deloitte & Touche and Nicholas Stadlen QC leading for the Bank. Dozens of other junior barristers and solicitors trailed in their wake. Court 73 was packed with a battery of computer and video screens. A stack of over 200 lever arch files, containing countless thousands of Bank and BCCI documents, was piled up between the two legal teams; it soon became known as 'The Berlin Wall'.

It was a trial of suitably grand proportions. Mr Pollock's opening statement lasted a total of seventy-nine days, the longest in English legal history. In his first few remarks, he laid out his case against the 'once-revered institution' of the Bank. His principal argument was that the Bank of England's banking supervisors knew that BCCI was corrupt but declined to investigate it or close down what was 'an unsupervised monster on the loose'. Pollock brandished documents which allegedly showed that the Bank's head of banking supervision was at pains not to assume responsibility for BCCI because it would be 'massively inconvenient', while another junior official, who later left the Bank in exasperation, warned that BCCI 'should have been strangled at birth'.

When Mr Stadlen finally got his chance to speak for the Bank it was July. He told the Court that there was 'a fundamental thread of implausibility running like a faultline' through the liquidators' case and mocked Pollock's 'wildly exaggerated definition' of the tort of misfeasance. Stadlen noted that the test in proving misfeasance was having a 'wilful disregard as to a serious risk of loss' and contended that Deloitte & Touche's case fell woefully short of proving this. Turning to the question of the twenty-two Bank officials' alleged failings, he said: 'The idea that these twenty-two people, independent of each other, hit upon this wicked and disgraceful conduct is fanciful.'

After a summer break, the court reconvened in late September and Stadlen continued with his opening submissions, taking them to a total of 119 days – a new record, smashing Pollock's. It was not until June 2005, therefore, that a weary but determined Bank called Brian Quinn, head of banking supervision at the time of BCCI's collapse, as its first witness. Quinn, who had since become chairman of Celtic Football Club, was asked to answer the accusations of his 'deliberately misleading, deceiving and concealing information' from the Bank's governors in the years running up to BCCI's collapse. Quinn told the court: 'Mistakes get made but I did not lie and did not deceive, and to say that is to misunderstand the culture of the Bank.' In September, the Bank called its second witness, Peter Cooke, who had been Quinn's predecessor and the man responsible for granting BCCI its original banking licence. As

Cooke's cross-examination proceeded, it also emerged that Deloitte had made three attempts to settle the case, all of which had been batted away by the Bank. The Bank was resolute: 'We have always made it clear that there would be no deal and no negotiations.'

On 2 November, as Cooke prepared to face a further day of cross-examination, Deloitte & Touche's team suddenly announced that its clients were discontinuing the action. The longest and most expensive trial in English legal history collapsed like a pack of cards. For Mervyn King, who was sitting at the back of the court that day, it was a moment of triumph. His legal team was equally victorious. In a statement prepared for such an eventuality, Stadlen said: 'It is time for the spotlight to shift to the other side of the court and for scrutiny to be brought to bear on the manner in which this hopeless case has been prolonged, long after its utter hopelessness was apparent for all to see.' Hopelessness had a price, of course, and the Bank's legal costs, comprising its solicitor Freshfields' fees for its own small army of lawyers and the instruction of three silks and three junior barristers, came in at £73.6m, plus £1.7m in interest. The other side duly paid up.

The more-or-less final chapter in the BCCI case came in April 2006, when Mr Justice Tomlinson delivered his 86-page written judgement. It exonerated the Bank and its employees. Tomlinson summed up as follows:

I became so concerned about the case that I decided both to consult and to warn the Lord Chief Justice about it. I told the Lord Chief Justice, then Lord Woolf, that the case was a farce … I told the Lord Chief Justice that the case as it was being pursued before me bore little or no relation to that which the House of Lords had considered fit to proceed to trial. I warned the Lord Chief Justice that the case had the capacity to damage the reputation of our legal system.

Tomlinson allowed himself some post-mortems, which gave an indication of the frustrations of the case:

> Although the Liquidators also provided a considerable volume of disclosure, the Bank quickly took the view that this was very largely useless, both in terms of its relevance to the case and the impenetrably poor way in which it had been listed and disclosed ... Indeed, one of our assistants memorably looked into one box of disclosure to find that it only contained a broken chair leg [extract from a letter from the defendant's solicitors dated 17 November 2005].
>
> Mr Pollock was only infrequently rude to me and I ignored it. Not everything said by Mr Pollock is intended to be taken seriously and sometimes his offensive remarks are the product of a well-intentioned but ill-judged attempt to lighten the mood.

He added:

> Mr Pollock's sustained rudeness to his opponent was of an altogether different order. It was behaviour not in the usual tradition of the Bar and it was inappropriate and distracting. I should have done more to attempt to control it, although I doubt if I should have been any more successful than evidently were Mr Pollock's colleagues whom on at any rate one occasion I invited to attempt to exercise some restraining influence. Whether this is a ground upon which an award of indemnity costs should be considered I do not need to decide.

To King's huge relief, the matter was finally closed. His splendidly irritable final word on the matter, appended to the Bank's press release on the day of Tomlinson's judgment, was: 'The Judge's words speak for themselves. It doesn't need any further comment from me.'

£££

Outside the Bank, business was booming, fuelled by what King referred to as 'a decade of unparalleled stability of both growth and inflation'.[125] The City, which enjoyed famously 'light touch' regulation, attracted a raft of overseas banks and other financial institutions (among them, Lehman Brothers, the American investment bank, which set up shop in Canary Wharf beneath a plaque unveiled by Gordon Brown). Indeed, in its first decade, the Monetary Policy Committee operated in an environment of 2.8 per cent annual economic growth and did not witness a single quarter of negative growth. It performed, outwardly at least, like a well-oiled machine: the average deviation of inflation from its central target was just minus 0.08 per cent.

The all-powerful committee continued to be the hub of much of the Bank's activities and to attract a cadre of distinguished economists. But some were unimpressed by the Bank's heavy weaponry and its generals. One such was Professor David Blanchflower, an economist at Dartmouth College, New Hampshire, who had become well known as a specialist in the economics of 'happiness'. Appointed to the MPC in June 2006, he became decidedly unhappy with the methodology behind the Bank's quarterly economic prognoses:

> Governor Mervyn King controlled the hiring and firing of the fore-cast team, who did his bidding. They had to produce a result that was consistent with King's views, or else they would be history … King always emphasised the importance of top-down judgements, which means you can just make stuff up as you go along. Worryingly, this was often only loosely based on the workings of the real world. Such glorified guesswork operated reasonably well during the boom years, but failed miserably when the recession hit.[126]

The Governor continued to rule more or less absolutely. As King's changes worked their way through Threadneedle Street, the cleverest among his immediate circle realised that in order to get anything past him, in the words of one colleague, 'you had to pretend it was subordinated to monetary policy.' If an idea was mooted, it was often framed in terms of being supportive of the MPC's work or contiguous to it. Anything which appeared remotely connected with financial regulation would be batted away impatiently. Even King's closest allies sometimes found it difficult to contain their exasperation.

There was something of a reshuffle at the top of the Bank in October 2005, when Sir Andrew Large, deputy governor with responsibility for financial stability, headed for the exit, citing his desire to return to the private sector. King wrote to Gordon Brown, with his suggestions for a replacement for Large. The Governor tactfully reminded the Chancellor that the Bank 'is now a smaller and much more focussed organisation'[127] than it was before 1997 and that the new deputy governor needed to wear three hats: those of deputy governor, member of the MPC and senior manager. King's list of candidates was divided into three: 'private sector, public sector and "imaginative candidates"'.[128] The list has not come down to us, but Brown evidently plumped for the second category. The role was taken by Sir John Gieve, a civil servant, who brought a certain amount of baggage with him from the Home Office, where he had been Permanent Secretary and served three Home Secretaries (Jack Straw, David Blunkett and Charles Clarke) within the space of five years. It had not been an altogether happy time and after Gieve's departure, in January 2006, the National Audit Office had sensationally declined to sign off the Home Office's accounts. Gieve found the Bank a different proposition, but not without its own challenges.

Although the Bank was enjoying relative 'peacetime' in the

years 2003 to 2007, it did at least go through the motions of planning for 'war', whether it might come from a terrorist threat or from a financial crisis. After the attacks on the World Trade Center, in New York, on September 11 2001 (when the Bank drew on an emergency $30bn swap line from the Federal Reserve to allow UK banks to settle their US dollar transactions) it had overhauled its security measures. The Bank instituted, among other things, a secure, web-based 'chatroom' in which it could talk to its counterparts at the Treasury, the FSA and to major financial institutions when other communication channels were closed. The chatroom was activated, for example, on the day of the terrorist bombings in London on 7 July 2005.

Three months later, in October 2005, the Bank carried out a number of 'war games' or crisis scenario tests with its Tripartite colleagues, up to deputy level. The exercise identified weaknesses in the legislative framework for failing banks – in other words, who would have ultimate responsibility for rescuing them *in extremis*. In the same year, King told the *Financial Times* that in November 2004 the Bank had come across a situation where 'there could be a problem in a particular institution which isn't terribly big, which may for completely unpredictable reasons turn out to pose a liquidity problem to a very big institution'.

While this institution was never identified and it did not seem to trouble the Bank unduly, nevertheless, by late 2006, the weaknesses in the legislation it had identified had been escalated into 'key issues' and classed as 'urgent' by the Treasury. There were further crisis scenario 'war games' and King later noted that 'at the end of that exercise Callum McCarthy, myself, Ed Balls as Government Minister and Treasury officials, all agreed that a key part of the future work programme was to work on these issues, and that programme was indeed put in place.'

Part of that 'programme' was the responsibility of the Bank's grandly named Financial Crisis Management Division, part of its Financial Stability arm, which was headed by Ian Bond, a Bank 'lifer' with 30 years' experience in Threadneedle Street. It was Bond who led a British Bankers' Association workshop at Pinners Hall, in the City of London, on 26 October 2006, which gave an interesting insight into the Bank's preparedness for 'a bank-specific crisis'.

Bond told his audience that 'we take a resolutely tripartite approach to crisis management in the UK: central bank, regulator and government (in the form of the Treasury) all have roles to play. But they are distinct roles, and need to be clearly understood by all parties so that there is no confusion "on the day" about who is responsible for what.'[129]

He went on to rehearse the various responsibilities of the Tripartite authorities and then to outline what would 'actually happen' in the event of a bank-specific crisis. Support operations for a failing bank could be selectively employed, with each of the Tripartite authorities feeding their assessments into the Treasury and, ultimately, to the Chancellor. It would be a collaborative effort, with information shared 'freely'. The system would encourage better decisions 'and it is likely to be clearer, after the event, why they were taken and whether the advice was reasonable, given what was known at the time'.[130]

On a practical note, Bond made mention of two particular initiatives at the Bank. First was the 'factbooks project' – databooks about financial institutions which the Bank intended to share with the Treasury and the FSA: 'The idea of assembling key information in advance, and being open about what additional information might be called for "on the day", has obvious attractions. That is what factbooks are all about: they are a tool for mobilising and sharing information quickly between the Tripartite authorities.' Second was the Bank's new money market arrangements and, specifically, the standing facilities which could offer unlimited capacity to borrow from the Bank 'and so make the provision of emergency liquidity much more straightforward'.[131] Bond concluded: 'That should reduce the risk of a short-term liquidity problem developing into a full-blown crisis.'[132]

At the end of Bond's workshop, chatting over coffee and biscuits, the participants would have certainly felt reassured that the Bank's Financial Crisis Management Division was a force to be reckoned with. From Bond's description, it resembled nothing so much as a fire crew in a constant state of readiness for what might happen 'on the day'. But the reality was rather different. The day, as it turned out, was closer than Bond and his colleagues in Threadneedle Street imagined. And all the Bank's preparations came, in the end, to nothing.

THE LONG RUN

Chairman (John McFall MP): *'Is there anything that keeps you up at night and makes you rush for the Rennies?'*
Hector Sants: *'I think we should always be focused on issues, but, as I have said, I do not think there is one thing that is particularly keeping me up at night at the moment in the context of this discussion.'*
Chairman: *'What about you, Jon?'*
Jon Cunliffe: *'Nothing.'*
Chairman: *'What about you, Sir John?'*
Sir John Gieve: *'The thing that worries me most is coordinating an international financial crisis, but at the moment that does not seem imminent and so I am sleeping all right.'*
Treasury Select Committee, 1 February 2007

John McFall MP: *'Sir John [Gieve], you sit on the FSA [board]; were you having a sleep in the back of the shop while a mugging was taking place in the front?'*
Treasury Select Committee, 20 September 2007

In the early summer of 2007, Mervyn King had an important appointment to keep and, for once, it was not on the Bank's business. During the weekend of 26–27 May he flew to Helsinki to marry his long-term partner Barbara Melander, an interior designer from Finland's Swedish-speaking minority. King and Melander, who is one year his junior, had first met in the 1970s but Melander subsequently married a Finnish businessman, remaining with him until 1996. In the following years, she renewed her friendship with King, although it was not until December 2005 that they were seen together in public, when they attended the Nobel Prize Committee's Royal Banquet in Stockholm. King's associations with the Nordic countries – and Finland in particular – were longstanding. He was busy writing for the *Journal of the Economic Society of Finland* as early as 1975 and often visited the region, expressing his admiration for the prudence with which it regulates its banking system.

On their wedding day, there was a simple ceremony in a small church in the centre of Helsinki, at which the bride wore a green dress and the groom one of his many dark suits. A champagne reception for eighty of the couple's family and friends followed. Returning to London after a short honeymoon, Mrs King turned a professional eye to her husband's bachelor flat in Notting Hill, west London, and to their converted oast house, in a hamlet near Canterbury, in Kent. The house was altered to accommodate the sauna, which no self-respecting Finn – and perhaps no self-respecting, modern Governor of the Bank of England – goes without.

Unlike the Governor, the Bank remained resolutely independent. May 2007 also witnessed the tenth anniversary of its independence, although it did not trouble its kitchen staff or the night guards. But while there was no banquet or firework display, there was, of course, a speech. A few days before the actual anniversary, which fell on a Sunday, the Royal Bank of Scotland hosted an evening reception at its London headquarters for the Society of Business Economists, an influential convocation of economists from academe and the City. Two hundred of its members came to hear King reflect on a decade of economic prosperity and the maturation of the MPC. How had it fared? The Governor offered a succinct historical summary:

> Since its inception, the MPC has met 120 times. At those meetings it raised Bank Rate seventeen times, lowered it on seventeen occasions, and left it unchanged eighty-six times. Bank Rate has varied between 3.5 per cent and 7.5 per cent. The MPC has changed interest rates at just over a quarter (28 per cent in fact) of its monthly meetings. Companies, households, trade unions and financial market participants can see that we change interest rates in response to news about the inflation outlook. That anchors inflation expectations. In the jargon of economists, people understand that we have a 'reaction function' – we react to the economic data in order to keep inflation on track to meet the target.[133]

King was clear about the MPC's singular achievement over the decade:

> The crucial achievement of the MPC is to have anchored inflation expectations. But, as the saying goes, we are only as good as our last meeting. We fully recognise that we must keep our eye on the ball if we are to continue to anchor inflation expectations on the 2 per cent target.[134]

After the 'nice' decade, it was supposed to be, in King's words, the 'not-so-bad decade' with 'not-so-bad' being the acronym for the 'not of the same order but also desirable',[135] a phrase coined in 2004. Three years on, however, it seemed too good to last. As the spring gave way to summer, there were signs of problems in the United States, where hedge funds had taken large, leveraged bets on 'sub-prime' mortgage securities, which were poorly rated and, in retrospect, highly likely to default. Scattered examples of hedge funds which had overextended themselves began to emerge. In early June, for example, the New York-based High-Grade Structured Credit Strategies Enhanced Leverage Fund – whose name encapsulated all the financial exotica of the time – got into difficulties, reporting double-digit losses. The fund was largely underwritten by Bear Stearns and as ripples of unease spread out into the wider market, other investment banks that had exposure to the hedge fund threatened to dump Bear Stearns's own collateral, a blunt method of recouping their losses on the hedge fund. This prospect caused near panic and was averted only when a deal between the banks was agreed.

In London, these events did not go unnoticed, to be sure, but they were perceived as the problems of a rarefied stratum of the investment community. Hedge funds, largely unregulated and freewheeling, were a law unto themselves. The banks which extended credit lines to them knew – or thought they knew – the risks of doing so. And, in this case, Bear Stearns was still a bit-part player in the wider drama. Although it was long established and well known on Wall Street, it had rarely troubled British institutions, let alone its central bank.

It was unsurprising, therefore, that when Mervyn King got to his feet on Wednesday 20 June to give his annual speech at the Mansion House banquet, he did not mention the events in New York specifically. His first comments were addressed to Gordon Brown, who was making his last appearance there as Chancellor before taking the Prime Ministerial reins. King congratulated him on his 'record-breaking period in office' and on his bold plan ten years earlier to give the Bank of England its independence. The Governor then turned to financial stability and, in particular, the boom in credit lending and concomitant securitisation of debt:

More than one banker and merchant in the City has said to me recently, 'I cannot recall a time when credit was more easily available'. How worried should we be?[136]

King noted that securitisation was 'transforming' banking from the traditional model in which banks originated and retained credit risk on their own balance sheets into a new model, in which that risk was distributed around a wide range of investors. This was no bad thing:

> As a result, risks are no longer so concentrated in a small number of regulated institutions but are spread across the financial system. That is a positive development because it has reduced the market failure associated with traditional banking – the mismatch between illiquid assets and liquid liabilities – that led Henry Thornton and, later, Walter Bagehot to promote the role of the Bank of England as the 'lender of last resort' in a financial crisis.[137]

Although securitisation certainly dispersed risk around the market, the ever more exotic derivatives being dreamt up to distribute the debt were becoming notorious. King was aware that there was danger lurking in their complexity:

> Exotic instruments are now issued for which the distribution of returns is considerably more complicated than that on the basic loans underlying them. A standard collateralised debt obligation [CDO] divides the risk and return of a portfolio of bonds, or credit default swaps, into tranches. But what is known as a CDO-squared instrument invests in tranches of CDOs. It has a distribution of returns which is highly sensitive to small changes in the correlations of underlying returns which we do not understand with any great precision. The risk of the entire return being

wiped out can be much greater than on simpler instruments. Higher returns come at the expense of higher risk.[138]

He also cautioned on the wave of cheap credit being offered to all and sundry. (The Governor had received one recently himself: 'We have the solution, Mervyn, for your bankruptcy.') Then he presented his audience with a now-fabled analogy:

The development of complex financial instruments and the spate of loan arrangements without traditional covenants suggest another maxim: be cautious about how much you lend, especially when you know rather little about the activities of the borrower. It may say champagne – AAA – on the label of an increasing number of structured credit instruments. But by the time investors get to what's left in the bottle, it could taste rather flat.[139]

Finally, he addressed the practicalities of understanding – and, more particularly, unwinding – highly levered portfolios, especially when many players wish to reduce their leverage at the same time. Liquidity in such circumstances, said King, 'is unpredictable': 'Excessive leverage is the common theme of many financial crises of the past. Are we really so much cleverer than the financiers of the past?'[140]

King's speech did not go unnoticed or unreported by the Press, but it was, in retrospect, not nearly enough. It echoed down the next three years as a warning about excessive dependence on credit and credit structures which seemed half hearted, even lighthearted. It would come back to haunt the Governor, not only during the financial crisis but in the long-drawn-out post-mortems, when it was cited as a classic example of the Bank 'not shouting loud enough'[141] about the dangers building up in the financial system.

If the guests at the Mansion House needed an example of some of King's strictures, they did not have to wait long. Far from the splendours of its Egyptian Hall, back, some might say, in the real world, Northern Rock – a building society-turned-bank on a windswept business park in Gosforth, near Newcastle upon Tyne – was putting together its interim results. Exactly a week after King's speech, Northern Rock released a statement via the London Stock Exchange that its profits would fall short of the City's expectations. Although the shortfall was modest – a 15 per cent rise rather than the anticipated 17 per cent – the accompanying commentary was more than enough to spook the market. Adam Applegarth, Northern Rock's chief executive, pointed to a 'mismatch' between the wholesale money market, which it used to borrow money, and the base rate, on which its own customer lending was based. 'Over the last five months the gap between the two has been getting steadily wider to the extent it was sixty-nine basis points [0.69 per cent] at one stage,' he said. 'That means that as interest rates rise our margins get trimmed. Conversely, when they fall they flatter our margins.' This veiled warning of trouble ahead caught the eye of analysts and they lost little time in marking down Northern Rock's shares; they fell 10 per cent, wiping £390m off the value of its equity.

The effects of the simple pivot – the mismatch between the wholesale rates and the base rate – which now threatened Northern Rock's profits were all the more alarming because the bank had been doing so well. In January, it had reported record pre-tax profits of £627m for the year ending December 2006. In April, it reassured investors that its lending performance was well ahead of the previous year and that it had 'a strong pipeline of business'. But now the City realised Northern Rock's margins would only be 'trimmed' further if interest rates rose again. Applegarth again reassured the markets that 'the medium term outlook for the company is very positive'. Others were not so sure, and Northern Rock's share price continued to fall steadily over the next few weeks.

If the Bank noticed this ebbing away both of liquidity and of investor confidence it did not seem to register. Despite its unique dependence on securitisation, Northern Rock appeared on no Bank watch-list, nor did its plummeting share price trigger any Bank equivalent of a 'stop-loss'. The Bank's regional agent for the North East, whose job it was to contribute to the monthly survey of 700-odd businesses across Britain which, in turn, feeds into the MPC's decision-making process, made no report of the gathering doubts in Northern Rock's boardroom. The Bank's machinery ground on. The MPC met on 5 and 6 July, voting (six for and three against) to increase Bank Rate by 0.25 per cent to 5.75 per cent.

As ripples of uncertainty continued to fan out in the market, they began to register in the Bank's Markets Division. From the beginning of July, Paul Tucker and his team spent an increasing amount of time analysing what he later referred to as 'the channels of strain',[142] a gnomic term for bottlenecks which were starting to appear, primarily in the wholesale markets. In particular, he was concerned about 'spillover' into the asset-backed commercial paper market, known colloquially as ABCP. Meanwhile, Mervyn King's diary that month was full of rather Pooterish dates: he spent two days in the West Midlands, making a presentation of a banknote at the Elgar Birthplace Museum, near Worcester, and visiting local companies, including Duncan Fearnley, the manufacturer of cricket bats. He was also in the South West to be interviewed by the *Western Morning News* and to visit Ginsters, the makers of motorway service station pasties. Back in London, the Governor gave a reception at the Bank for Gérard Errera, the French Ambassador, and visited Glyndebourne for a performance of Rossini's *La Cenerentola*.

In King's absence, it fell to his deputy Sir John Gieve to keep the Bank's speech-making apparatus ticking over. On 24 July, he appeared at the Barbican Centre to address an audience of City executives on 'uncertainty, policy and financial markets'.[143] In his speech, he addressed some of those uncertainties afflicting the credit markets. He noted the collapse of the Bear Stearns-backed hedge funds, but observed that 'underlying economic and corporate fundamentals remain encouraging' and that 'within financial markets, liquidity remains high overall'. Nevertheless, a thread of unease ran through his text, particularly about the state of sub-prime investments in the United States and the possible knock-on effects. It was, he said, 'a particular area of uncertainty'.

When the MPC met again, on 1 and 2 August, it voted unanimously to keep Bank Rate flat at 5.75 per cent. The holiday season was well under way and the Bank's deliberations merited little comment. As the City emptied, those left behind kept half an eye on their Bloomberg terminals. When the week of 6 August began, however, some traders noticed a marked deterioration in the liquidity of their holdings. At one investment house – BNP Paribas Investment Partners (BNPP IP) – fund portfolio managers were concerned enough to seek guidance from their chief executive, Gilles Glicenstein. Three funds – Parvest Dynamic ABS, BNP Paribas ABS EURIBOR and BNP Paribas ABS EONIA – together worth €1.6bn had extensive holdings in asset-backed securities, including sub-prime mortgages, and were rapidly becoming illiquid. On Tuesday 7 August, Glicenstein took the drastic and unprecedented decision to suspend the funds' net asset value calculations, thereby leaving them 'unpriced' and effectively freezing redemptions by investors. Glicenstein said in a later interview: 'We saw that we had apparently reached a problem … and we couldn't price our products properly. We had the choice to either do a fire sale, or take a little time, find some liquidity and protect our clients, which is what we did.'[144] As BNP's worried investors digested Glicenstein's decision, the company issued a blunt statement: 'The complete evaporation of liquidity in certain market segments of the U.S. securitisation market has made it impossible to value certain assets fairly regardless of their quality or credit rating.'[145]

The next morning, as news of BNPP IP's decision seeped into the market, Mervyn King and Paul Tucker were in front of the small corps of economics correspondents that follows the Bank's quarterly *Inflation Report*, for the routine press conference which accompanies its publication. There was no reference to BNPP IP and only the briefest mention from the Governor of 'tremors in financial markets' and 'developments in spreads', which he thought reflected 'a more realistic pricing of risk and that's to be welcome'.[146] There was, however, an acknowledgement of the need for vigilance. Tucker assured the journalists that:

> one of the tests that the Governor and I set each other a few years
> ago was that if anything went wrong we probably wouldn't be
> able to spot it but we should aim to be able to understand it if
> and when it happened.[147]

Tucker's words proved all too prophetic. It did not take long for news of BNPP IP's decision to work its way around the system and the next day, Thursday 9 August, there was a cataclysmic snapping shut of both the interbank lending market in the UK – the wholesale market used by banks and building societies – and the market for the sale of asset-backed bonds, such as those in BNPP IP's funds. The markets effectively closed for business. As King himself put it, looking back a month later: 'The markets and the securities that many banks and others had been creating suddenly dried up.'[148] As the global bond and equity markets began to buckle under the effects of this devastating development and indices dropped by hundreds of points all eyes turned to the central banks.

Officials at the European Central Bank (ECB), in Frankfurt, were quick to respond to the crisis. Jean-Claude Trichet, its President and King's opposite number, interrupted his holiday in Saint-Malo, on France's Brittany coast, to authorise the injection of almost €95bn into the reserve accounts held by forty-nine financial institutions at the ECB, giving them at least temporary respite and much-needed liquidity. The funds were to be followed by further tranches – €61bn the next day, €48bn the following Monday and a final sum of €25bn on the Tuesday.

American markets also opened sharply lower that Thursday and banks' requests for emergency funding prompted the Federal Reserve's Open Market Trading Desk – known as 'The Desk' – to announce it was pumping $24bn into the American banking system. The following day it made further interventions totalling $35bn, the largest such action undertaken since the days following September 11 2001. In all cases, these huge injections of liquidity – the Fed's $35bn increased the size of banks' reserve accounts by a factor of four – were made in the form of 'repurchase agreements' ('repos'), which gave banks funds in the form of a short-term loan, with collateral posted as surety, to be repaid within a day, a week or by agreement.

While the ECB and the Fed fought their way through that Thursday, in London it was a different story. King himself spent this most torrid day watching the England cricket team play India in the opening day of the Third Test at the Oval, in Kennington, as a guest of Paul Sheldon, the then chief executive of Surrey County Cricket Club. King takes his cricket seriously and, according to a senior colleague at the Bank, the Governor had left strict instructions that he was not to be contacted unless it was an emergency;

as the day wore on, the definition of 'an emergency' became a matter of some debate at the Bank. Under normal circumstances, King's two deputy governors, Sir John Gieve and Rachel Lomax, would have held the fort. That day, however, Gieve was in Scotland making funeral arrangements after a family bereavement. Lomax was at her post in Threadneedle Street, however, and joined a series of teleconferences with the other central banks, but she gave no indication that the Bank was minded to follow the lead set by the ECB and the Fed and offer liquidity assistance to UK-based financial institutions. Paul Tucker and his colleagues in the Markets Division, where the serried ranks of Bloomberg terminals showed a sea of red, were rather less sanguine. Tucker called a meeting of the entire Markets team, which crowded into the Bank's Sterling Room to discuss the catatonic state of the markets. According to one senior member of staff who was present, the discussion was, however, very much about diagnosing the problem, rather than a council of war about proposals to deal with it. Questions were asked about what action the Bank might take, but the answers were to the effect that the Bank had just undertaken its routine weekly money market operations and there was no immediate need for any special intervention. When the Governor, still enjoying the cricket at the Oval, was eventually alerted to the situation, in a phone call from either Tucker or his own private secretary, his reaction, according to other staff, was one more of annoyance than surprise. He feared the ECB's massive interventions would spook the markets even further and make a bad situation worse. Above all, so the argument went, it was a euro and a dollar problem, not a sterling one.

The Bank did nothing.

A few months later, when the BBC's Robert Peston asked King whether 9 August had been 'a big day' at the Bank of England, the Governor floundered:

Peston: 'Was August 9th a big day at the Bank of England? Were you aware of what had happened within banking markets?'

King: 'Well, certainly we couldn't have said with certainty that the events over the next couple of months would pan out as they did, no, but it was certainly an important day, there's no question about that. And it began with the revelation of losses in a major French bank's investment funds and it followed with a very large injection of liquidity by the European Central Bank. And many people were surprised by that and asked a question: well, what do they know that we don't? So in markets that day there was a very big disturbance, and almost immediately contacts between the central banks around the world started and we would not normally be in daily contact – regular contact, yes, but not daily contact. But from that day onwards daily contact pretty well started.'[149]

The Bank's absence from the drama being enacted by other central banks went entirely unchallenged in Whitehall. Alistair Darling, who had been Chancellor of the Exchequer for just two months, was on holiday in Majorca and – astonishingly – only heard about the market collapse and the ECB's unprecedented interventions from the headline on a copy of the *Financial Times* he picked up from a newspaper kiosk. Horrified, Darling immediately recognised that it was 'inconceivable'[150] that London-based banks would not be affected by the liquidity squeeze:

It was infuriating. Why hadn't I been phoned? It was one of those cases when the civil servants dealing with the matter were so close to the problem that they did not see it for the crisis it was about to become.[151]

On his return to London, the Chancellor wasted no time in insisting that the Bank of England and the FSA work with the

Treasury to identify any immediate problems in the banking system. And in the days which followed, British banks duly began to beat a path to the authorities' doors with requests for assistance. At the FSA they received a sympathetic hearing and the promise that their concerns would be communicated to the Bank. There, eventually, they encountered a stony-faced King. Their requests were for additional liquidity, at no 'penalty rate', and an increase in the range of collateral against which the Bank would lend. King demurred. The Bank stuck resolutely to its existing system whereby banks requiring additional funds would continue to pay the penalty rate – one percentage point above Bank Rate – and the strict criteria for eligible collateral remained firmly in place.

The Governor later explained his reasons in a letter to the Treasury Committee. They were threefold: first, that 'the banking system as a whole is strong enough to withstand the impact of taking onto the balance sheet the assets of conduits and other vehicles.' Second, 'the private sector will gradually re-establish valuations of most asset backed securities, thus allowing liquidity in those markets to build up.' Third, there would be a risk of 'moral hazard':

> In essence, this 'moral hazard' argument is that, should the central bank act, and effectively provide extra liquidity at different maturities against weaker collateral, markets would, especially if the liquidity were provided at little or no penalty, take it as a signal that the central bank would always rescue them should they take excessive risk and get into difficulties. Such a signal would lead to ever more risk taking, and the next crisis would consequently be greater than it would otherwise have been.[152]

King's views were not shared by everyone at the Bank or, indeed, in Westminster. It was obvious to many there that the money markets were 'a shambles' and had been heading in that direction since the spring of 2007. 'We saw disjuncts in the market and there were signs of distress in the wholesale market in particular,' said one former Bank official. 'The Bank's attitude throughout to the bank CEOs and chairmen who came to see us was "it is moral hazard – fix it yourself". Mervyn just dug his heels in.' Many argue that just as 9 August marked the beginning of the financial crisis, at least in the public perception, it was also the day on which the Bank made a fatal mistake in failing to address a collapse in market confidence.

King's attitude had not changed by late August when the Bank's switchboard started lighting up with further calls from banks, including Lehman Brothers and HSBC, with an urgent new request. The banks needed advice, and fast – Lehman Brothers went so far as to send a limousine to pick up a senior member of the Bank's staff and whisk them down to Canary Wharf. The bankers wanted to know whether the Bank would lend its assistance to a restructuring of the asset-backed commercial paper (ABCP) market, the cause of Paul Tucker's earlier concern, which had all but seized up. Specifically, they wanted support for a so-called 'Montreal Accord' for banks domiciled in the United Kingdom. The request referred to an agreement which had just been struck in Canada: participants in the ABCP market there, worth some $32bn, had put together a 'standstill' agreement, which allowed time for their short-term securities, which had become irredeemably (in every sense) stuck, to be swapped for longer-term ones. The deal allowed for the largest structured credit restructuring in history and prevented a cataclysmic meltdown which would have spread very quickly to Europe, where many of the banks which had provided assets for the vehicles – including Deutsche Bank, HSBC and UBS – were headquartered. As it was, banks in London were sufficiently worried to seek out the Bank of England. Their question was: would the Bank support a Montreal Accord here? The answer was a flat 'no'.

The issue caused some debate at the Bank. A somewhat subversive paper, produced by its Financial Markets Law Committee, noted that one of the leading architects of the Canadian Montreal Accord had '"knocked heads" together in order to broker the deal', adding: 'This prompts the question: is there any reason, in principle, why a central bank such as the Bank of England could not engage in a similar "head-knocking" exercise?'[153] Although there were legal issues to consider, it concluded: 'Those obstacles are, with sufficient care and planning, surmountable ... There are, in the UK at least, usually ways in which these restrictions may be circumvented for the purposes of crisis control.'[154]

Indeed, some bankers with long memories might have hoped for a more sympathetic hearing from King on this occasion, given his previous involvement with a joint project between the Bank and – coincidentally – the Bank of Canada to put together a framework for financial crisis resolution. The project culminated in November 2001 with a paper called *The Resolution of International Financial Crises: Private Finance and Public Funds*. King and Paul Jenkins, his opposite number in Canada, wrote the foreword, while their respective colleagues Andy Haldane and Mark Kruger provided the bulk of the text. In it, there is much discussion of 'standstills' – exactly as embraced in the Montreal Accord – as 'a way of enhancing the crisis management process'. The paper went on to outline the numerous benefits of standstills, including the fact that they can 'promote creditor coordination', 'align creditor and debtor incentives' and 'help ensure that payment stoppages are orderly'.[155] It concluded: 'The decision to call a standstill lies with the debtor. But the official sector can play a useful supporting role.' But it was not, apparently, a role which the Bank of England was minded to play for the anxious bankers who sought its help in August 2007.

£££

For Northern Rock, the catatonic state of the interbank lending market, on which it depended so heavily, spelt disaster. When Adam Applegarth, Northern Rock's chief executive, heard from the company's traders of 'a dislocation in the market',[156] he quickly recognised that if the bank could no longer access the wholesale market it would sound a death knell for the company. Matters came to a head during the weekend of 11–12 August, after an intense discussion among its board. It was decided that Dr Matt Ridley, the company's chairman, should discuss the situation with the Financial Services Authority on Monday 13. Ridley, an aristocrat (the son and heir of Viscount Ridley, and nephew of the late Lord Ridley, the former Conservative minister) and a well-known author of books on environmental issues, is an unlikely man to find himself in conversation with the powers that be about the rescue of a bank with £100bn in assets. Nevertheless, his conversations with the FSA were deadly serious: if there was a continued deterioration in the wholesale money market, Northern Rock would collapse. To compound matters, its shares, already heavily shorted by hedge funds, looked as though they were teetering on the edge of an abyss.

At the FSA, Sir Callum McCarthy and Hector Sants recognised the gravity of Northern Rock's situation and quickly passed its information to the Treasury and to the Bank. A conference call between deputies – Sir John Gieve for the Bank, Hector Sants for the FSA and a senior Treasury official – took place on Tuesday 14 August. Gieve informed Mervyn King about the call. The FSA team introduced the codenames 'Elvis' for Northern Rock and

'Memphis' for Newcastle, fearing – rightly as it turned out – that news of the negotiations would leak.

Two days later, on 16 August, the matter had been escalated and Ridley found himself on the telephone to Mervyn King. Although King mentioned the 'theoretical possibility'[157] of emergency support for Northern Rock, King's instinct was very clear: the Bank should not be drawn into the affairs of individual commercial banks. As Ridley's colleagues were later informed, King was remarkably sanguine. He was convinced that the trouble in the wholesale markets would soon blow over and that Northern Rock would manage to get a crucial securitisation away in September. If anything, he was worried that Northern Rock itself might spook the market by giving the impression of actually needing assistance. Northern Rock's board, in the thick of its very real funding crisis, was taken aback.

Notwithstanding King's apparently relaxed attitude – one which was not shared by some of his senior colleagues in the Bank – it became clear that Northern Rock's best chance lay with a new owner, the so-called 'safe haven' option. The same day, 16 August, its executives and advisers set about the task of preparing information memoranda and drawing up a shortlist of potential acquirers. As Ridley put it later: 'We picked up the phone to anyone and everyone.'[158] Their timing was not good. The City was greatly preoccupied with the final stages of a protracted and bloody contest for ABN Amro, the Dutch bank, which effectively removed RBS, Barclays and Santander from the list of Northern Rock's likely buyers. Barclays, which had been squeezed out of the ABN Amro process – fortunately, as it turned out – was in no mood for another. The obvious candidate was Lloyds TSB and it duly emerged as Northern Rock's strongest suitor. The process of due diligence ahead of a possible transaction began in earnest and within a few days nearly one hundred people from Lloyds

TSB and its advisers were installed in a data room, scrutinising Northern Rock's accounts and its loan book.

In the midst of this process, on Thursday 30 August, Ridley and Sir Ian Gibson, Northern Rock's senior non-executive director, had an audience with King in the Governor's Office at the Bank. They found him alone except for a note taker. Ridley and Gibson were seeking the Governor's reassurance that the Lloyds deal could indeed go ahead. But, for a second time, according to former employees of Northern Rock, King surprised them. He spent a full forty minutes telling the two men that they should not do a deal with Lloyds and that they should remain independent. The Governor's view was in stark contrast to that of the FSA, where McCarthy and Sants seemed equally convinced that a deal with Lloyds could and should happen.

Four days later, on Monday 3 September, unbeknown to Northern Rock, there was a meeting between the Tripartite authorities, at which a decision was taken that Northern Rock would be granted a support facility in the event that neither a securitisation nor a takeover by Lloyds proved possible. By 5 September, however, Lloyds had decided that the deal to acquire Northern Rock was fraught with risks. It decided to seek a guarantee, or 'backstop',[159] facility, which might amount to some £30bn to make sure they had sufficient liquidity to cover Northern Rock's own liquidity issues. The discussion about such a facility began with the FSA, but was soon channelled to the Bank and, indeed, to the Governor's Office. King was sceptical:

> They wanted to know first, before putting a bid on the table, whether it would be possible for them to borrow about £30 billion without a penalty rate for two years, and I said, well, the Bank of England does not normally lend £30 billion to a going concern.[160]

King made it clear that, from the Bank's point of view, a Bank guarantee was a non-starter, not least because any such facility would essentially constitute 'state aid':

> So I said to the Chancellor that this was not something which the Bank of England would do. My advice, clearly, was that this was not an operation which either central banks or governments normally did. If it were to go ahead it would require an indemnity for the Bank of England from the Treasury. Our legal advice was that this was clearly state aid and (and this was perhaps most important of all) it would be quite impossible to make an offer of a loan of that kind to one bank to buy Northern Rock without making it quite clear to other potential bidders that they too would have access to it, and I think, as the Chancellor said when he came to you before, the idea that if he stood up and said, 'I am willing to lend £30 billion to any bank that will take over Northern Rock' – that is not the kind of statement that would have helped Northern Rock one jot or tittle.[161]

By Sunday 9 September, when King was at his monthly meeting of central bank governors in Basel, the crisis engulfing Northern Rock prompted a telephone conference call between the Governor, McCarthy and Darling. Darling was alarmed not only by Northern Rock's perilous state, but also by the increasing calls from other banks for increased liquidity. Much to Darling's annoyance, King stuck resolutely to his dictum of 'moral hazard' and the need for a penalty rate to be attached to any assistance provided by the Bank. Darling found King's insistence that 'normal judgements could still apply in what were obviously deeply abnormal circumstances'[162] particularly hard to take:

My frustration was that I could not in practice order the Bank to do what I wanted. Only the Bank of England can put the necessary funds into the banking system; indeed, that is one of the core purposes of a central bank. The Bank was independent and the Governor knew it. We did not agree what to do.[163]

While Darling's realisation of the full implications for the government of the much-vaunted independence for the Bank of England make this moment something of a historic one, the more immediate fact that the Tripartite could not agree on how to handle the crisis soon began to influence events. As news of these fractious conversations filtered down to Lloyds' board, its interest in Northern Rock began to wane and it ordered its advisers to stand down. In the words of Applegarth, 'our corporate activity ceased'[164] at the beginning of the week of 10 September. Northern Rock was effectively on its own. That day there was a call from Sir John Gieve, King's deputy, to Applegarth, to discuss an emergency facility for Northern Rock in the absence of a takeover by a third party. The facility was now a reality, but by the Tuesday the Bank's strong preference for a 'covert' operation was, for legal reasons, deemed impossible. This occasioned much debate between the Bank and the Treasury. Ultimately, according to a senior Bank employee, the Treasury's lawyers 'told' the Governor that the Bank could only conduct an overt operation, although many other legal experts later queried this. King informed his colleagues of the direction and it was decided that the facility – an 'overt' operation – would be announced on Monday 17 September, the week's delay being partly to allow the company to batten down the hatches and brace itself for its customers' reaction. It went so far as to plan increased bandwidth for its website to cope.

On Wednesday 12 September, while the anxious negotiations over the fate of Northern Rock continued, King sat down at his desk and wrote a letter. He was due to appear before the Treasury Committee a week later and wished to give John McFall MP, its chairman, the text of his opening statement. Since the last session, King said in his letter, 'the turmoil in financial markets, which continues, has clouded the outlook.'[165] He added that 'I am conscious that in sending you this statement I am taking a snapshot of a fast moving situation with a long exposure camera.' King enclosed his opening statement, which was entitled 'Turmoil in Financial Markets: What Can Central Banks Do?'. It resembled nothing so much as the considered response to a particularly knotty exam question. It is noteworthy that even as the Bank barrelled towards what would be the first run on a British bank since Victorian times, King's 'long exposure camera' seemed strangely detached from the events unfolding in Newcastle. He did, however, allude to the situation:

Central banks, in their traditional lender of last resort (LOLR) role, can lend 'against good collateral at a penalty rate' to an individual bank facing temporary liquidity problems, but that is otherwise regarded as solvent. The rationale would be that the failure of such a bank would lead to serious economic damage, including to the customers of the bank. The moral hazard of an increase in risk-taking resulting from the provision of LOLR lending is reduced by making liquidity available only at a penalty rate. Such operations in this country are covered by the tripartite arrangements set out in the MOU between the Treasury, Financial Services Authority and the Bank of England. Because they are made to individual institutions, they are flexible with respect to type of collateral and term of the facility. LOLR operations remain in the armoury of all central banks.[166]

King's statement ended on an optimistic note, manifestly not reflected by current events: 'The current turmoil … has disturbed the unusual serenity of recent years, but, managed properly, it should not threaten our long-term economic stability.'[167]

The ink was barely dry on King's letter (later described disparagingly by the committee as 'an eloquent essay on moral hazard'[168]) before the Bank's ability to 'manage properly' the unfolding crisis was tested to the full. Not for the first time, the real world intervened to upset King's careful and logical analysis of the situation. The very next afternoon – Thursday 13 – the Bank started to hear what King later described as 'rumours in the market'[169] which suggested it had guessed – or been informed – about a possible support operation for Northern Rock. At 4 p.m., there was a hastily convened meeting of the standing committee of deputies. In the light of the 'leaks in the market',[170] it decided to bring forward the announcement of the Bank facility to 7 a.m. on Friday 14. There was a flurry of activity while arrangements were put in place and the Bank's Court was asked to prepare itself for an emergency meeting that evening in Threadneedle Street. At that meeting, King spent forty-five minutes outlining the terms of the facility to be granted to Northern Rock and sought the Court's approval. As he fielded the directors' questions, however, the Bank's control over events was quietly unravelling. At the BBC's Television Centre, in White City, west London, programme directors were in urgent discussion with Robert Peston, the BBC's business editor and a former *Financial Times* journalist, who had been tipped off that Northern Rock had received emergency assistance from the Bank. In fact, the terms of the emergency 'lender of last resort' facility were still being hammered out between the Bank and Northern Rock's treasurer and company secretary in Threadneedle Street and would not be finalised until the small hours of the next morning. But the gist of Peston's story was correct. At 8.30 p.m., to the consternation of King and his colleagues at the Bank, the news was flashed across the BBC's News 24 channel.

Later King was reflect that 'the nature of a bank run is that it is a knife edge: it might happen, it might not.'[171] In this instance, it happened. The Bank's emergency facility was finally – and officially – announced at 7 a.m. on Friday:

> The Chancellor of the Exchequer has today authorised the Bank of England to provide a liquidity support facility to Northern Rock against appropriate collateral and at an interest rate premium. This liquidity facility will be available to help Northern Rock to fund its operations during the current period of turbulence in financial markets while Northern Rock works to secure an orderly resolution to its current liquidity problems … In its role as lender of last resort, the Bank of England stands ready to make available facilities in comparable circumstances, where institutions face short-term liquidity difficulties.[172]

The Bank's announcement had virtually the opposite effect of what it intended. As Northern Rock's executives were later to confirm, its use of phrases such as 'lender of last resort' and 'liquidity problems' caused further alarm rather than reassurance. Panicked by the BBC's news story, large numbers of Northern Rock's customers had already jammed its telephone lines and caused the bank's website to crash as they attempted to withdraw their money. By Friday morning, many more were heading to its branches. The sheer extent of withdrawals from Northern Rock – £1bn on that Friday alone – meant that the facility the Bank had extended, intended as a backstop, had to be called on immediately. The media followed the crisis hour by hour.

It was the Bank's darkest hour. A run on a British bank had not occurred since 1866, when Overend, Gurney & Co., a wholesale discount bank, collapsed (it had requested assistance from the Bank of England, which had refused) and crowds of anxious investors besieged its offices in Lombard Street. A hundred and forty-one years on, in August 2007, there was a sense of bewilderment at the Bank and at the Treasury. The Governor and the Chancellor of the Exchequer were, however, elsewhere that Friday. Both had flown to Oporto, in Portugal, for a meeting of finance ministers and central bank governors, chaired by Fernando Teixeira dos Santos, Portugal's Minister of State and Finance. The day's session, held in the Palácio da Bolsa, produced little more than a statement of the obvious: 'We are experiencing a period of volatility and reappraisal of risk in global financial markets...'[173] Away from the conference proceedings, King and Darling stood in thc hall transfixed by pictures on a giant television screen, which showed queues of worried Northern Rock savers waiting outside its branches. Darling recalled:

> As we gazed at this horrifying spectacle playing out in the Friday sunshine half a continent away, my companion leant over: 'They're behaving perfectly rationally, you know.' It was not what I wanted to hear, even if it was Mervyn King, the Governor of the Bank of England, who was telling me.[174]

Back in Britain, the weekend provided no respite from the crisis engulfing Northern Rock. It was clear that drastic action would have to be taken to stop the run and to prevent a more widespread panic in the market. On Saturday, King spoke to Nick Macpherson, the Permanent Secretary of the Treasury, and arranged to see Alistair Darling again on Sunday morning. They discussed the extent of the facility the Bank had granted Northern Rock but also the possibility of a more dramatic intervention – a government guarantee of deposits in the bank. As King later recalled:

Over the weekend a lot of debates took place about a range of issues: the bid, a guarantee, people had different views to what the right answer might be, as the Chancellor made clear at the Treasury Committee. The view that I expressed to him was that we needed a government guarantee, but of course one of the practical problems of doing this, and the reason why it could not be done in a matter of hours, was to work out what the phrase 'there is a government guarantee' actually meant.[175]

The intricacies of financial and regulatory intervened many times that weekend, according to King: '[The] lawyer said, well hang on a minute, make sure you know exactly what it is that you're guaranteeing before you go on television and tell people.'[176] King had another conversation that weekend, with Adam Applegarth, in which he confirmed that the facility granted to Northern Rock might, in fact, be transferable. As King put it later: 'I confirmed very quickly that we would roll over the lender of last resort facility to any bidder.'[177] In other words, it might provide the security which a bidder – Lloyds was exhumed as still being the most likely candidate – could take comfort from. The prospect of a guarantee linked to a sale was discussed at length over the weekend, with Darling's strong preference for a deal. As the hours ticked by, however, the prospect of a safe haven with Lloyds seemed to evaporate once more.

On the morning of Monday 17 September, King called staff together in the Bank's conference centre to address them in a so-called 'Town Hall' meeting. According to one who was present, the Governor was at his most headmasterly, 'explaining the Northern Rock situation in words of one syllable, as though we were children'. Over in Downing Street that day, Darling had the unenviable and embarrassing task of putting the finishing touches to the proposed government guarantee in the presence of Hank

Paulson, the beefy US Treasury Secretary, who was visiting London. Much of their discussions in the sitting room at No. 10, according to Darling, 'centred on the Americans' perception that the Bank of England was not taking the unfolding drama seriously'.[178] Paulson's dry observation on the Governor was that 'Your guy Mervyn has a high pain threshold.'[179] As the day drew to a close, with Paulson still by his side, Darling held a press conference in Downing Street. Faced by a hostile crowd of journalists, the Chancellor was at least able to confirm the government guarantee:

> In the current market circumstances, and because of the impor- tance I place on maintaining a stable banking system and public confidence in it, I can announce today that following discussions with the Governor and the chairman of the FSA, should it be necessary, we, with the Bank of England, would put in place arrangements that would guarantee all the existing deposits in Northern Rock during the current instability in the financial markets. This means that people can continue to take their money out of Northern Rock. But if they choose to leave their money in Northern Rock, it will be guaranteed safe and secure.[180]

Darling's promise was confirmed a few days later into an actual guarantee – covering 'future interest payments, movements of funds between existing accounts, and new deposits into existing accounts'.[181] In fact, it guaranteed 100 per cent of such deposits (supplementing the Financial Services Compensation Scheme's £35,000 limit), suddenly making Northern Rock the safest place in Britain to park funds. This reassured the public and the run on Northern Rock was, in large part, stemmed. But the damage – and cost – was considerable. Whereas Northern Rock's origi- nal shortfall had been put by the company at only £2–3bn, by late October it had been forced to draw down £14bn from the

Bank's facility. Even that large sum proved insufficient. A couple of months later, Northern Rock disclosed that it had borrowed a total of £25bn from the Bank, the bulk of it in a second facility which was covered by a floating charge over, as King dramatically put it, 'all the assets of Northern Rock, the whole lot, right down to the paper clips'.[182]

While the market digested the government guarantee, King and his colleagues at the Bank reflected on the events of the past week. Perhaps they should have acted more swiftly alongside the ECB and the Federal Reserve? In Threadneedle Street there was a change of heart. King hurriedly called a confidential meeting of leading bankers to discuss their need for additional liquidity. Two days after the Chancellor's Downing Street press conference, the Bank made the following announcement:

> The Bank of England announces that it plans to conduct an auction in which it will provide funds at a 3-month maturity against a wider range of collateral, including mortgage collateral, than in the Bank's weekly open market operations … The size of the initial auction will be £10 billion; the size of future auctions will be decided in due course. This measure is being taken in order to alleviate the strains in longer-maturity money markets.[183]

This dramatic U-turn, which King described as 'a balance of judgement',[184] threw a liquidity lifeline to banks and building societies which had reserve accounts at the Bank and to those with access to its standing facilities. They could now post hitherto unacceptable assets – specifically, mortgages – as security against short-term Bank funds. Despite this relaxation of the Bank's stringent requirements, it seemed more of a face-saving gesture than a coordinated plan. It looked like policy-making on the hoof.

The following day – barely a week after the beginning of the run on Northern Rock – King, Sir John Gieve and Paul Tucker found themselves in front of the Treasury Committee, chaired by John McFall, a plain-speaking Scottish MP. The session, held in the Wilson Room of Portcullis House, opposite the Palace of Westminster, had a surreal air about it, with the wreckage of Northern Rock floating around the participants. The eight MPs were in particularly combative mood and never more conscious that the media were hanging on their every word. They were determined to nail the Governor and his deputy. King brazened it out, taking the long view:

> The most important point I want to make is to ask yourselves how would the Bank of England have dealt with this in earlier years. How would it have dealt with this in the 1990s? The first way it might have dealt with it was to invite the directors of Northern Rock and prospective purchasers into the Bank or the FSA for a weekend to see if that could be resolved and a transfer of ownership agreed over the weekend such that the depositors in Northern Rock would have woken up on Monday morning to find themselves depositors of a larger and safer bank.[185]

This route – essentially, the Lloyds option – was stymied, King maintained, because Northern Rock, as a publicly quoted company, was subject to the Takeover Code, which imposed a 'long and prolonged timetable' on any change of ownership. King continued:

> The second way in which the Bank would have preferred to do it in years gone by, and did do it in the 1990s, and the way that I would have wanted to do it on this occasion, is to have acted covertly as lender of last resort, to have lent to Northern Rock without immediately publishing that fact, publishing it after the

operation had been over so that you and others could hold us
accountable for the operation itself.[186]

This, too, had proved impossible. King insisted that the Bank's
efforts to save Northern Rock had been fatally hobbled by the
interaction between four apparently unconnected pieces of legislation, namely the Takeover Code, the Market Abuses Directive,
the rules governing retail deposits in a bank in administration and
those concerning deposit insurance.

The committee brushed this aside. The crisis had exposed a
grievous lack of coordination between the Tripartite authorities
and a vacuum of communication. This observation gave rise to
the immortal exchange between King and Michael Fallon MP:

Fallon: 'Who was in charge?'
King: 'What do you mean by "in charge"? Would you like to
define that?'
Fallon: 'What our constituents want to know given this mess is
who is in charge of it, who is responsible?'[187]

King's answer – 'we are each responsible for the various responsibilities that we have been given under the MoU' – while perfectly
correct, did not inspire confidence in the Tripartite. It was the first
of many nails in that particular coffin.

The committee reserved its strongest criticism for Gieve, who,
besides being a deputy governor, was also on the board of the FSA.
He was accused not only of 'having a sleep in the back shop while
a mugging was taking place in the front', but of complacency
in the face of 'market chatter' about the deteriorating state of
Northern Rock and of ignoring a great many warning signs in the
market. His absence from the Bank for two weeks at the height
of the crisis merely added to the catalogue of alleged ineptitude.

Even Tucker, who barely managed to get a word in edgeways, was accused of 'obfuscation' by one of the committee when he tried to explain the intricacies of Northern Rock's funding model.

Despite King's relatively calm demeanour before the committee, it was clear that the Bank's reputation had been badly damaged. As he left the poisonous atmosphere of Portcullis House and returned to the Bank, that week's edition of *The Economist* was appearing on newsstands; it summed up the general mood, with a cover picture of a Blimpish King and the excoriating headline: 'The Bank that failed: how Mervyn King and the government lost their grip'. Its leading article – an unprecedented attack on a Bank Governor – did not make pleasant reading, saying that 'the charge against Mr King is that his purism turned a crisis into a fiasco.' The newspaper's conclusion was blunt: 'He has lost credibility; and a central banker without credibility is not much use.'[188] All in all, it was a black day for the Bank.

King clearly felt the lack of heavyweight advice during the crisis. Particularly noticeable by his absence was Alastair Clark, a Bank 'lifer' with thirty-six years' service to his name, who had retired with immaculate timing only six months before. Although they had had their differences, King had valued Clark's work at the Bank. Now the Governor picked up the telephone and asked Clark to come back. It was a 'one last job' call. The gravity of the situation was not lost on Clark and he arrived back at Threadneedle Street in late September. He spent the next year at King's side, wrangling with the unfolding financial crisis, before retiring again in the autumn of 2008. (He was hauled back for a second time, in 2011, to bring his experience to bear on the new Financial Policy Committee set up by the Treasury).

Although its fate now lay largely with the Treasury, Downing Street and the small army of investment bankers from Merrill Lynch hired to find a buyer for it, Northern Rock continued to haunt the Bank of England. The Governor did his best to project an image of business as usual, but there was no escaping questions from the journalists who gathered in the Bank's conference centre in mid-November for the press briefing occasioned by the quarterly *Inflation Report*. After an hour or so of back and forth about the gloomy economic outlook, the session neared its conclusion. It fell to Brian Swint, a reporter from Bloomberg News, to ask a final question of Mervyn King:

> Swint: 'Governor, the first run on a UK bank took place under your watch. Have you considered resigning?'
> King: 'No.'[189]

While questions about King's own future were being asked in the Press and, as it turned out, in Downing Street, the spotlight remained firmly on the object of all the trouble: Northern Rock. The government guarantee in August 2007 gave way to resignations by its senior executives and a disorderly queue of prospective purchasers for the company's assets. A number of bidders emerged, including Sir Richard Branson's Virgin Group, J. C. Flowers, the American private equity firm, and Olivant, a group led by Luqman Arnold, a former leading light of UBS and of Abbey. Lloyds, Northern Rock's most persistent suitor, re-emerged with a suggestion that the government nationalise Northern Rock and then immediately sell it on to them. The entire process was opportunistic, bad tempered and expensive, with Northern Rock racking up advisory fees of some £40m. Ultimately, many of the interested parties required the government to take the lion's share of the risk and provide a suitably watertight indemnity. Outright nationalisation of the stricken bank seemed to be the only route: Darling and Brown eventually resigned themselves to drawing up plans for such a move, which was finally announced in mid-February 2008.

This grim process was interrupted by the publication of a 180-page Treasury Committee report, jauntily entitled *The Run on the Rock*, which laid bare the whole sorry saga. The report drew many conclusions from the affair, but at its core were damning assertions that there was little or no leadership structure within the Tripartite arrangement of Bank, FSA and Treasury and certainly no communications strategy which could be drawn on in times of crisis. The Bank and the FSA had drifted apart and, while the Treasury remained reasonably close to both, there was a singular lack of what is known in Whitehall as 'joined-up thinking'. More worrying was the disconnect which had been identified between the Bank and the City. Alistair Darling, for one, found himself fielding calls from bankers complaining about the Bank. It dawned on the Chancellor that the Governor had become more or less detached from the chief executives of London's leading financial institutions: 'In particular, by the autumn of 2007, I was being told time and time again by bank chief executives that the Bank simply did not understand the nature of the problem they were facing, which was lack of liquidity.'[190]

The fallout from the Northern Rock debacle rumbled around Westminster, the City and Canary Wharf. At the FSA, there was a shake-up of the senior management team, although only one senior executive, Clive Briault, lost his job as a result. Briault had been managing director for Retail Markets, which had put him at the epicentre of the Northern Rock crisis. He had arrived at the FSA at its inception in 1998, with eighteen years' experience at the Bank of England. His departure from the FSA was reportedly cushioned by a £612,000 severance package, including £202,500 in compensation for loss of office. Some commentators found a £30,000 'performance-related bonus' particularly galling. (The FSA was to suffer a slew of other departures in subsequent months, bidding farewell to David Kenmir, the organisation's chief operating officer, who had taken over Briault's brief, and, in 2010, to Jon Pain, head of supervision, and Sally Dewar, head of risk.)

As 2007 drew to a close, there were further dramas in the market. On 12 December central banks, including the ECB, the Federal Reserve and the Bank of England, reached into their vaults once more to alleviate pressures in the short-term interbank lending markets, which essentially oiled the wheels between banks. The Bank raised the size of its reserves offer from the scheduled £2.85bn to £11.35bn and, for a second time, extended the range of collateral it would accept against Bank funds. The Fed poured in $40bn in two tranches, while the ECB produced a further $20bn. While this was to prove only a temporary respite, there was a palpable sense that the central banks had a coordinated approach to the problem.

A week later, King and Gieve were back in front of the Treasury Committee, which, terrier-like, was still determined to get to the bottom of the machinations before, during and after the run on Northern Rock. The session was, however, rather less gladiatorial than that in the previous September and ranged widely over the Bank's role in ensuring financial stability. King and Gieve were more self-assured, with the Governor even allowing that he wished he had 'spoken out' in August, to explain the strictures placed upon the Bank by the existing money market operations. But this cut little ice with Philip Dunne MP, who was more interested in King's own somewhat precarious future:

> Dunne: 'Do you believe that it is important for the confidence of the financial system in this country that central bankers serve their full term?'
> King: 'I have no idea. In general, I think central bankers should be appointed and serve whatever part of that term they wish to see through.'

Dunne: 'If you were offered a second term, would you expect to serve it in full if your health allowed?'

King: 'What a depressing thought. That is something we will return to after Christmas.'

Chairman [John McFall]: 'Have a good Christmas.'

King: 'Thank you very much.'[191]

With these festive thoughts ringing in his ears, King took his leave of the committee. Back in Threadneedle Street that evening, he joined his senior colleagues in the Executive Team for their Christmas drinks party. There was little to celebrate, but much to reflect on. Above all, as he had intimated to the MPs in Westminster a few hours earlier, the Governor knew that the measures taken to help prop up the financial system over the past few months were not an end to the crisis; in fact, there might be far worse to come.

A CRISIS OF CONFIDENCE

'It was like a spark falling on tinder. The diffused though slight discredit caused by known bad speculations, and the uncertainty who might be mixed up in them, was at once aggravated into malignant fear … no one knew who was sound, and who was unsound.'

Walter Bagehot, 'The Panic', The Economist, May 1866

The ninety-minute Swiss flight from London City Airport to Basel on Sunday 6 January 2008 gave Mervyn King time to look through his papers for a meeting at the Bank for International Settlements. The central bankers congregating at the Tower building in Centralbahnplatz for their bi-monthly get-together had much to discuss. The first week of the new year had opened with grim economic data from the United States and continued frenetic trading in oil, its lifeblood, which had breached the $100-a-barrel mark for the first time. King had other matters on his mind, too. As Philip Dunne had alluded during the Treasury Committee hearing, his five-year term as Governor would expire in the coming June and the issue of his reappointment had become a vexed question. In Downing Street, there were serious doubts about a second term. Alistair Darling had deep worries about the 'strains' in his relationship with the Governor, which had come to the fore during the Northern Rock debacle. Gordon Brown was even less keen on the Governor and there was, according to Darling, 'a growing antipathy between them'.[192] (This was to boil over spectacularly the following year, when the notoriously volcanic Brown became so angry as he watched King give evidence at a televised Treasury Committee hearing that he suggested that Darling march in and stop the Governor in mid-flow. Darling declined.)

For his part, King had also been canvassed as to whether he wished to go forward for a second term. It seems that he hesitated. But as he weighed up the pros and cons, the torrid events of the previous months did not loom particularly large. Although Northern Rock had been nothing short of a disaster for the Bank, King had, to a large extent, rationalised it. He firmly believed that the single biggest reason for the Bank's inability to act as it wished was the lack of 'a statutory resolution process' and not any fundamental failure of leadership or oversight. It did not greatly influence his decision-making. Rather, it was the overwhelming pressure of the job of Governor which gave him pause. But in the manner of a batsman determined to get to his century, it was, it seems, his unapologetic obsession with the inflation target which persuaded him to stay; he was grimly determined to put in place the structures which would keep inflation in line. So far, he had managed this. Only once since becoming Governor in 2003 had he been obliged to write to the Chancellor explaining why inflation had missed its 2 per cent target and, by any standards, his record on monetary policy was a good one.

Under these circumstances and in the absence of any other appropriate candidate, it was not deemed the right moment to ease King out of the Governor's chair. Reluctantly, Brown and Darling gave their agreement to his reappointment. There was an uncomfortable meeting between Governor and Chancellor, during which Darling suggested that the Bank needed to redouble its efforts to keep recalcitrant bankers in check. One can only guess at King's reaction to Darling's other suggestion, that the Bank's Paul Tucker should be given '[his] head more often'[193] to mitigate some of the more autocratic aspects of the Governor's rule. These pleasantries dealt with, the Treasury duly announced King's reappointment on 30 January. The Treasury Committee went through the motions of sending the Governor a question-naire covering 'the challenges for his second term', quizzed him briefly on his record and then let him get back to his labours in Threadneedle Street.

King struck a sombre tone in his first public speech of the year, at a joint Institute of Directors/CBI dinner in Bristol in late January. He predicted that the coming year would pose great economic challenges – 'more so than at any time since the Bank of England was given its independence in 1997'.[194] King noted that the Bank faced twin buffeting winds, 'one from the west and one from the east':

> They correspond to what economists call demand and supply shocks. The former is the credit crunch which has blown across the Atlantic, and threatens a sharp slowing in output growth. The latter is the rise in energy and food prices, reflecting continued strong growth in Asia that, together with rising import prices, threaten to lift inflation noticeably above target in the coming months.[195]

Spelling out his message, King rehearsed the grim news of Britain's own stalled housing market, a sudden decline in consumer spend-ing and dramatic rises in fuel and food costs. He anticipated that 'inflation could rise to the level at which I would need to write an open letter of explanation, possibly more than one, to the Chancellor'.[196] The speech was a blunt exercise in managing expectations and aimed squarely at both Whitehall and the media.

While the Bank's focus remained squarely on the vagaries of the economy, fissures in the banking system, particularly around banks which had weak capital bases, continued to exercise King and his colleagues. They were worried, not only about liquidity, which had been partly addressed, but also about solvency. It was all too apparent how interconnected the banks were, depending on each other to honour counterparty risk, which meant that Britain's banks were susceptible to headwinds from abroad, particularly from the United States. There, weak economic data, interest rate cuts and demands for higher collateral requirements in the banking system set off a chain of events which claimed its first major casualty in mid-March. In scenes reminiscent of Northern Rock's imprecations to the Bank of England, the Federal Reserve found itself fielding desperate calls from Bear Stearns, a longstanding but weakly-capitalised Wall Street brokerage. On Monday 17 March, London awoke to the news that the firm had collapsed into the arms of J. P. Morgan for the paltry sum of two dollars a share, or $250m. This valuation, later revised upwards, reflected J. P. Morgan's famously hard-nosed bargaining skills, as well as something more visceral: fear.

King pondered the events unfolding in New York as he and his then private secretary, Chris Salmon, made their way to an off-diary lunch with another group of Americans, gathered in London. King and Salmon were the guests of Robert Tuttle, the then American Ambassador, and Robert Kimmitt, the deputy Secretary of the US Treasury, who was visiting Britain that week. For King, it was a timely opportunity to communicate his wider concerns about the financial system to the upper echelons of the American administration.

Kimmitt was an important catch. A much-decorated Vietnam

veteran, a lawyer by training and a former US Ambassador to Germany, he had decades of experience in public policy, not least on the National Security Council and at the US Treasury. In 2007, he had been a contender to become president of the World Bank. Although those laurels eventually went to Robert Zoellick, Kimmitt remained at the centre of US economic policy and its interaction with Wall Street, with which he was intimately acquainted. Ironically, as it was to prove, in a career break from public service in the mid-1990s, he had been a managing director at Lehman Brothers.

King knew his comments over lunch with Kimmitt would find their way back to Washington quickly. Ambassador Tuttle duly obliged, sending a confidential cable to the US Treasury and the State Department, as well as to his diplomatic colleagues in Brussels, on the evening of Monday 17 March. In his cable, Tuttle made it clear that King was serious about a radical approach to addressing seizures in the banking system: 'The King proposals were not casual ideas developed in the course of luncheon conversation. It was clear that his principal objective in the meeting was to outline his outside-the-box thinking for Kimmitt.'

King did not mince his words, as Tuttle's cable reported:

King said there are two imperatives. First to find ways for banks to avoid the stigma of selling unwanted paper at distressed prices or going to a central bank for assistance. Second to ensure there is a coordinated effort to possibly recapitalise the global banking system. For the first imperative, King suggested developing a pooling and auction process to unblock the large volume of financial investments for which there is currently no market. For the second imperative, King suggested that the U.S., UK, Switzerland, and perhaps Japan might form a temporary new group to jointly develop an effort to bring together sources of capital to recapitalise all major banks.

King's first proposal was for some sort of 'auction system', as Tuttle reported, where banks could move paper they wished to sell, if necessary at a low price, without the rest of the market taking this as a sign that the bank was in trouble. 'King said, however, he did not know yet how to structure such an auction.'

The second proposal concerned King's frustration with the G7 meetings, which, Tuttle said, King thought 'almost dysfunctional on an economic level', not least because the group did not include key economies in its deliberations. King had been in Tokyo for the latest G7 meeting barely a month before and had apparently found it to be little more than a talking shop. He suggested an entirely new international group, which could even include sovereign wealth funds, to provide resources for the recapitalisation of the banking sector. He apparently suggested that 'Japan might not be included because it has little to offer', although including the Japanese 'might force their hand in finally "marking to market" impaired assets'. Kimmitt hummed and hawed over this proposal, saying he was cautious about starting new groups 'because of the inevitable debate around whom to include'.

The meeting with Kimmitt highlighted King's frustrations with the heavy and unwieldy machinery of international economic policy, as well as his belief that the way to achieve real policy change lay in the gift of a few top officials in Washington, London and Zurich. Three weeks later, on 11 April, King was in Washington himself to attend another meeting of G7 central bank governors at the US Treasury, hosted by King's old friend Ben Bernanke. Whether Ambassador Tuttle's cable containing King's description of the group as 'almost dysfunctional' had reached Bernanke is not known.

£££

King's comments to Kimmitt about the imperative to find ways 'for banks to avoid the stigma of selling unwanted paper at distressed prices' were not idle ones. That very week, King sat at the home computer in his Notting Hill flat and worked up a draft plan to meet this imperative head on. The plan was discussed at length with Alistair Darling, who had been with King at the summits in Tokyo and Washington. The initiative was announced on 21 April as the Special Liquidity Scheme (SLS), whose aim was to improve the rapidly deteriorating liquidity position of UK banks. Under the scheme, Britain's banks and building societies were able to swap high-quality mortgage-backed and other securities for UK Treasury bills. The Bank noted that 'financial markets are not working normally' and that 'across the world, there is a lack of confidence in assets created from packages of bank loans, most notably mortgage-backed securities'. These markets were closed and the assets untradeable. The SLS would attempt to alleviate the 'over-hang' of such assets on banks' balance sheets, by lending the banks money with their mortgage assets as security. The 'money' in this case was to be highly liquid Treasury bills, which were essentially a cash equivalent. The hope was that with the overhang, in part, cleared, the banks would, in turn, start lending to one another again and liquidity would return to the market. Final approval for this ambitious plan had come from Darling in the form of a four-line letter sent by Dan Rosenfield, his principal private secretary, giving a government guarantee for the facility. Prior to the announcement, King had dispatched Paul Tucker and Alastair Clark to the City, where they held private meetings with the chief executives of the major banks to sell them the idea. It was made clear to them that any assets deposited in the SLS would have to be 'historic' ones, acquired before the beginning of the crisis.

The SLS was no small undertaking. The Bank envisaged that the banks' initial use of the scheme would be some £50bn. The Treasury bills to equal this large sum came from the Debt Management Office (DMO), which lent them to the Bank in a stock-lending arrangement (in other words, the Treasury bills were not issued first). This was the first major engagement between the Bank and the DMO of the financial crisis, which found its fullest expression in the programme of Quantitative Easing a year later. The SLS was a different animal, however. Firstly, it was explicitly ring fenced from the Bank's own money market operations and therefore not an influence on its monetary policy. Secondly, it had a defined timespan: by October 2011, the Bank said, 'assets will have been returned to the banks, all Treasury bills to the Bank of England, and the Scheme will close.' In addition, the Bank would not accept just any old rubbish from the banks. It demanded assets worth 'significantly more than the Treasury bills they have received in return' and it would not accept 'raw mortgages' or securities backed by US mortgages.

Equally, the banks had a few reservations. In particular, they did not want to be seen as the 'next Northern Rock' if they used the SLS and it became known that they had done so. King, still smarting from his failure to conduct a covert operation during the Northern Rock debacle, now managed it, at least partially. The SLS, it was decided, would not appear on the Bank's balance sheet, as standard Bank facilities were not being used. As the Office for National Statistics later noted there was, in its words, 'avoidance of disclosure': 'One reason that the scheme was designed as a "collateral exchange" was to avoid statutory disclosure requirements.'[197] This was at the heart of the scheme, confirmed by a meeting between Sarah Breeden, then head of the Bank's Risk Management Division, and officials from the US Embassy a couple of months later. The embassy's record of the meeting indicates how important the issue had become:

A request is taken as a sign that a bank is in serious financial difficulty. Accordingly, banks have been reluctant to utilise the BOE as a funding source. Breeden said it took over four months to develop the SLF [sic] and much attention was paid to avoiding the stigma associated with borrowing from the BOE. The BOE chose to use asset swaps because there is no requirement to disclose even aggregate data on the number and size of swaps. The BOE hoped that non-disclosure by the BOE combined with strict confidentiality agreements with participating banks would eliminate the stigma issue. While the SLF is still new, Breeden said that this key objective of the SLF has been achieved.[198]

The SLS rolled into action with the Governor and his colleagues at the Bank working on the assumption of a take-up of around £50bn. Little did they suspect that in the nine months following its launch the SLS would become the vehicle for no less than £185bn in funding – for which it received £287bn of illiquid assets – for the banks. The gargantuan numbers indicated the eventual extent of the malaise which, by January 2009, had seen a total of thirty-two banks and building societies take refuge in the scheme. The Bank did not do all its work for nothing. As its 2009 Annual Report showed, for the period from the start of the scheme to 28 February 2009, it made a whopping £573m post-tax profit in relation to the SLS. The DMO, for its part, received a payment of £54m from the Bank for the loan of its Treasury bills.

The SLS provided a much-needed fillip for the Bank's Governor. In the press conference held to announce the scheme, he took much of the credit for its genesis: as the *Financial Times* put it, he 'implicitly asserted copyright over the idea of swapping Treasury bills for mortgage-backed securities'.[199] While this may have been partly the case, the final scheme was rather more of a joint effort than King cared to admit. Darling, who was on a visit to China on the day the SLS was announced, later recorded that 'I had worked on this for several months and put a great deal of effort into persuading the Bank to agree to it ... That it was announced when I was on the other side of the world was a bit odd.'[200]

£££

While the Bank and the Treasury busied themselves with these sweeping initiatives to prop up the banking system, at the FSA, Adair Turner and Hector Sants were anxious not to get left behind. On 4 June 2008, they announced the appointment of Jeremy Bennett, a former colleague of Sants's at Credit Suisse First Boston, where Bennett had been co-head of fixed income for Europe. Bennett was appointed as a senior adviser to the FSA's wholesale and institutional business unit, along with Simon Stockwell, a corporate advisory banker from Lehman Brothers, and David Smith, a forensic accountant from KPMG. The trio were quintessential 'grey panthers', the term used for industry talent which the FSA brought in periodically to give it some advice from the real world. On this occasion, the implication of the three appointments was clear: the FSA needed banking expertise, and quickly. It was horribly clear to Sants and Turner that if the problems afflicting financial institutions intensified there was no 'Plan B'.

Bennett's initial brief was a brutally simple one: to draw up plans to deal with a full-scale banking crisis if, as one insider recalls, 'things got ugly', or indeed, uglier. Bennett, whose particular expertise was in credit derivatives, understood all too well the dangers of toxic assets infecting the balance sheets of banks and other financial institutions. He set about drafting not only a putative Plan B, but also Plans C, D and E, which envisioned increasingly apocalyptic scenarios. All of Bennett's plans, many of which explored the idea of equity injections into failing banks, were pitched first to Sants and then sent on to the Treasury, where they landed heavily on the desks of Tom Scholar and his colleague Nikhil Rathi, both of whom were to find themselves at the eye of the storm in the coming months. Scholar – of the Bank's gold sales fame – had left Gordon Brown's office after just six months for the balmier climes of the Treasury, where he was now managing director of the department which oversaw banks' activities. But, while Bennett's plans were studied, it was clear to him and his new colleagues that they ranked low in the Treasury's list of priorities. For the Bank's part, its view was that its role should be confined to providing liquidity, rather than fundamental equity, to troubled institutions.

There were other distractions in Threadneedle Street in June, sparked by the departure of Rachel Lomax, the Bank's deputy governor with the prized monetary policy brief, who had decided to pursue other interests at the end of her term. This created a vacancy for deputy governor. The two obvious internal candidates were Charlie Bean, the Bank's chief economist, and Paul Tucker, its executive director of the Markets Division. It was an open secret that Tucker badly wanted the job but that Bean was the Governor's favoured candidate. In Whitehall, Treasury mandarins also had their views and lobbied hard for someone with City experience such as Sir James Sassoon or Paul Myners to fill the post. Ultimately, there was another victory for the 'MA Way' and Bean was duly appointed and took his place at the Bank's top table. Before he took up his new post, he did, however, face the House of Commons Treasury Committee; it was an uncomfortable session, the tone set by John McFall MP's opening:

Chairman [McFall]: 'Some commentators have said you are the Governor's choice, an inside job, it is all a screw-up: discuss.'

Professor Bean: 'I am not sure describing it as an inside job is appropriate. What is true is that of internal candidates the Governor did consider that I was suitable for the position, but of course this is an appointment that the Treasury makes and it was a Treasury process.'[201]

Storm clouds also gathered over the other deputy governorship, held by Sir John Gieve. Gieve had not fared well in the post-mortems conducted after the Northern Rock debacle, which some of his colleagues thought unfair, given the fact that Gieve had been one of those around the Governor who had urged him to act swiftly to prevent the crisis. Despite this, he was in danger of becoming a scapegoat for the Bank; he was all too often at loggerheads with King and had few allies among the Bank's Court or at the Treasury. The final blow came after his involvement in discussions with the FSA and the Treasury over one of the key measures proposed in the new Banking Act 2009, which was designed to deal with failing banks. This was the so-called Special Resolution Regime (SRR), which allowed for distressed banks to be sold in whole or in part. After a weekend of intense negotiations led by Gieve, responsibility for the SRR was secured for the Bank, giving it a central role in its execution. It was hard won, with one Bank insider describing the discussions between the Tripartite as 'a power struggle'.

In the crowning irony of Gieve's time at the Bank, the new responsibilities which came with the SRR gave the Treasury an opportunity to look again at the deputy governor's role. Treasury officials made it clear to Gieve that the new brief was sufficiently different to his pre-SRR role that he would have, effectively, to reapply for his job and start a new five-year term. In the event, he baulked at the idea of a fight with the Treasury and, on 18 June, he submitted his resignation, which it was agreed with the

Treasury would be announced the following day. That evening Sir John had one last engagement, in the form of the annual Mansion House banquet. It was during dinner that the news of his impending resignation was leaked to the Press (some pointed the finger directly at the Treasury). Gieve was observed frantically working his BlackBerry as his assistants at the Bank tried to rush out an official press release. It was an undignified episode. But if he was bitter about how he had been elbowed out, Gieve kept his counsel. He served out his notice for a few months at the Bank, but the long shadow cast by John McFall MP's stinging question – 'were you having a sleep at the back of the shop?' – followed him out of the door.

The Bank did not have long to reflect on the resignations of Lomax and Gieve. In the same month, King and his colleagues watched with dismay as a new casualty of the credit crisis was wheeled in. Bradford & Bingley, Britain's largest buy-to-let mortgage lender with a loan book of £42.2bn, had announced a profits warning in May, followed by a £400m rights issue which was subsequently restructured three times in the face of increasing investor scepticism. By the time the shambolic fundraising neared its closing date, in mid-August, Bradford & Bingley had lost its chief executive, who had fallen ill, and the support of its largest shareholder, TPG Capital, the private equity group. As Bradford & Bingley's share price plummeted and Citigroup and UBS, who had underwritten the rights issue, were faced with the prospect of heavy losses, it was beginning to look dangerously as though it was heading for an endgame: a repeat performance of Northern Rock.

Just as Lloyds TSB had emerged as a suitor for Northern Rock, so did the Spanish bank Banco Santander for Bradford & Bingley. But it also requested an assurance regarding the mortgage lender's portfolio of toxic assets, principally sub-prime mortgages; again, no guarantee was forthcoming.

Matters came to a head during a long weekend of 27–28 September. On the Saturday morning, the teams from the Bank and the FSA met their Treasury colleagues to discuss the plight of 'Badger' – their codename for Bradford & Bingley. They rapidly came to the conclusion it was no longer a viable concern capable of meeting its 'threshold conditions' as a deposit taker. It was effectively bust. The rescue package, announced on 29 September, was a mixture of commercial deal-making and institutional Machiavellianism. The lender's £20bn savings business and branch network was sold to Abbey National, owned by Grupo Santander. The remainder, comprising the huge mortgage book, personal loan book, headquarters and its wholesale liabilities, were nationalised, with the company's shares passing immediately to the Treasury. On Bradford & Bingley's website, its Frequently Asked Questions for shareholders included the not unreasonable query: 'What's happened to my shares?' (Ultimately, Bradford & Bingley plc, the newly nationalised entity, was deposited in UK Financial Investments Ltd, the government's equivalent of a lost children's tent, where it would be in the company of Northern Rock. Ordinary shareholders in Bradford & Bingley received no compensation for their loss.)

The legal teams for the Treasury (Slaughter and May) and for the Bank (a forty-strong team of solicitors from Freshfields led by Michael Raffan) had been at pains to ensure that it was Bradford & Bingley's fellow banks which bore the brunt of the bill for its failure. The collapse had triggered the Financial Services Compensation Scheme (FSCS), to which the banking industry subscribed. It was, however, unprepared for a bailout amounting to many billions of pounds. In the event, under a very hastily drafted Transfer Order ('Made at 7.40 a.m. ... Laid before Parliament at 11.00 a.m.'[202]), the FSCS paid out £14bn to ease the transfer of retail deposits to Abbey National, with the Treasury topping this up with a further £4bn. The FSCS's funds came directly from the Bank of England in the form of a short-term loan which, as anyone in need of short-term loans knows, does not come cheap: the Bank expected the FSCS's first repayment of interest, and any proceeds from the wind-down of Bradford & Bingley's business, to be made in September 2009 and to amount to some £450m. Freshfields' lawyers had done their work with clinical precision and the Bank's modesty had been spared; the banks themselves had been left in no doubt that it was they who would underwrite the rescue of one of their own, as well as paying the Bank handsomely for its pains. Above all, King's *bête noire* of 'moral hazard' had been kept at bay.

£££

The tender mercies administered to Bradford & Bingley were, of course, overshadowed by the cataclysm visited upon a much larger and rather more metropolitan financial institution: Lehman Brothers. September was dominated by its collapse and, on Monday 15 September, its filing for bankruptcy protection – events which proved so seismic that they achieved instant historical importance. 'Pre-Lehman' and 'Post-Lehman' quickly became market shorthand for 'relatively normal' and 'extremely abnormal'. Lehman was an American bank, but had a large presence in London's Canary Wharf, where it employed 5,000 people. The emergence of Barclays Capital as a possible bidder for the failed business brought it into the British Tripartite authorities' field of vision. The FSA was, however, reluctant and refused to allow Barclays to guarantee Lehman's outstanding trades. The deal foundered, much to the Americans' dismay. In the end, Barclays did secure some of Lehman's core assets, notably its investment banking and broking arms, although there was a protracted tussle over the deal. In the meantime, the American bank's collapse precipitated further wild gyrations in stockmarkets, particularly among the shares of banks and other financial institutions. At the Bank of England, there was an urgent need to address what it called 'current disorderly market conditions'.[203] It extended access to the SLS and, on 18 September, announced it had agreed a 'reciprocal swap agreement', commonly called a swap line, with the Federal Reserve to finance US dollar liquidity, in the form of $40bn in overnight funds against eligible collateral. This was a coordinated response with the Fed, the ECB and the central banks of Japan, Canada and Switzerland. The 'interconnectedness' of global financial institutions, with all the dangers that it entailed, could at least be tackled by similarly large-scale currency swaps between the central banks. While the Bank of England's Markets Division scrambled to put these arrangements in place, King was whisked to Downing Street for early morning discussions with Gordon Brown and Alistair Darling on what the increasingly beleaguered Prime Minister's spokesman called the 'main economic and financial issues' facing the country.

As King's Executive Team at the Bank watched developments anxiously, outwardly at least they preserved *sang froid*. The same week as Lehman's collapse stunned investors, Spencer Dale – Corporal Jones to King's Captain Mainwaring – was in Dover giving a workmanlike analysis of house prices and the inflation outlook to the Dover and District Chamber of Commerce. Although he chose a rather groovier text than Jones's 'Don't panic!' (his speech was entitled 'All Along the Watchtower', a nod to Jimi Hendrix), he stressed the need for increased vigilance in uncertain times. In reality, it was too late. In the next few months, the businessmen and women of Dover, along with the rest of the country, watched their investments plummet and the banks at their very street corners threaten to stop working altogether.

September came to a close in dramatic fashion. In the last few days of September, the Bank became aware of the dire situation in which the UK banks found themselves, in particular HBOS and RBS. The two banks, which had a combined balance sheet worth some £3 trillion, more than double the UK's entire annual GDP, were going bust, and fast. While RBS owned NatWest, one of the largest retail chains in the country, HBOS was Britain's largest mortgage lender. The latter's stability had been dealt a severe blow by rumours that it was seeking government support; its share price swung wildly – up to 40 per cent in a single day. On 19 September, a merger between HBOS and Lloyds TSB, brokered personally by Gordon Brown, was agreed at short notice and waved through without referral to the competition authorities. A week later, on 26 September, Mervyn King sought out Adair Turner and Alistair Darling for a private meeting, at which he laid out the stark reality that unless the banks – in particular, RBS and HBOS – were recapitalised, there was a severe risk of a domino effect. The prospect of such large and systemically important banks failing was too awful to contemplate. The Governor had also met with Paul Tucker and Sir Nick Macpherson to discuss the looming crisis. It was, as Tucker said later, 'a dire emergency'. His sentiments were echoed by Macpherson, who put it as follows: 'Over a period of days there emerged a very considerable risk that the banking system would collapse altogether.' They rapidly reached the conclusion that an operation of the greatest secrecy was necessary to avoid two further bank runs, which would have been on a far greater scale than Northern Rock. The same day, 26 September, Darling gave the order for work to start at the Treasury, the Bank and the FSA on a scheme which became known as ELA: Emergency Liquidity Assistance. The scheme, which was essentially 'owned' by the Bank, was put together in five days.

In the middle of this process, Darling called together the principal banks' chief executives for an evening meeting at the Treasury on Tuesday 30 September. Six o'clock saw them troop in: Sir Fred Goodwin (RBS), John Varley (Barclays), Eric Daniels (Lloyds TSB), Dyfrig John (HSBC), Peter Sands (Standard Chartered), Graham Beale (Nationwide) and Antonio Horta-Osorio (Banco Santander). Arranged on the other side of the table, literally and metaphorically, were Darling, King, Turner, Paul Myners (then Financial Services Secretary, essentially Labour's City minister) and a posse of Treasury officials led by Sir Nick Macpherson.

The meeting was inconclusive, partly because the planning taking place for the ELA scheme was not disclosed to the bankers. Instead, they were asked for their views on the crisis, how much of it devolved to the need for additional liquidity and how much for core capital. Many of them focused on the former, in particular for overnight liquidity, which was the purlieu of the Bank. King insisted that the Bank stood ready to provide funds; the bankers knew this invariably came at a high price.

When it began, on 1 October, the ELA scheme was remarkable both for its entirely covert nature and for its scale. King was, according to Macpherson, 'clear that for emergency liquidity assistance to be successful secrecy was of the utmost importance'. The Bank used 'its powers'[204] to suppress the existence of the ELA from its 2009 Annual Report and it was not finally disclosed until a full year after the scheme's inception, in November 2009, when the Treasury Committee received a piece of paper headed 'Additional Information'. As Jim Cousins MP said at that hearing: 'This morning the Committee found some very interesting information on the table in front of it.' In its submission, the Bank defended itself thus:

In most cases, confidence can best be sustained if the Bank's support is disclosed only when the conditions that gave rise to potentially systemic disturbance have improved to a point where the disclosure itself should not be a cause of such disturbance.[205]

The size of the ELA was unprecedented: facilities were put in place to allow RBS and HBOS to draw down tens of billions of pounds. At its peak, on 17 October, RBS would borrow £36.6bn, while on 13 November, HBOS drew a maximum of £25.4bn on the facility.

The Bank's operations were partly financed by four swap transactions between the Bank and the Federal Reserve in the United States. But the Bank started the ELA essentially 'naked', with only the prospect of the banks' collateral to fall back on. As the amount of borrowing by the two banks increased dramatically, the Bank suddenly lost its nerve. It sought out the Treasury once more and requested an indemnity against possible defaults. On 13 October, the Treasury granted an £18.1bn indemnity, for which the Bank paid a fee, which eventually equated to £18.9m. (The indemnity, incidentally, created a contingent liability for the Treasury, which the government should have disclosed to Parliament. Macpherson, the Treasury's Permanent Secretary, advised the Chancellor of this obligation, but Darling chose not to do so, fearing it would blow the gaff on the whole affair and trigger runs on the two banks.)

The total use of the ELA facility peaked at £61.6bn on 17 October, when the Bank's already frayed nerves began to give way. As a result, on that day, the two banks provided it with collateral in the form of a ragbag of residential mortgages, personal and commercial loans and gilts with, according to the Bank, 'a total value in excess of £100bn' – a large margin of surplus collateral, reflecting the indeterminate quality of the assets being posted. In a comment which highlighted the breakneck speed at which the Bank had to move, King was later to say: 'We had to take raw mortgages and [had] no means of investigating their merits.'[206] The Bank charged RBS and HBOS substantial fees for the ELA facility, although the size of these has never been disclosed. Paul Tucker was asked whether the terms given to the banks were not 'tough stuff'? He agreed:

> It was tough stuff; it was an absolutely classic lender of last resort operation where the only point of doing it was whether it bridged to something. This applies to every single lender of last resort operation that has ever been carried out. Either you bridge through some panic that will pass and the organisation can resume its life or you bridge to some private sector purchase of it, which was not remotely available to RBS in these circumstances, or some state equity support, which was where we ended up. Can lender of last resort buy time? Yes, it can. It was very effective in buying time. It would have been a great mistake not to buy time. Can lender of last resort make all the problems of the world go away? No, it cannot.[207]

Ultimately, although the Press professed outrage and alarm at the secrecy around the ELA, the Governor and his team took pride in the fact that it had been conceived and delivered, the facilities repaid (in December and January) and the banks' collateral returned, all in the space of a few months. It was all the more remarkable, given the other grievous matters piling up on the Bank's doorstep.

£££

In the same week as the ELA was sanctioned there came news from an unexpected quarter – Iceland – which threatened to heap further catastrophe on the banking system and decimate the British public's savings. Large Icelandic banks, which had made audacious forays into British retail banking, suddenly appeared to be in trouble. First to fall was Heritable Bank, swiftly followed by Kaupthing. The Bank, the Treasury and the FSA hurriedly convened, along with lawyers from Freshfields. Two of the latter, Ken Baird (Freshfields' head of restructuring and insolvency) and his colleague Katharina Crinson, recalled the gravity of the situation in an interview (now used by Freshfields to illustrate the firm's work to incoming employees), which lends the air of a thriller to the proceedings:

Ken Baird: 'The worry was systemic risk – if one bank collapses, they all collapse, and there was a real terror that everybody was going to withdraw their money from the Icelandic banks. One person does it, everyone does it – suddenly the bank can't afford to repay so it collapses. The thing the government in the UK needed to ensure was that all those savers could get access to their money.'

Katharina Crinson: 'There was always the possibility of Kaupthing's parent in Iceland bailing it out.'

KB: 'But until that happened it was just pure speculation. This job really kicked off big style, 6 p.m. on Friday 3 October. We got yet another call from [the] Treasury saying: "Can you please come down for a meeting?" These meetings of course had people from the Bank of England's side, people from the Treasury side, and people from the Plan B side, and that's where we came in.'

KC: 'We needed to start putting together a team of people who could be ramped up quite quickly.'

KB: 'We'd been there three or four times before but this time was for real, we started doing the planning for two banks failing in the next week. That only gave us twenty-four hours, thirty-six hours to prepare. On the Tuesday we were in court to put into administration a bank called Heritable Bank [owned by Landsbanki Islands hf since 2000].'

KC: 'At that point it became very clear there's probably not going to be any other solution for Kaupthing than administration as well.'

KB: 'We got back to the office that day and were told "another meeting tonight, ten o'clock" at the Treasury. The next day Kaupthing, one of the biggest banks, also were into a process. Two banks in two days is something quite unique in my experience. The scale of the problem we faced here was tremendous. We had a bank with tens of thousands of customers, we needed overnight, virtually, to give them access in another bank to the same money, the same information, the same accounts, in a seamless way as if there was no problem at all, all in the middle of the biggest financial crisis we'd ever faced.'

KC: 'We worked incredibly hard to ensure that transfer was quick and was smooth. And that, in turn, meant that there wasn't a run on the bank. And that people's confidence, at least partly, their confidence in the banking system wasn't as shattered as it could have been had that transfer order not been made.'

KB: 'That avoided what would have been a systemic collapse of the financial system.'[208]

At the Bank of England, it fell to Nigel Jenkinson, then executive director for financial stability, to cope with a situation which bore all the hallmarks of another Northern Rock. Besides the army of lawyers from Freshfields and from Slaughter and May, the Bank decided to send two of its own employees to Iceland. There was a moment of high drama in Jenkinson's department when staff were asked which of them had a passport to hand; two were found and promptly dispatched to the airport to catch the first flight to Reykjavik, along with officials from the Treasury and the FSCS. On 13 October, the Bank provided a short-term secured loan of up to £100m to Landsbanki to assist British savers.

The FSCS went into overdrive. While it paid out just over £1bn in the seven years from its inception in 2001 to September 2008, in the subsequent five months alone it paid out some £20bn for five bank defaults (Bradford & Bingley, Heritable Bank, Kaupthing, Landsbanki and London Scottish Bank).

£££

Despite the very real danger, only narrowly averted, that there could have been a run on one of its banks with British customers, Iceland rapidly became a sideshow, as the precarious position of Britain's own banks became alarmingly obvious in the first few days of October. The Bank's secret Emergency Liquidity Assistance facility was providing just that – liquidity – but it was clear that the banks – in particular, RBS, Lloyds TSB and Barclays – might need a much more fundamental rescue package.

Matters came to a head in the first weeks of October, when the Bank found itself cast as a deal maker, negotiating both with the banks and with the Tripartite. King, Andrew Bailey and Andy Haldane found themselves at the heart of a complex set of transactions, largely being driven by the FSA and the Treasury. It was unfamiliar territory and much more the preserve of corporate financiers than economists and central bankers. Those corporate financiers did exist in Whitehall but they were in short supply. They were certainly not, as ex-Treasury man Sir James Sassoon later noted bluntly, at the Treasury: 'HM Treasury's group of special advisers and senior officials with direct responsibility for financial services lacked any significant financial market experi-ence.' The few financial practitioners there were had been diverted to agencies such the government's Shareholder Executive, where they had spent the past few years busily sizing up state-owned assets for sale. As it was, both the Bank and the Treasury had to lean heavily on their external lawyers and bankers for advice, racking up huge fees in the process.

The week of Monday 6 October opened with a further meeting at the Treasury, hosted by Darling, for all the banks' chief executives, at which it became clear that a full rescue package to bolster the liquidity being provided by the secret ELA was required.

Tuesday saw another collapse in bank share prices – and that of RBS in particular. It shares were suspended twice during the course of the day's trading, signalling that selling had become disorderly. Investors were dumping RBS stock at any price they could get. Darling heard this grim news in Luxembourg, where he was attending a meeting of Ecofin, the boring-but-necessary convocation of European finance ministers. In London, the Bank and the FSA braced themselves. At RBS itself, it faced the final denouement in its tortured recent history. Sir Tom McKillop, its chairman, telephoned Darling to warn him that the bank had only a matter of hours left before it went under.

At the Bank, King was left in no doubt that the government and the Treasury would not allow RBS to go down. Macpherson told King that the Bank was to do everything in its power to provide sufficient funds to RBS, which would allow the stricken bank to get to the end of the day, not least after the US markets opened in the afternoon. There was simply no alternative, given the size and reach of the Scottish bank, on which so many other financial institutions both in Britain and across the world depended. The Bank obliged. RBS got to the 4.30 p.m. London market close in one piece, but still desperate for funds.

That Tuesday evening proved to be a historic one. King, Andrew Bailey and Andy Haldane made their way to the Treasury, which had assumed the air of a war room – a war which was, by any stretch of the imagination, going badly. While King discussed the latest developments with Darling, now arrived back from

Luxembourg, and Adair Turner, Bailey and Haldane got to work on the detail of what would be a rescue package, both for RBS and for the other banks, of unprecedented scale. At the Treasury, the Bank officials found Tom Scholar and his colleagues Nikhil Rathi and Mridul Hegde, along with a number of FSA executives, including Hector Sants and Jeremy Bennett, the former Credit Suisse banker. Jeremy Heywood, the Downing Street Permanent Secretary, sat alongside them. 'It was not calm,' one of those present recalled, 'there was a real sense of wartime.'

Scholar orchestrated a rolling series of meetings and corralled the various teams in separate rooms. As the evening wore on, the eight banks' chief executives – Goodwin, Varley, Daniels *et al.* – arrived and were corralled into Darling's room on the second floor, told in no uncertain terms to take the terms of the proposed rescue package or leave them. The principal elements of the bailout were non-negotiable. Much of the detail was, however. Advisers from Credit Suisse, UBS and J. P. Morgan Cazenove, later joined by another team from Citi, found themselves giving off-the-cuff tutorials about the various tiers of bank capital, which appeared to be an entirely new ground for many at the Treasury. As one of the bankers present put it: 'No one at the Treasury had any idea about bank capital.' For some in the Treasury that night, in terms of getting a deal done between the various parties, 'complexity became our friend'.

The plans worked up by Jeremy Bennett and his colleagues at the FSA were laid out and scrutinised. The FSA had hired Credit Suisse to do due diligence on the banks and a grim consensus had formed that it was going to be necessary to intervene at the banks' equity level – essentially recapitalisation – to stabilise their gyrating share prices and restore confidence in the system. Scholar concentrated on getting the FSA and the Bank to agree a deal. One of the first proposals was for 'contingent equity', which was essentially a drawdown facility, whereby Treasury funds would be drip fed into the banks as they needed it and convert into equity. The FSA team initially proposed that the facility would be 'uncapped', without an official limit. Bailey and Haldane relayed this to Mervyn King at the Bank. He bridled at the idea of an unlimited facility and was equally sceptical when a figure of £100bn was suggested; it seemed that contingent equity, was, at least for the Bank, a non-starter. It was back to the drawing board, but reluctantly. According to one who was present, there was a palpable sense that, while the FSA and the Treasury officials tried to work things out, the Bank's attitude was 'destructive' and 'obstructive'. The simmering animosity between the Bank and the FSA haunted the proceedings and tempers frayed. 'What does Mervyn actually *want*?' was the exasperated cry at one point, as suggestions and rejections flew back and forth. The others observed Haldane adopt a somewhat Machiavellian role, chipping away at the Governor to get his agreement on key clauses, while a diplomatic Bailey tried to move the broader issues along to some sort of conclusion. For the FSA and the Treasury the biggest challenge was how to get King on side. One of those present observed: 'We got the impression he felt a sense of responsibility for what was happening. He knew there was a crisis, but he wanted a "small" crisis.'

Gradually, plans coalesced and compromises were found. While the various teams continued to work at the Treasury, Alistair Darling convened a meeting at 11 Downing Street with King, Macpherson and Baroness (Shriti) Vadera, who shuttled between Downing Street and the Treasury. Their principal task was to formulate the messages which would eventually be relayed to the media and the public and the text of the broad terms of the bailout; by the end of the night the latter ran to thirty pages.

The final package amounted to £500bn, of which £400bn was essentially new money, and the whole was directed at Britain's eight largest financial institutions: Abbey National, Halifax Bank of Scotland, Barclays, HSBC, Lloyds TSB, Nationwide Building Society, Royal Bank of Scotland and Standard Chartered Bank.

The three elements of the deal were further liquidity support from the Bank of England, a series of loans and a new bank debt guarantee scheme. The Bank's main contribution was to increase the size of the SLS, which it had set up the previous April, by £100bn. Despite the size of this increase, especially since the SLS had originally been planned to be 'only' £50bn, it was a relatively straightforward addition, providing Treasury bills in return for the banks' unwanted loans and mortgage securities. Secondly, the Treasury offered the banks £25bn to draw on in order to increase their core Tier 1 capital – essentially a buffer of core funds by which their financial integrity is measured. Although all eight banks and building societies committed to increases in this capital ratio, by March 2009 it appeared they had not needed the Treasury's own facility. The third element of the package was a Treasury facility which provided guarantees up to £250bn, at commercial rates, of new short- and medium-term debt issuance to assist banks in the refinancing of maturing, wholesale funding obligations – essentially, to encourage them to start lending to each other again.

Wednesday 8 October arrived and with it the 7.30 a.m. announcement of the bailout. That morning, while the Treasury officials watched the City and the media analyse their efforts, the Bank team was still hard at work. A special meeting of the MPC was convened for mid-morning and a series of conference calls were orchestrated with the Bank's counterparts at the Federal Reserve, the European Central Bank and the Bank of Canada. At midday, the Bank and its peers played a blinder, announcing a joint emergency 0.5 per cent cut in interest rates. In the Bank's case, this was its largest cut since November 2001 and took Bank Rate to 4.5 per cent.

The bailout did not end there. A few days later, on Monday 13 October, a fourth element of the rescue package was announced: the injection of £50bn to recapitalise the banks, in return for permanent interest-bearing shares, or PIBS. While the SLS and Credit Guarantee Scheme seemed other-worldly in their size and complexity, the idea of the government taking more or less straightforward equity, albeit with an eye-watering coupon of 12 per cent, in the banks had a certain sex appeal. A new company, UK Financial Investments Limited, was hastily assembled to hold the government's new equity portfolio, along with its holdings of Northern Rock and Bradford & Bingley, and RBS, Lloyds TSB and HBOS were eventually shepherded in.

RBS raised a total of £20bn, of which £5bn was issued to the government and the rest, in the form of a rights offer, was under-written by the Treasury. In the event, the government bought nearly all these shares. For its part, HBOS raised £11.5bn, of which £3bn was in preference shares to the government (subsequently converted into Lloyds TSB shares after its shotgun marriage with that bank) and the rest in a rights offer which, again, was mostly taken up by the government. Lloyds TSB suffered the same fate, raising £5.5bn, of which £1bn was in preference shares and £4.5bn was in a rights offer which, for a third time, was almost all purchased by the government. The bald facts were that all three rights offers had failed and the government had ended up with large stakes in Britain's bombed-out banks.

£££

As 2008 – an *annus horribilis* if ever there was one – drew exhaust-edly to a close, there were housekeeping matters to attend to back at the Bank. Some six months after the untimely resignation of Sir John Gieve, its deputy governor, Alistair Darling finally prepared to announce his successor. The deputy governorship had, for the first time, been publicly advertised and attracted no less than thirty-three completed applications. Each included a short essay on what candidates believed they could bring to the role. The Treasury worked with a firm of headhunters to whittle down the candidates to a shortlist of five or six. Finally, the shortlisted individuals faced an interview panel chaired by Sir Nick Macpherson, the Permanent Secretary.

Despite this elaborate and gruelling process, it came as no great surprise that Paul Tucker, now fifty years old, a veteran of twenty-eight years at the Bank and a member of the MPC for six, eventually got his reward. His appointment was confirmed on 10 December and he took up the second deputy governorship in March 2009. According to colleagues in Threadneedle Street, Tucker had made it abundantly clear that if he was not appointed deputy governor, he would be off. King was, perhaps, pragmatic and recognised the value of Tucker's contacts in the City – never more valuable than now – and that his expertise in financial stability would continue to play well outside the Bank. Furthermore, having had a clutch of external deputy governors foisted on the Bank, with mixed results, King was said to be keen that it should be an internal appointment. His letter to the Treasury pointed officials firmly in the direction of a skillset which was obviously Tucker's. When it finally came, his appointment completed the realignment of the top tier of the Bank: Lomax and Gieve were gone; in their place, Bean and Tucker. Bean was King's man and a known quantity who was happiest fine-tuning the Bank's suite of macroeconomic models. Tucker was an entirely different matter; his elevation to the deputy governorship at last put him within sight of the summit.

There was, however, little time for empire-building in late 2008. By the turn of the year, it was clear that, for all the authorities' efforts, the package of measures announced in October was not working, at least for Britain's banks. In fact, there was chaos. Confidence was at rock bottom and it seemed that all-out nationalisation was becoming a distinct possibility. Furthermore, although the Bank of England's expanded SLS had been busy taking troubled assets from the banks in return for Treasury bills, the strict criteria for acceptance meant that the banks were running out of 'good' assets to park there; and they were still encumbered by vast quantities of 'bad' assets. Above all, the spectre of a rerating – downwards – of Britain's 'AAA' status was looming ever larger, particularly in the corridors of Threadneedle Street.

In mid-January 2009, the Bank, the FSA and their investment banking advisers found themselves back at the Treasury, closeted in a meeting room and wondering what exactly they should do next. It was widely felt that the equity injections into the banks had failed. They wanted something 'big enough to deal with the problem, which didn't involve taking equity again', according to one of those present, and something akin to a 'circuit breaker' to end the banks' repeated crises. There was much debate about the pros and cons of nationalisation. By this stage, the Bank was very clearly of the opinion that it was the only option. Indeed, making a further £80–100bn of equity available to the banks was tantamount to this, because the government would end up owning the banks outright. Others were not so sure. They were alarmed that the discussions were only about the banks' equity. What about their liabilities? After all, the three main banks had balance sheets of some £5 trillion. Did the government really want to take these onto its own national balance sheet? There was a distinct silence while the enormity of this sunk in.

As enthusiasm for nationalisation faded rapidly, an alternative plan was laid out which had been worked up by Jeremy Bennett, the former investment banker who had worked on the October bailout. It was suitably ambitious, a programme which envisaged a facility to allow the banks to offload all of their toxic assets into a safe haven. This was to be the Asset Protection Scheme (APS) and it was essentially a vehicle to provide banks with insurance against loan defaults. The banks were to pay the government a flat fee – similar to an 'excess' – and in return would be insured against 90 per cent of possible losses. The plan had several advantages: firstly, the scheme was large enough for the market to believe it would work; secondly, it allowed the banks themselves to decide what to put into it; and thirdly, it gave them breathing space of several months to do so. It was no time for small measures. The APS had to be able to accommodate the most toxic 10 per cent of the banks' combined £5 trillion balance sheets. So Bennett's suggestion was that the facility would be no less than £500bn, which would represent by far the largest single transaction in the Treasury's history. There were sceptics in the room who asked Bennett: 'Are you absolutely sure about this?' Bennett insisted the scheme could work, saying: 'You've got to trust me.' In the end, Bennett, the credit derivatives expert from the City, won the day and the APS was given the go-ahead. Even in the first hours after its conception, it offered hope that a line could be drawn under the banking crisis and that banks could divest themselves of their toxic assets and provided a halo of stability. In a sense, it represented capitulation on both sides. 'Finally,' said one person involved in the discussions, 'it was "give us all your shit".'

The team spent the night of 18 January drafting a seven-page term sheet and a briefing note for Alistair Darling. The Chancellor duly announced it on the cold, rain-soaked morning of 19 January. Bundled with a number of other measures, the full magnitude of the APS was somewhat diluted by the announcement of an extension of the Bank of England's Credit Guarantee Scheme and the first green light for Quantitative Easing. To the media it was simply a 'blank cheque' for the banks; the Treasury was too exhausted to disagree. After all, the APS effectively put the government and the British on the hook for many billions of pounds of potential losses and, to all intents and purposes, made them assume £5 trillion of risk. What mattered more than public perception, however, was that the City bought into the idea. That same morning, Tom Scholar, Jeremy Bennett and Paul Myners, the City minister, held a briefing for banking analysts in the Churchill Room, at the House of Commons. As they filed in, the three men were far from sure what sort of reception the analysts would give the APS. In the event, it was broadly welcomed.

The Bank of England reserved its judgement, however. At first, it 'pooh-poohed' the idea and regarded it as 'too complicated', according to an insider. Although Andrew Bailey attended the 'APS Steercom' meetings, the Bank largely left the Treasury and Slaughter and May, the City lawyers, to do their work. The result, apart from a £22m bill to the Treasury from Slaughter and May, was a monster 800-page prospectus which captured the Byzantine detail of the scheme. At the end of February, RBS became the first bank to join the APS, paying a fee of £6.5bn for the right to have insurance protection on £325bn of assets and agreeing to bear the first loss of up to £19.5bn (later revised to £282bn and £60bn). For its part, Lloyds Banking Group initially signed an 'agreement in principle' to place £260bn of assets – out of a total balance sheet of £1.1 trillion – in the scheme, paying a fee of £15.6bn and agreeing an 'excess' of £25bn. Lloyds subsequently withdrew from the agreement, but paid a fee for the implicit protection it had received. Barclays considered participating in the APS but in the end decided against it.

The Bank of England was eventually reconciled to the APS and King conceded that if confidence was to be restored in the banks, it was imperative that the toxic assets on their balance sheets were identified and isolated. Thankfully for the Bank, responsibility for this – and the management of the APS – remained squarely with the Treasury, which set up the Asset Protection Agency, billeted alongside the Debt Management Office in the City. Crucially, the APS bought time for the financial institutions; it gave them a breathing space, during which the Treasury spent many long hours examining their asset registers, as Sir Nick Macpherson later recalled:

> When we were doing the Asset Protection Scheme, we had liter-ally 100 people working on it day and night – poring over the assets, doing the calculations and so on.[209]

Macpherson's colleague Nikhil Rathi was one of them, as he explained to the Treasury Committee in March 2009:

> Part of the reason for the scheme is the huge uncertainty that exists around these assets and their value and how they are going to perform in different economic scenarios going forward. Much of the work we are doing at the moment is on an asset-by-asset basis to get some understanding precisely of the risk transfer that has been passed to the taxpayer.[210]

As the APS found its feet and the deals were struck with RBS and Lloyds, there was a moment for the weary Tripartite teams to reflect on the work they had accomplished. Scholar, his Treasury colleagues, Bennett and others went out for a curry in Brick Lane, in London's East End, at the end of several months' slog on the project. As they toasted their success at getting this extraordinary scheme off the ground, they noticed a group of young City traders sitting at the next table. They were from one of the very banks which had so nearly ended up bust, broke and nationalised. As the evening progressed the traders became more and more drunk, rowdy and obnoxious. One of the APS team recalled ruefully: 'We did wonder whether, in the end, we had really changed anything at all.'

£££

The coda to these gargantuan efforts to tackle the financial crisis was that the Bank gradually assumed more power. In July 2008, the Bank, the Treasury and the FSA had presented their ideas on financial stability and depositor protection to Parliament. They provided the bones of the Banking Act 2009, which received Royal Assent on 12 February 2009 and which substantially increased the powers – as well as the responsibilities – of the Bank. The Banking Act filled a large hole which had been only temporarily plugged by the Banking (Special Provisions) Act 2008, passed in February of 2008, and which had been a hasty attempt to establish a regime for dealing with failing banks. The new Banking Act 2009 was an altogether more grown-up affair. First, the Act created a permanent Special Resolution Regime (SRR) to deal with distressed banks; second, it gave the Bank of England a statutory financial stability objective and established a Financial Stability Committee to oversee that objective. Mervyn King gave this a half-hearted welcome; in the Bank's 2009 Annual Report, he wrote ruefully: 'I regret that the new responsibility has not been accompanied by any new powers to deal with banks before they fail. Responsibilities and powers need to be aligned.'[211]

The SRR was an exercise in 'lessons learned' and there were many echoes of the Northern Rock and Bradford & Bingley debacles in its pages. It set out in legal form three 'stabilisation options' for a failed bank, namely transfer to a private sector purchaser, transfer to a so-called 'bridge' bank and transfer to temporary public sector ownership. The Act was clear that the first two options would be the Bank of England's responsibility – it would have to conduct the sale of a failing bank or establish new, wholly owned subsidiaries to act as a 'bridge' bank; the Treasury would take the lead on any transfer into public sector ownership. Separately, the Act also established a new bank insolvency procedure, to allow for a prompt winding up of a failed bank and payments to depositors under the Financial Services Compensation Scheme. The net result was that the Act formalised the Bank's hitherto *ad hoc* rescue packages, which had so exercised its Governor and his legal advisers and given a great many lawyers and investment bankers many long nights.

PART III

THE PARADOX OF POLICY

'That is what I call the conventional unconventional purchases.'
Mervyn King, evidence to the Treasury Committee, 24 March 2009

'It is clear to us that the only real financial discipline that is currently imposed on the Chancellor is the opinion of the gilt market on the sustainability of the public finances.'
House of Commons Treasury Committee Report on the Budget 2009

A cartoon by Peter Brookes, which appeared in *The Times* in March 2009, now hangs in the well-appointed lavatories of Brooks's, Sir Mervyn King's club in London's St James's. It depicts the Governor and Gordon Brown as two colourful playing cards – a King and a Joker. King is gleefully wielding a sword on which Brown's testicles are impaled, while Brown is doubled up in agony, clutching his crotch. Above this scene are the words 'Stimulus Package'. The cartoon was published as King issued a stern warning to the Labour government that, given the parlous state of its finances, Britain could ill afford further rounds of fiscal stimulus – the temporary cut in VAT, to 15 per cent, for example, had been a grand but expensive gesture. The cartoon also points to the fact that in the spring of 2009 King's relations with

Brown had reached rock bottom. The government was exhausted, impoverished and now, with King's intervention, emasculated.

The Bank, meanwhile, was in the throes of one of the occasional *grands projets* which central bank Governors dream about. This was its programme of Quantitative Easing – monetary, rather than fiscal, stimulus – which ultimately became a £275bn bet on getting Britain's economy going again in the midst of the worst recession in living memory. QE, as it rapidly became known, was highly experimental, of uncertain consequence and unknown conclusion. It was that thing rarely observed in the Parlours of the Bank of England: a gamble.

QE had its genesis in the dark days of December 2008. While the Bank was working with the Treasury to address the danger of collapse in the banking industry, it was also becoming increasingly alarmed by the deteriorating state of the wider economy. The Bank's network of regional agents, who fed data, news and anecdotal evidence into Threadneedle Street, had provided ample evidence that 'demand' – the appetite for goods and services – had all but stalled across the country. Their December report was particularly gloomy, noting, among other things, that 'demand for a range of consumer services had continued to shrink. Most notably, there were widespread reports of lower spending on services associated with housing, financial services, and on entertainment outside the home.'[212] Overall, Britain's GDP had fallen by a whopping 6 per cent during the recession; it was to fall a further 2.5 per cent in the first quarter of 2009.

King and his colleagues watched the data roll in with dismay. He recalled later that 'For the first time in my life, the amount of money was growing too slowly.'[213] The 'amount of money' he referred to is what is known among economists as Broad Money (or 'M4'). It represented the very lifeblood of the economy.

In more normal times, the Bank might have lowered interest

rates, which would have had the effect of increasing the money supply, to counter this ebbing away of demand. But it had already lowered Bank Rate from 5.0 per cent in September 2008 to just 1.0 per cent, the lowest in its history. The Bank's economists peered anxiously at their models and wondered what would happen if Bank Rate was taken even lower, to 0.5 per cent, the so-called 'lower bound'. 'We wondered whether the money market would stop functioning altogether,' recalled one. The situation presented very real dangers. One Bank insider put it bluntly: 'We had reached the point where we would try anything. There was a real threat that the recession would turn into a 1930s-style depression. It was a very serious situation.'

In the weeks leading up to Christmas 2008, the anxious conversations between senior officials at the Bank and the Treasury coalesced into something resembling a workable plan. A joint team began working 'intensively'[214] on a transmission mechanism, whose purpose would be to pump very substantial amounts of cash back into the economy. This mechanism gained a name – the Asset Purchase Facility (APF) – and a cloak of the greatest secrecy.

Dave Ramsden, a familiar face at the Bank in his capacity as Treasury representative on the Monetary Policy Committee, took the lead for the Treasury. At the Bank, King made Paul Fisher, head of the Bank's Foreign Exchange Division (but earmarked for Markets), and Spencer Dale, the Bank's chief economist, joint chairmen of an APF steering group. They were joined by Sarah Breeden, the feisty head of the Markets Division's Special Projects who is known as 'Mrs Fixit' in Threadneedle Street. Breeden, who knows her Bagehot and is highly regarded by the Governor, had led the Bank's Northern Rock team during that crisis and been intimately involved in the implementation of the Special Liquidity Scheme. From 1 January 2009, Graham Nicholson, the Bank's chief legal adviser, newly arrived from Freshfields, also came on board.

These senior Bank executives gathered a further twenty staff, including their best analysts and econometric modellers from the Markets and Monetary Analysis divisions. The group convened in the Bank's Sterling Room and began work in earnest, fleshing out the bones of the scheme. Several of those who worked on it during those long winter days remember the design of the APF – and, specifically, how it would interact with its counterparties – being uniquely challenging and by far the most complex of their careers at the Bank.

At the heart of the APF was, as its name suggested, the intention to buy 'assets' – specifically, debt securities – from large financial institutions such as pension funds and other asset managers; this would provide them with cash, which, so the argument went, they would spend on other, 'riskier', assets. It was called 'portfolio rebalancing'. That, at least, was the theory and Quantitative Easing was still, with the odd historical precedent, a theory, drawn from the pages of economists' academic literature. Such 'unconventional measures' – the Bank's preferred phrase – had, however, been broached in the Bank before. Paul Tucker had speculated on QE's attractions back in July 2004:

> Faced with a liquidity trap, the Bank could in principle make purchases of securities to inject base money, which would be within our vires and technically would be 'excess reserves'.

Tucker raised a couple of caveats which, as it turned out, were to exercise the Bank later on:

> We would need to do so in a way that preserved the integrity of our balance sheet. The second point is that, in such circumstances,

there would potentially be a need to coordinate with government debt management, since that by definition also involves the exchange of securities for cash.[215]

Four and a half years later, Tucker found himself discussing this with his colleagues again. But, in late 2008, as the APF steering group hurried to make QE a reality, divisions between the Bank team and the Treasury team rapidly appeared. The arguments turned on which assets the APF should actually buy. The Treasury was adamant that it should be used to buy corporate bonds from financial institutions and, in doing so, unblock the credit markets. This, the Bank pointed out, would not technically be Quantitative Easing, since it would not involve increasing the money supply. The Bank was equally adamant that it should be designed for 'textbook' QE, which it envisaged as creating new money and buying solely government debt.

'Politically, the Treasury wanted us to buy corporate assets,' recalled a Bank insider. 'The government felt it was both necessary and desirable that that it was seen to be assisting corporate credit.' But while some at the Bank, including, it is said, Spencer Dale, were in favour of the corporate credit route, the Governor and others were equally determined that any programme should concentrate on government bonds, or gilts. It was anathema to King that the Bank's balance sheet should be exposed to corporate 'credit risk'. There was a strong sense, one person close to the discussions recalled, that 'the Governor did not want to go down in history as the one who lost a lot of money on corporate bonds.' This rationale was later given voice by Professor David Miles, an external member of the MPC:

The advantage of gilt purchases is that the market for gilts is liquid and deep, and there is no credit risk. The homogeneity of gilts (in terms of credit risk) means that the MPC is not drawn in to making credit allocation decisions between issuers and deciding which firms get funding and which do not.[216]

Besides the wrangling over which assets to buy, there was also the matter of exactly how much the APF should spend. 'The Treasury wanted to make a big splash,' said one Bank insider. 'They came up with the number £50bn. We never saw that figure as a target. We were just trying to work out what exactly the problem was we were trying to solve.'

King was at great pains to ensure that if the proposed scheme was envisaged as being overtly part of the Bank's monetary policy, decisions should remain with the Monetary Policy Committee. Effectively, the MPC was to be handed an enormous sum of money and told to go shopping – and quickly. But there was a further very important twist. Although the Bank insisted that the MPC should be able to vote to turn the tap of Quantitative Easing on or off, it would not decide which assets the programme would acquire. As King pointedly reminded the Treasury Committee a few months later: 'The choice of the individual instruments and the precise methods has been delegated to the Executive of the Bank by the Chancellor, not [to] the MPC.'[217] In other words, it was to be the Governor and his team who would ultimately decide on how the programme was carried out. The devil was in such details.

While the wrangling between the Bank and the Treasury went on, the APF steering group grasped the nettle and set up a working group to build the actual machinery – the econometric models, the auction process whereby bondholders could sell their securities to the Bank and the framework which would govern the APF's putative counterparties. As the pieces of the jigsaw gradually fell into place, those involved were left in no doubt about the seriousness of the scheme and about King's ownership of it. 'It became a very big deal and very personally associated with the Governor,' said one. By mid-January 2009, after many weeks of hard slog, the mechanics of Quantitative Easing had finally been worked out and there was a palpable sense of achievement. Fisher and Dale took their team for a celebratory beer in a pub round the corner from the Bank.

As the Bank and the Treasury prepared to unveil the Asset Purchase Facility, news of the possibility of Quantitative Easing began to seep out to the media. It lost no time in canvassing the opinion of George Osborne, the Shadow Chancellor:

> The very fact that the Treasury is speculating about printing money shows that Gordon Brown has led Britain to the brink of bankruptcy ... Printing money is the last resort of desperate governments when all other policies have failed. It can't be ruled out as a last resort in the fight against deflation, but in the end printing money risks losing control of inflation and all the economic problems that high inflation brings.[218]

Undaunted, the Treasury made its official announcement on 19 January 2009. It stuck to its entirely arbitrary figure of £50bn and the APF was introduced as a scheme which would allow the Bank to 'purchase high quality private sector assets', predominantly corporate bonds, syndicated paper and asset-backed securities to 'increase the availability of corporate credit, by reducing the illiquidity of the underlying instruments'. In addition, there was a crucial nod to the Governor: the Treasury would also allow the Bank's Monetary Policy Committee to use the APF for 'monetary policy purposes' should the MPC conclude that this would be 'a useful additional tool for meeting the inflation target'. Ultimately, this would be summarised by the Bank as follows:

The objective of Quantitative Easing is to boost the money supply through large-scale asset purchases and, in doing so, to bring about a level of nominal demand consistent with meeting the inflation target in the medium term.[219]

The inner workings of the APF were all news to the media and the public. After two years of grappling with stories about derivatives, bank capital ratios, the mysteries of the Interbank market and other financial exotica, they were never going to enjoy Quantitative Easing. Even the term, which had emerged from the economic swamp of 1990s Japan, was a mouthful. The Bank of England preferred its own Kafkaesque phrase 'unconventional measures'. The newspapers' headline writers rapidly plumped for the abbreviation 'QE' and this settled itself hazily in the popular consciousness.

In the City, QE was greeted with a good deal of scepticism, particularly before the programme became associated, rather erroneously, with a 'feelgood' factor which would give a fillip to the markets. The Bank sent Paul Fisher and his colleagues on a roadshow to explain the APF's ambitions to leading asset managers, pension funds and dealers. Many of them did not like the sound of it, despite the fact that the Bank was essentially offering to buy their bonds at good prices and, potentially, in vast quantities. Senior banking figures puzzled over the announcement, too. One chief executive recalled that it seemed 'highly controversial' for the Bank to embark on such an audacious move. It also seemed to reflect a Doomsday scenario and the question was asked in the City: what does the Bank know that we don't?

Rather than have the large sum of £50bn attached directly to its own balance sheet, the Bank set up new a vehicle to make its actual purchases. The Bank of England Asset Purchase Facility

Fund Limited (BEAPFF) was incorporated on 30 January 2009; Paul Tucker and Spencer Dale appointed as its first directors (Tucker was replaced by Paul Fisher on 1 March). Despite their presence on the board of BEAPFF, the company's accounts were not to be consolidated with the Bank's own accounts and therefore, technically, the Bank had no economic interest in the fund; it was agreed that any losses would be indemnified by the Treasury – and any profits would accrue to it. BEAPFF would, therefore, 'never show a profit or a loss'.[220]

BEAPFF's remit was, in crude terms, to start spending as fast as possible. But where was the new company's money to come from? The Bank agreed with the Treasury that the putative £50bn would be financed by a loan to BEAPFF from the Bank, initially 'through the issuance of Treasury bills'. In effect, the Bank's corporate bond purchases were financed by a loan from the UK Debt Management Office (DMO), an executive agency of the Treasury, which is responsible for managing government debt and, as part of this task, issuing Treasury bills. This arrangement was to continue until 6 March, when the Bank began to create its own money.

In the event, after all the fuss, the APF's much-vaunted corporate bond purchases came to virtually nothing. Over the first few months of 2009, the Bank sulkily bought a total of just over £1.6 billion of such bonds, repeatedly claiming that the corporate bond market was too small for the Bank's purchases to have the required effects. The remaining £48.4 billion of the £50 billion facility lay unused. It was still there in the early autumn of 2011, when George Osborne reminded the Governor that he was still at liberty to use it to assist the credit markets. The Governor's distaste for it had not diminished with the passage of time. Finally, the death knell came in November 2011, when the following paragraph was slipped into the Chancellor's Autumn Statement:

It has been shown over the life of the APF that its objective to ensure the normal functioning of corporate capital markets can be delivered by undertaking asset purchases of substantially less than the ceiling of £50 billion set in 2009. The ceiling on private sector asset purchases is therefore being reduced by £40 billion to £10 billion. This provides scope for the Government to announce a package of credit easing interventions.

The last sentence was, of course, a complete nonsense. The APF's original £50bn, while pretty spurious, was always intended to be used to acquire corporate bonds issued by large, blue-chip companies, never to 'ease' the credit sought by small and medium-sized private companies (the much put-upon small and medium-sized enterprises, or SMEs). Its reduction to £10bn did not provide 'scope' for the government, it simply retired the facility.

£££

By 5 February, when the Bank's Monetary Policy Committee met for its usual monthly deliberations, full-blown Quantitative Easing was firmly on the menu. The MPC decided that the moment had come to undertake asset purchases for 'monetary policy purposes'. The committee agreed that such purchases would help boost inflation, which it feared would slam into reverse as deflation, and bring it back in line with the Bank's all-important 2 per cent medium-term target. The Committee's minutes recorded that its members agreed unanimously that King should write to the Chancellor 'to seek authority to conduct purchases of government and other securities, financed by the creation of central bank money using the APF'.[221] Government securities were, of course, gilts. The minutes noted that 'it would be crucial for the Chancellor to ensure that the Government's debt management policy would be consistent with the monetary policy actions of the MPC. The Committee recognised that the impact of such operations was both uncertain and subject to time lags.'

Twelve days later, on 17 February, King wrote to Darling, in somewhat gnomic terms, to make the Bank's request:

> To the extent that the facility could be used to buy gilts on the secondary market financed by central bank money, this could be similar to the current implementation of monetary policy, except that the instrument of policy would shift toward the quantity of money provided rather than its price.[222]

This paragraph would not win any prizes for plain English, but it did contain the first official mention of gilts as the target of the APF. Reassuringly, King's letter went on to say that if the facility were to be used for 'monetary policy purposes, purchases of assets would be financed through central bank money, rather than by the issuance of Treasury bills'. He returned to the MPC's concern about whether the purchase of gilts would be 'consistent' with the work of the DMO:

> If the facility were to be used to purchase gilts, it would be important that the Government's debt management policy remain consistent with the aims of monetary policy. It should not alter its issuance strategy as a result of the transactions that are taken through the Asset Purchase Facility for monetary policy purposes.[223]

Darling responded to King's letter on 3 March. He was able to 'authorise the MPC to use the Asset Purchase Facility to purchase UK Government debt on the secondary market'. In addition, he was increasing the scale of purchases of all eligible assets very considerably, to up to £150bn. There was another, vain effort, incidentally, to interest the Bank in corporate credit: 'In line with the current arrangements and in recognition of the importance of supporting the flow of corporate credit, up to £50bn of that should be used to purchase private sector assets.' The balance – up to £100bn – was sanctioned to buy gilts. Interestingly, having dropped this huge new number of £100bn into the proceedings, Darling's letter then took a rather defensive turn, spending several paragraphs outlining the work, goals and ambitions of the DMO.

It is worth noting that, by now, the MPC, the Governor and the Chancellor himself had all strenuously insisted that the Bank's gilts purchases should be consistent with the DMO's gilts issuance strategy. The problem was this: QE laid the Bank open to the charge, predicated on the inarguable facts that gilts are government debt and that the Bank is 100 per cent owned by the government, that if the Bank bought gilts, albeit on the secondary market, would the country not be put in the invidious position of buying its own debt?

£££

The Debt Management Office, the object of the Bank's gnawing concern, is based in unremarkable modern offices in Philpot Lane, in the heart of the City of London, a stone's throw from the flame-topped Monument to the Great Fire of London and a few hundred yards from the Bank itself.

Here, a hundred staff toil on the vital, but rather thankless, task of managing the government's borrowing, which in turn fuels the public finances. Each year, the DMO receives the *Debt and Reserves Management Report*, known as the 'Dreamer', from the Treasury. This document outlines the government's cash requirements and the amount of debt financing it will need to raise in the market. The debt – cumulatively, Britain's national debt – is manifested in the form of gilts (properly 'gilt-edged securities' or 'gilt-edged stock'). These are guaranteed by the government, issued by the DMO and sold into the market by so-called gilt-edged market makers, or GEMMs, drawn from the leading investment banks.

Like many other sorts of debt security, gilts pay a modest amount of interest until the government gets around to paying back the principal. Gilts come in various flavours, mostly dictated by their maturity dates: so-called Treasury bills have maturities of anything up to twelve months, 'short-dated gilts' have one- to seven-year maturity dates, 'medium-dated' gilts have seven to fifteen years, while 'long-dated' gilts are fifteen years and over. Between the time they are issued and the time they are redeemed, gilts' prices fluctuate as they are bought and sold in the market. And, in all cases, gilts' yields have an inverse relationship with their price. So, when a gilt's price in the market falls, its yield rises and *vice versa*.

It is tempting to see the DMO in Dickensian terms, as a great, clanking engine room, producing monstrous swathes of debt. The reality is more prosaic. Its offices are calm and open plan, with serried ranks of desks, computer screens and Bloomberg terminals. The walls are hung with mementoes of its illustrious predecessor, the Bank of England's Gilt-Edged Division: long-forgotten, but possibly still outstanding, debt in the form of framed Treasury bills, black and white photographs of whiskery old gentlemen and a couple of wax seals of the Exchequer. Otherwise, it is a highly sophisticated trading room. Over £4 trillion in debt and cash market transactions passes through its dealers' terminals each year. In charge of this formidable operation is Robert Stheeman, a former investment banker who spent sixteen years in the Debt

Capital Markets Division of Deutsche Bank, in London, before joining the DMO in January 2003. Stheeman – known in the market as 'Mr Gilts' – has the responsibility to carry out the DMO's mission:

> The primary objective of UK debt management is to minimise, over the long term, the cost of meeting the Government's financing needs, taking account of risk, whilst ensuring that debt management policy is consistent with the objectives of monetary policy.

While there is a relationship with the government's 'monetary policy' – the jealously guarded preserve, of course, of the Bank of England – the DMO's prime roles remain to raise debt and manage debt. In the fourteen years since its creation, as the public finances have deteriorated, it has been getting gradually busier. In its first financial year (1998/99) the DMO issued just £8.2bn of gilts, conducting its auctions manually and largely without computers. The following year, gilt issuance was £14.2bn, but in 2000, the government received a £22.5bn windfall from the sale of 3G mobile phone spectrum licences – £19.5bn more than had originally been forecast. It was suddenly awash with cash and for a moment it seemed that, having gone to all the trouble of setting up the DMO, it might not be needed after all. In the event, the windfall was quickly soaked up and there was £10bn of gilts issuance in 2000/2001. From here on in, the annual issuance figure began to rise sharply, climbing to £49.9bn in 2003/2004. Over the next few years there was something of a plateau before a spike to £62.5bn in 2006/2007 and £58.5bn in 2007/2008. The following year, things began to unravel in the UK economy and the government's need to raise funds became more urgent. The DMO's original remit for 2008/09 was for gilt sales of £80bn. This was revised upwards by £30bn, to £110bn in October 2008.

Barely a month later, in November 2008, the Pre-Budget Report prompted a revision to the revision. This increased the sum by a further £36.4bn, to a dizzying £146.4bn.

By the time the Bank was planning QE, therefore, the DMO was issuing more gilts than at any time in its history. Strangely, it was not party to the principal discussions at the Bank about the APF, which was just about to become the biggest buyer by far of its gilts and which would, as an unintended consequence, cause a great deal of stress in the gilts market.

£££

When the Bank's Monetary Policy Committee met on 5 March, it considered two proposals. First, that Bank Rate should be cut by 0.5 per cent, from 1.0 per cent to 0.5 per cent, a motion carried unanimously. Second, that the APF should now begin its work. The committee's minutes record some debate about the quantum of funds the facility would deploy, but ultimately the figure of £75 billion was settled on. There was then a certain amount of twisting and turning about the switch from corporate bonds to gilts.

> The Committee noted that the Bank would continue with its purchases of private sector assets in order to improve directly the functioning of corporate credit markets … However, it was likely that the purchases of private sector assets over the coming months would be significantly less than the £75 billion target for overall purchases. In part that was because the size of those private sector asset markets was relatively small. But in addition, the first objective of those purchases was to reduce spreads and to improve the flow of credit. As such, the scale of purchases by the Bank in those markets was not the primary objective. Given

these considerations, the Bank would also need to buy substantial quantities of conventional gilts in the secondary market in order to meet the Committee's objective for overall asset purchases.[224]

The committee agreed that its gilts purchases would be made 'from the domestic non-bank financial sector rather than from banks' for the reason that such institutions 'were likely to use some of the proceeds from asset sales to buy other assets' and therefore spur the 'portfolio rebalancing' effect which the QE programme hoped to achieve. Finally, it was decided that the Bank would not purchase gilts with very long-dated maturities of twenty-five years and above, because this might cause problems for pension funds, which were holders of large amounts of such gilts.

As these resolutions fell into place, all eyes around the committee table turned to Paul Fisher, who was attending his first MPC meeting, having been appointed a member of the committee just four days previously. As head of the Bank's Markets Division, Fisher was directly responsible for carrying out the gargantuan gilts purchase programme. Amid the shuffling of papers as the MPC meeting closed, there was, apparently, a quip from the Governor to the effect 'all yours, Paul; off you go'. The momentous economic experiment had finally been given the go-ahead.

But the Bank bungled it.

At twelve noon precisely, the MPC's decisions were transmitted from Threadneedle Street to the market. It said that the Bank would begin its gargantuan gilts-buying programme by acquiring 'medium- and long-maturity conventional gilts'.[225] The gilts market knew this meant everything from seven years' maturity to fifty years' maturity. It traded on this basis for the next 2 hours and 22 minutes, in which time fortunes were made, and perhaps lost, for gilts investors around the world. Then, at 2.22 p.m., the Bank issued a clarification. What it had actually meant to say was that it would be buying gilts in the 5- to 25-year maturities. The unmistakeable impression this left, according to senior figures in the London market, was that the Bank understood so little about the gilts market that it did not even have a grasp of the basic terminology.

The market, in the words of one GEMM, 'went haywire' as traders scrambled back into the 5- to 25-year range, immediately causing the gilts on either side to drop dramatically. This temporarily fractured the yield curve, the bond market's yields-over-time backbone, which, given the significance of the curve's integrity, is something You Just Do Not Do. The gyrations of the market caused consternation, too, at the DMO, whose own dealers found themselves in the eye of the storm.

At 4 p.m., many of the GEMMs were called into the Bank. Paul Fisher, looking somewhat dishevelled according to one who was present, managed to clarify further the Bank's intentions and lay out its plans for further purchases. He agreed, incidentally, that there would be 'questions' about the relationship between the Bank's gilts purchases and the DMO's gilts issuance strategy. The GEMMs left wondering what else the Bank would spring on them.

It was not a good start. By the time the APF made its first actual purchase of gilts, on 11 March, the market had run up prices in the Bank's selected range of gilts to the extent that traders were already booking very substantial profits. There was, for example, an unprecedented seventy basis points (0.7 per cent) move in the yield on the ten-year gilt (from 360bps to 290bps) between the day before the asset purchase programme was announced and one week after it. A trader who held, say, £100m of gilts on the most sensitive part of the yield curve – the five-year mark – would have cleared a profit of some £2m in the week that QE was announced.

In spite of these unintended consequences, once it had started its £75bn programme the Bank did not waste time. By 9 April, it had purchased no less than £26bn of gilts. A month later, on 7 May, it increased its target purchases by a further £50bn to £125bn. This was followed by a further £50bn on 6 August and another £25bn in November, bringing the total to £200bn.

To put these figures into perspective, there were a total of £537bn conventional gilts outstanding at the beginning of 2009. The Bank's purchases were, therefore, by any standards, massive interventions in the gilts market. The Bank made its purchases in twice-weekly operations, during which it selected a particular maturity range of gilts – either those with a five- to ten-year range, or those between ten and twenty-five years. The actual mechanics of the purchases made by the Bank were described thus:

> The Bank purchases these assets predominantly from non-banks, but banks act as intermediaries in the process. The Bank pays for the assets purchased by creating central bank reserves and crediting the accounts of the banks that act as intermediaries. Those banks will in turn credit the accounts of the non-banks from whom they obtained the assets.[226]

In plain English, this means that the Bank's 'printed' money rarely actually leaves the Bank. When it buys a gilt from, say, a pension fund, it credits that pension fund's bank account. That bank account will invariably be with one of the main clearing banks, which will be one of the Bank's own reserve account holders. So, the transaction is little more than a simple transfer of funds from one part of the Bank to another. A purchase has, however, been made, a transaction has occurred and money has changed hands. The pension fund is now free to put the proceeds to work in the wider economy.

King and his colleagues made the process of QE sound all very easy. In fact, the opposite was the case, as Paul Fisher revealed in October 2010, when he addressed an audience of West Country businessmen at a hotel near Stroud, in Gloucestershire. In his speech – 'An Unconventional Journey' – Fisher gave a candid account of some of the problematic mechanics of QE. For a start, he said, the Bank relied heavily on market makers to find it enough gilts to buy. The commercial banks, the Bank's first point of call, were not suitable. Fisher recalled:

> Although commercial banks act as market makers for gilts, and were thus the immediate conduit for the gilt purchases, they typically held only a very small amount on their own balance sheets as part of their liquidity portfolios. Market makers had to source gilts in the market before selling on to the Bank.[227]

The other large holders of gilts were insurance companies and pension funds, many of whom seemed reluctant to part with them:

> There were market participants who told us that this would not be possible as the asset managers would not be able to move away from their benchmark holdings (the initial target being £75bn). Once the programme was announced, the Bank took steps to proactively discuss our operations with market participants, to allay that initial scepticism. In the weeks that followed the announcement in March 2009, we called in our contacts at the Gilt-Edged Market Makers and many of the larger asset managers, to explain the operations and to encourage them to participate.[228]

Having persuaded some of these parties to sell their gilts to the Bank, Fisher was particularly concerned that its purchases were made at 'a fair market price':

> We had to consider this against the backdrop of a heavy UK government issuance programme: we were alert to the risk that market participants might buy direct from the government's Debt Management Office (DMO) and attempt to sell the same gilts to the Bank at a higher price.[229]

In a masterstroke to thwart such dastardly deeds, which every gilts trader in the City had realised instantaneously, the Bank had decided to set 'a targeted rate of purchases initially three times higher than the DMO were issuing'. Leaving aside the comic vision of the Bank furiously buying gilts three times faster than the DMO could issue them, there were more ingenious plans to frustrate the spivs: firstly, the purchases were designed as competitive auctions; secondly, the Bank bought bundles of gilts, rather than individual stocks, to mitigate the danger of a bottleneck in any one particular gilt; and finally, according to Fisher: 'We eliminated from the operations any gilts which we knew the DMO were about to issue or had issued in the previous week.'[230]

A sceptical member of Fisher's audience, ruminating over the coffee and mints in Stroud, might have concluded from all this that the Bank's forays into the gilts market were proving far more difficult than the Bank had first envisaged. Fisher acknowledged this: 'I don't want to imply that implementing and maintaining our programme of asset purchases was straightforward operationally. Far from it.'[231]

Indeed, it was heading for potential disaster.

The biggest difficulty, besides actually sourcing enough gilts and desperately trying not to trip over the DMO's own issuance programme, was that the Bank of England's vast gilts purchases caused considerable dislocation in the gilt market. The stress principally derived from the ensuing shortage of gilts in the market: the Bank was, after all, on course to own a staggering 29 per cent of the entire free float of the entire amount of gilts in issue. A more forensic analysis revealed an even larger Bank exposure in certain gilts. The Bank rapidly reached a situation where, in Fisher's words, '[it] started to hold more than 70 per cent of some of the gilts in issue'.[232] This was an astonishing concentration, by any standards.

At the DMO this caused real alarm. By the late spring and summer of 2009, the DMO's dealers began to see what are known as 'fails' in the gilts market. A 'fail', or 'delivery failure', is essentially an unsettled trade, when a transaction between a seller and a prospective purchaser does not complete. In these cases, it was because of a persistent lack of gilts liquidity. Fails are rare: in normal times, there might have been one a month. Now, however, the DMO was witnessing multiple fails each day. This was exacerbated by a series of 'repo squeezes', in which the borrowing and lending of gilts between market counterparties became severely disrupted. The DMO was forced to activate its Standing Repo Facility and, on 22 May, its Special Repo Facility. The latter, according to the DMO, is only employed when there is 'evidence of severe market dislocation or disruption'.[233] In plain terms, these facilities allowed the DMO temporarily to create extra gilts, to allow trades to settle smoothly, albeit at a penalty rate. This was not a case of topping up the available supply with a handful of additional gilts: so stressed did the market become that the Standing and Special Repo Facilities were used repeat-edly, making available hundreds of millions of pounds worth of 'extra' securities. (Interestingly, this situation had been envisaged by the Bank of England itself in an internal crisis-planning brief in 2003, which referred explicitly to a DMO emergency facility: '[The facility] could be of use following an event of major opera-tional disruption if much of a particular Government stock is temporarily removed from the market (this would cause liquidity problems as Government stock is commonly used as collateral in payment systems).'[234])

Faced in the summer of 2009 with this precise situation, which one person involved described as 'desperate', not least because it had begun to interfere with the DMO's own issuance strategy, the Bank and the DMO convened an urgent meeting. On 6 August they issued a joint statement announcing that the Bank would lend the DMO further huge amounts of gilts 'to relieve any undesirable frictions in the functioning of the market':[235]

> The amount available will be at least 10% of the APF's holdings of each stock, and more where the APF's holding is greater than 50% of the free float. In addition, the Bank will be prepared to make the APF's gilts available for use in the DMO's Standing Repo Facility and in any relevant DMO Special Repo Facility in specific stocks...[236]

This *Alice in Wonderland* scenario, in which the Bank would lend back gilts it had just bought, albeit at one remove, so that the DMO could reuse them in the market, may give economists of the future pause. At the time, it was the only way to solve the problem. But while the unprecedented amount of 'fails' and the chaos caused by 'repo squeezes' were the most serious unintended consequences of the Bank's QE programme, they were not the only ones. At one point, it became clear to the London market that because the Bank was announcing which gilts it was going to buy before it actually made its 'buybacks', some traders were, despite the Bank's best efforts, successfully 'spivving' the market.

Each week, ahead of the days on which the Bank was to make its purchases, certain gilts would trade expensively – the 5 per cent 2014 gilt, for example, was cited as a particular target by gilts traders – their prices spiking out of the normal market curve. Because such issues were scarce, there would often be few sellers – and the only buyer in town at such high prices was the Bank. At 2.45 p.m. on the Bank's appointed buyback days, its own traders would take a snapshot of the market and decide on their purchases, which were, in part, informed by the lowest relative discounts available from the sellers. By this time, an unscrupulous trader would have discounted heavily the price spike he had created, meaning his block of, say, £100m gilts did indeed offer the best 'relative' value and could be more or less certain to be included in the Bank's purchases.

This sort of irregular activity was not lost on the Bank. It took to excluding certain gilts from its buybacks with no warning, to second-guess these unscrupulous traders and leave them holding overpriced gilts. Occasionally, the Bank would call the GEMMs in, warning them that it was able to see all their trades and dropping hints about their regulator. Eventually, the Bank resorted to rejecting 'expensive' bonds altogether.

£££

On 24 March 2009, Mervyn King's official diary held an unusual entry, sandwiched between appearances before the Treasury Select Committee and the House of Lords' Economics Affairs Committee: 'Audience with Her Majesty The Queen'.

As he was led through the halls of Buckingham Palace, he could reflect that this was the first time in her 57-year reign that the Queen had held an audience with a Governor of the Bank of England. It was an uncomfortable interview with the headmistress, as it were, but also perhaps a moment for King to reflect on another staging post on the extraordinary journey of the boy from an anonymous suburb in the Black Country. For half an hour, they sat alone together to discuss the parlous state of the nation's economy. The Queen's interest, which no doubt extended to her own bruised and battered £100m investment portfolio, had been piqued a few months previously, when she paid a visit to the London School of Economics. On that occasion, she famously asked Professor Luis Garicano, a director of research, why 'nobody noticed it' – the 'it' being the gathering storm cloud of the credit crisis. Garicano recalled: 'She was asking me if these things were so large, how come everyone missed it.' His reply to Her Majesty was that 'at every stage, someone was relying on somebody else and everyone thought they were doing the right thing.'

The pattern of King's interview with the Queen has never been revealed, although King has hinted that, in answer to her question, he explained that in fact people did see a crisis brewing but no one could be sure where and when it would appear. He used the analogy of an earthquake zone and the need to prepare for future shocks: '[We] should be trying to build buildings in ways which are more robust.'[237] The matter did not end there. A few months later, King's old friend Peter Hennessy wrote a letter to the Queen to tell her that the British Academy, a scholarly body of indeterminate purpose, had convened a forum to debate her original question. It had concluded that

> the failure to foresee the timing, extent and severity of the crisis and to head it off, while it had many causes, was principally a failure of the collective imagination of many bright people, both in this country and internationally, to understand the risks to the system as a whole.[238]

While the Queen might have been forgiven for thinking that the Bank of England's senior team were among the 'many bright people', Hennessy was at pains to point out that the Bank had issued 'many warnings' about financial imbalances, and that, regarding inflation, 'the Monetary Policy Committee had helped deliver an unprecedented period of low and stable inflation in line with its mandate.' Finally, Hennessy reassured the monarch:

> Given the forecasting failure at the heart of your enquiry, the British Academy is giving some thought to how your Crown servants in the Treasury, the Cabinet Office and the Department for Business, Innovation & Skills, as well as the Bank of England and the Financial Services Authority might develop a new, shared horizon-scanning capability so that you never need to ask your question again.[239]

In fact, Her Majesty might have felt a question coming on the very next day. As if to confirm her worries about Britain's finances, news arrived at the Bank of England from the Debt Management Office. The DMO had held an auction of £1.75bn of the 4.25 per cent Treasury Gilt 2049, a long-dated bond. It received only £1.67bn in bids, a cover ratio of 0.93 times. Bluntly, there were not enough buyers for the government's bonds. It was the first time that a conventional bond auction had failed since 1995, when an auction was covered only 0.99 times. The failed – or 'uncovered' – auction had an immediate impact on yields, which rocketed twenty basis points to 3.53 per cent, as prices fell. Robert Stheeman told the *Daily Telegraph* that the uncovered auction was because of 'a volatile market', adding: 'I am not totally surprised by today's result ... I cannot rule out more uncovered auctions.'

£££

As the Bank's Quantitative Easing programme swung into action in the spring of 2009, Alistair Darling was having sleepless nights at 11 Downing Street. The Budget, presented on Wednesday

22 April, was a thoroughly messy and last-minute affair which was still being cobbled together forty-eight hours before the Chancellor rose to the Dispatch Box in the House of Commons. When he did, it described the bill for a string of disasters: the near-systemic failure of the financial system, the beginning of a deep and prolonged recession and a collapse in consumer confidence. As a result the government's borrowing requirements were truly astronomical:

> Our own figures for public sector net borrowing will be £175bn this year, or some 12.4 per cent of GDP. From 2010, as the economy starts to recover ... borrowing will fall to £173bn, then £140bn, £118bn and £97bn. As a share of GDP, our borrowing will be 11.9 per cent of GDP next year, and then, as we move towards balance, 9.1 per cent in 2011–12, then 7.2 per cent and 5.5 per cent in 2013–14. This downturn will inevitably mean sharp increases in national debt relative to GDP. UK net debt, which includes the cost of stabilising the banking system, will, as a share of GDP, increase from 59 per cent this year, to 68 per cent next, 74 per cent in 2011–12, 78 per cent and 79 per cent in 2013–14.

It became horribly clear that the government would have to borrow massively to balance its books. Having broken this grim news, Darling proceeded calmly to outline a series of plans to raise funds – a new 50 per cent tax rate for high earners, increased duty on alcohol and tobacco and efficiency savings in the public sector. (The headline-grabbing 50 per cent tax rate would, it was later calculated, raise a mere £2bn.) By any standards, it was a political and, indeed, cynical Budget. The *Debt and Reserves Management Report* was also published that day, revealing the coming year's instructions to the DMO. Ian Pearson, Economic Secretary to the Treasury, must have taken a deep breath before writing the following in the Foreword:

> Net gilt issuance in 2009–10 is projected to be £203.4 billion and gross gilt issuance is projected to be £220.0 billion.

In the absence of any official commentary, the reader was left to draw their own conclusions. They were horribly clear. The £220bn figure was a massive 50 per cent increase on the previous year. And, at a stroke, the entire current gilts market, which then stood at £713bn, would balloon by a third within twelve months. The £220bn number was news even to the gilts market itself. Consensus forecasts had been around £180bn, which was already regarded as a superabundance. The higher figure spooked the market, sending the benchmark ten-year gilt yields higher. The announcement elicited varying reactions from the Press. The headline in the *Financial Times* was 'Market gasps at record £220bn of gilts'. The newspaper quoted Stheeman as saying: 'The £220bn is a very, very large figure. It is unprecedented but I am confident that the gilts market is mature enough, deep enough and liquid enough to absorb this large amount of bonds.'[240] Others were less sanguine. David Page, an economist at Investec, described the issuance as 'a staggering amount, without peace-time precedent. It will test investors' appetite.'[241] Willem Buiter, the former member of the Bank's Monetary Policy Committee, took a particularly pessimistic view, in the same day's *Financial Times*:

> In a year that will see £200bn [sic] worth of gilts issuance, you will avoid spooking the markets only if you have fiscal credibility: markets and the public must believe you are willing and able to raise future taxes and/or to cut future public spending to stop the debt burden from becoming unsustainable. To be an effective

Keynesian in a slump, you need a reputation as a fiscal conservative. The UK government does not have this reputation.[242]

Buiter's verdict was a blunt one: 'It would help if Mr Brown – responsible more than anyone for this debacle – were to resign.'[243] Neither
Brown nor anyone else resigned; the government ground on.

By June 2009, King had become increasingly uneasy about
the government's handling of the economy and relations with
Darling had become strained. This came to a head as the two
men prepared to deliver their speeches at the annual Mansion
House banquet on Wednesday 17 June. According to Darling, the
Governor had declined repeated requests to let the Chancellor see
a copy of his speech in the weeks leading up to the event. Darling
was finally shown the speech a couple of hours before it was due
to be delivered. He was horrified at what he read:

> It was obvious that it would be seen as evidence of a deep division
> between him [King] and me. It was a blatant bid for the Bank to
> take over regulation of the banks – and what seemed to me to be
> a rewriting of recent history.[244]

It was to prove an uncomfortable evening. King's speech was a
direct attack on Labour's economic policies. He declared that
'fiscal policy too will have to change', noting that the measures the
government had taken to stabilise banks and the wider economy
had meant that debt 'has been transferred from the private to the
public sector' – and the result was a national debt which looked
dangerously out of control:

> Five years from now national debt, as a proportion of national
> income, is expected to be more than double its level before the
> crisis. So it is also necessary to produce a clear plan to show how

prospective deficits will be reduced during the next parliament, so returning to a gradually declining path for the ratio of national debt to national income.[245]

King's admonition to the Chancellor – 'to produce a clear plan' – clearly implied that he thought there wasn't one. For good measure, King added that it was no good the Bank having its statutory objective to ensure financial stability if it did not have the tools for the job; in the meantime, King said: 'The Bank finds itself in a position rather like that of a church whose congregation attends weddings and burials but ignores the sermons in between.'[246]

The Governor's remarks were seized upon by the Press, which gleefully reported them as an unprecedented 'rebuke' to Darling and noted the marked deterioration in relations between the two men. Darling was indeed furious at King's overtly political tone. He was convinced that King was exploiting the incumbent government's weakness 'in a way he would never have done if he had thought he would still have to deal with us after the next election'.[247]

Worse was to come. The following week, King used his appearance before the Treasury Committee to chastise the government further for its handling of the public finances. Noting that 'the scale of deficits is truly extraordinary', he urged the Chancellor to make clear how they would be reduced by more credible means than simply issuing vast quantities of gilts: 'Although we are finding it easy now to finance those deficits by issuing gilts, there could be problems down the road. We need a credible statement of what will guide the deficit reduction.'[248] King's comments broke the longstanding convention that the Bank does not comment on the government's fiscal policy, but confines itself to monetary policy. Accordingly, they did not go down well at either 10 or 11 Downing Street.

£££

QE was far from over. The juggernaut ploughed on into 2010 and by the end of January, the Bank of England had completed the grand total of £199.458 bn of asset purchases. In an internal document called Working Paper 393, the Bank's own analysts provided a summary of the breathtaking scale of the operation:

> Alongside separate liquidity support to the banking sector, these purchases have expanded the Bank's balance sheet as a proportion of nominal GDP to three times its level before the onset of the crisis in the summer of 2007, as large as at any point in the past two centuries. The Bank's gilt purchases represent 29 per cent of the free float of gilts (the amount of non-official holdings of gilts) and are equivalent to around 14 per cent of nominal GDP.[249]

A hugely swollen internal balance sheet, a giant-sized bite of the entire gilts market and that eye-watering equivalence to 14 per cent of nominal GDP were the fruits of the Bank's labours. Even its most ardent supporters blanched at extending the programme and there was a general feeling that it was time to take stock. In March 2010, the Bank dispatched Spencer Dale, its chief economist, to a conference at Trinity College, Cambridge, to give a speech entitled 'QE: One Year On'.

In his opening remarks, Dale noted that it had been a 'truly extraordinary year for our economy and for economic policy' before giving a defence of the QE programme, the genesis of which lay in academic economics and literature which Dale freely admitted was 'still in its infancy'.

It was clear that the Bank's economists had studied the 'insights' provided by this academic corpus and reached the conclusion that, as Dale put it, 'the financial crisis meant that we had to put these insights into practice.' Grasping the nettle, the Bank had identified three key channels of monetary transmission: 'the impact of imperfect substitutability and the portfolio rebalancing channel on relative prices, the role of financial market liquidity, and the importance of expectations'. In plain terms, this meant addressing the relative appetites of large insurers and pension funds for gilts or cash, a rebalancing of portfolios and the reassurance the market drew from the Bank's readiness to make substantial asset purchases.

There was too, a palpable element of machismo in the speed and force of the Bank's QE programme which, Dale suggested, bolstered confidence in the MPC and its commitment to the all-important inflation target. But having flexed its muscles so impressively, the Bank then had to ascertain the effects of the programme. Dale asked: 'So what impact have our asset purchases had to date?'

> That's the two hundred billion pound question. Unfortunately, it is hard to provide a definitive answer. To be clear this is no different from our inability to assess precisely the impact of the reduction in Bank Rate from 5 per cent to 0.5 per cent. Or indeed of any macroeconomic policy measure. Without knowing what would have happened in the absence of a policy action, it is not possible to identify its incremental impact. But what is different is that this policy instrument is relatively untried and untested. So the demand to provide some insight into its impact is that much greater. This demand is quite understandable, but difficult to satisfy.[250]

In other words: we don't know. In conclusion, Dale admitted that 'many academics questioned whether [QE] would have any impact at all', but from his own perspective, the decision to proceed had been 'relatively straightforward', given the 'likely' effects of the programme:

The inflation target provides a clear, numerical objective for policy. The outlook for inflation suggested further monetary stimulus was necessary to achieve that target. With Bank Rate close to its lower bound, this stimulus had to be implemented via alternative means. And there are clear and convincing economic arguments why – in the real world – injecting money directly into the economy is likely to provide a means of achieving that stimulus.[251]

So the best the Bank's chief economist could come up with was a 'likely'. To be fair, the impact of QE, for better or worse, will be felt in a longer timeframe than the year which Dale had to observe it. But the fact remains that, to date, nobody really knows whether QE is working, has worked or will work. It remains an enigma and, in the end, the Bank can – and does – fall back on the 'counterfactual', the last refuge of the economist. Charlie Bean, speaking a few months before his colleague, put it like this:

The truth is that we will probably never know exactly how effective the policy of Quantitative Easing has been, for the simple reason that we can never know with precision what would have happened in its absence. My only confident prediction is that academic economists and their PhD students will be poring over the topic for decades to come.[252]

£££

Throughout the second half of 2010 and the first half of 2011, the Bank continued to watch the incoming data closely to ascertain whether a further round of Quantitative Easing – 'QE2' as it quickly became known – would be required. 2011 was, in Mervyn King's words, 'the year of reluctant growth'[253] in the United

Kingdom and by September there emerged a distinct faction on the Monetary Policy Committee which favoured further Quantitative Easing by way of increased intervention in the gilts market.

Adam Posen, an outspoken member of the Monetary Policy Committee, led the charge from within, calling repeatedly for a further £50bn programme. His colleagues demurred, however. The minutes for the MPC's monthly meeting in the first week of September showed a vote of eight to one against a proposal to restart the QE programme. Despite this, external factors – principally, the sovereign debt crisis engulfing the Eurozone and downgraded growth figures for western economies – continued to pile pressure on Britain's central bank to 'do something'. In the absence of further rate cuts – although a 0.25 per cent cut to Bank Rate was also discussed in September 2011 – QE was increasingly seen as a way to boost confidence, even if its effects were uncertain.

Whether by accident or design, the arguments in favour of further QE were considerably bolstered that same month by the publication in the Bank's *Quarterly Bulletin* of a lengthy essay entitled 'The UK's Quantitative Easing Policy'. Three of the Bank's economists – Michael Joyce, Matthew Tong and Robert Woods – carried out a meticulous analysis of the policy, albeit one which was embroidered with the same caveats as before. It was still impossible to calculate the precise macroeconomic impact, beneficial or otherwise, of the programme, given the many other factors at work in the markets. Nevertheless, with a canny eye on the headline writers and after much summing, averaging and the liberal use of 'may' and 'could', the trio managed to quantify Quantitative Easing's impact, firstly on gilt prices, secondly on inflation.

For the former, Joyce, Tong and Woods reckoned that the

Bank's asset purchases pushed down gilts' yields (concomitantly raising the price of gilts) by about 1 per cent, and may have helped lower investment grade corporate bond yields by 0.7 per cent and junk bond yields by 1.5 per cent. This was partly calculated by a frankly odd attempt to gauge the 'size of surprise'[254] felt by market participants at the various announcements made by the Bank about its QE purchases. As the economists put it, the Bank analysed 'expectations regarding the total size of QE purchases to calculate *the amount of asset purchase news* in each announcement'[255] (my italics). The Bank acknowledged that QE's impact on the equity markets was even harder to determine, but plumped for 'an impact of around 20 per cent'.[256] It summed up with a claim which might have raised eyebrows in homes up and down the country: 'Combining these effects on government and corporate bonds and equity prices suggests an overall boost to households' net financial wealth of about 16 per cent.'[257]

Turning to inflation, the Bank economists' calculations 'suggest that QE may have raised the level of real GDP by 1.5 per cent to 2 per cent and increased inflation by between 0.75 to 1.5 percentage points'.[258] They noted that these estimates 'are clearly highly uncertain … but they do suggest that the effects of QE were economically significant'.[259] Despite the uncertainty, this was quite an admission, given the Bank's previous reluctance to acknowledge that QE was inherently inflationary and its insistence that much of the rise in inflation was attributable to surging energy and commodity prices. To put it into perspective, as the article pointed out, the inflation rise attributed to QE was 'equivalent to a 150 to 300 basis point [1.5 per cent to 3 per cent] cut in Bank Rate'.[260] It is noteworthy that a few months after the Bank's self-congratulatory essay came a more sober reflection from the Bank of International Settlements (BIS), in Basel.

In its own *Quarterly Review*, published in December 2011, the BIS questioned the downward pressure on gilt yields which the Bank had claimed. BIS economists estimated that, far from the 100 basis point fall in yields, QE had resulted in no more than a 27 basis point fall.

While some in the City of London expressed their scepticism about the Bank's analysis – 'Bank propaganda', according to one gilt-edged market maker – its *Quarterly Bulletin* certainly succeeded in helping to make the case for more QE. By Thursday 6 October, the MPC had entirely changed its mind about whether to recommend an extension of the facility; it voted unanimously for a further £75bn, to be dispensed over the following four months. In his letter to George Osborne that day, King made it clear that, despite the fact that inflation was running at around 5 per cent, the risks remained on the downside. Demand was so weak that deflation, or a fall in prices, remained a clear, medium-term danger:

> The deterioration in the outlook has made it more likely that inflation will undershoot the 2 per cent target in the medium term. In the light of that shift in the balance of risks, and in order to keep inflation on track to meet the target over the medium term, the Committee judged that it was necessary to inject further monetary stimulus into the economy. I am therefore requesting the authority to use the Asset Purchase Facility to purchase assets financed by the issuance of central bank reserves totalling £275 billion.[261]

QE2, like its predecessor, got off to a bad-tempered start, despite King's heavily scripted assurances to millions of television viewers that it was 'the right thing to do'.[262] Four days after the announcement, on Monday 10 October, there was something of a collision between the Bank's APF team and its counterparties, when gilts traders drove up the price of the 8.75 per cent 2017 gilt, an issue of which the Bank already held a substantial quantity. By early October, it had reached a price of £140.78, a significant premium to its original issue price of £100. For the first time since the start of QE in March 2009, the Bank declined to pay up. It made the following statement: 'The Bank has decided to reject all offers against the 2017 government bond following significant changes in its yield in the run-up to the auction.'[263] One market observer, John Wraith, director of fixed income strategy at Bank of America Merrill Lynch, told Bloomberg that traders had pushed the price of the 2017 bond up 'aggressively, obviously in the hope that they'd be able to sell it to the Bank of England'.[264] Wraith went on: 'The Bank of England rejected it and that might have given people a bit of a shock. There would have been some people who hoped that the Bank would be willing to pay significantly higher prices for the bonds.'

The Bank had had enough of being taken advantage of by opportunistic traders and made an 'example' of the 2017 bond. But it also faced a new challenge: actually being able to source enough gilts in the market. Although the 'free float' in gilts is theoretically around £600bn, in reality very few of them were for sale in the autumn of 2011. The overseas investors, who own a disproportionately large chunk of the gilts market, had been willing sellers to the Bank in the first round of QE; now they were distinctly reluctant. Equally, British pension funds and other asset managers were, if anything, seeking to buy gilts, rather than sell them, as a bulwark against declining confidence in other countries' sovereign debt. At the Bank this problem coalesced into the threat of 'uncovered buybacks' – a situation whereby the Bank might make a statement as to its intention to buy a certain amount of gilts, but be unable to meet its requirements in the market. Members of Fisher's team expressed this concern both to GEMMs and to colleagues at the Treasury. The response seems to have been 'pay up for the gilts you want or draw a line'. Not for the first time, the Bank found itself playing in the markets and, arguably, being outfoxed by them.

£££

Besides the question of whether dropping £275bn into the gilts market had any tangible effects, another niggle about Quantitative Easing continued to exercise its critics. Was it actually legal? Back in late 2008, when the scheme was first conceived, this question was addressed by the Bank's APF steering group. A 'legal stream', led by Graham Nicholson, was set up to examine the legal implications of QE. The key question was how the Bank, as a central bank, could buy government debt. The statute books confirmed that Article 123 of the Treaty on the Functioning of the European Union prohibits the financing of a government's budget deficit:

> Overdraft facilities or any other type of credit facility with the European Central Bank or with the central banks of the Member States (hereinafter referred to as 'national central banks') in favour of Union institutions, bodies, offices or agencies, central governments, regional, local or other public authorities, other bodies governed by public law, or public undertakings of Member States shall be prohibited, as shall the purchase directly from them by the European Central Bank or national central banks of debt instruments.[265]

It was the word 'directly' which prohibited the Bank from buying gilts in the primary market, from the DMO. Instead, it had to purchase them in the secondary market. As Paul Fisher

THE BANK

pointed out in his great Stroud speech, the Bank was scrupulous in its adherence to this rule and eliminated from its purchase programme any gilts recently issued by the DMO, albeit by one week.

The issue was also addressed by Charles Bean in a breezy Q&A – 'Your Questions Answered on Quantitative Easing' – on the Bank's website: 'Are you not simply monetising government debt? Is there any economic distinction between buying government debt in the secondary market from buying it directly from the Government?'[266] Bean's answer:

> The key point is that the Bank is not being forced to create money in order to cover the gap between the government's tax income and its spending commitments. *If it were carried out to finance the budget deficit* [my italics], it would be a violation of Article 123 of the Treaty on the Functioning of the European Union. Rather, the Bank is undertaking Quantitative Easing in order to meet the inflation target and will sell the government debt back to the private sector once the economy recovers, thus unwinding the original increase in the money supply.[267]

Bean is, of course, correct: the Bank was not forced into buying gilts to finance the government's budget deficit. But compare Bean's Q&A answer to the comment in his speech to the London Society of Chartered Accountants in mid-October 2009, when he was discussing the effects of the scheme:

> Gilt yields will be lower than they would otherwise have been during the period that they are held in the Asset Purchase Facility, *so reducing the cost of financing a given budget deficit* [my italics]. This needs to be factored into any calculations of the implications for the public finances.[268]

While this comment arguably blew the gaff on the highly nuanced pronouncements of the Bank, in truth the QE programme followed the letter of the law. But the Bank's purchases of prodigious quantities of government debt – to the point where, in late 2011, it held 29 per cent of the free float – may well give those future economists and their PhD students pause for thought as they ponder the tightrope the Bank walked, as it entered the gilts market on a gargantuan and unprecedented scale.

Finally, the question must be asked about QE: what is the endgame? By the end of February 2012, the Bank will have purchased some £275bn of government debt in the form of gilts. The Bank's exit – technically the 'unwind' of its positions – has exercised its senior economists and lawyers, not to mention the Treasury Committee and the DMO, from the very earliest days of the QE programme. The Bank realised, according to one member of the original APF steering group, that 'we were building a big exit problem.' One suggestion was that when the moment finally came, the holdings in BEAPFF, the Bank's acquisition vehicle, would be sold and the cash garnered simply destroyed, thereby neatly neutralising the whole exercise. Another possible scenario is that the Bank will take some, or all, of BEAPFF's gilts onto its own balance sheet and hold them to maturity.

Questioned on this by the Treasury Committee, King would not be drawn on the specifics of the Bank's plan, beyond saying that there was indeed an exit strategy, which would be guided by two things: the raising of interest rates and the tightening of monetary policy. If these stars aligned, it would be perfectly feasible to sell the assets it had acquired:

We will have to consult with the Debt Management Office and obtain their agreement to sell the assets, and that is reasonable because we got the Debt Management Office to agree that they would not offset our purchases through their issuance strategy. So the one thing that has to be done is that any operation we carry out with these asset purchases, perhaps subsequently sales, has to be coordinated with the Debt Management Office.

This statement is perhaps the single one which encapsulated the circularity of the DMO's issuance of gilts, and the Bank of England's purchase of and the prospect of a subsequent sale of those gilts. (It was also the first time anyone had admitted that a deal had been struck between the Bank and the DMO, whereby the DMO agreed, in King's words, 'that they would not offset our purchases through their issuance strategy'.)

By 2010, when Paul Fisher was addressing his West Country audience, the Bank's response to questions about an exit strategy for QE had acquired a little more finesse. Fisher was able to tell them that, when the time came to 'unwind' the purchases, the Bank's MPC 'will face a number of difficult decisions'. First, it will have to decide when is the best time to start selling. Second, the MPC will have to decide how fast to sell its gilts – Fisher reiterated his Governor's point about the need to coordinate any sales with the DMO, which, lest anyone forget, has its own vast programme of gilts sales.

This issue was broached a few months later, in May 2011, when the BIS published a report from a study group established by its Committee on the Global Financial System and chaired, coincidentally, by Paul Fisher:

When the time comes to sell the purchased assets, central banks will operate on the same side of the market as debt managers. Issuance rates at the time are likely to be still elevated, even if declining. Communication with debt managers on operational issues may become even more important when both are selling.[269]

The report went on:

> Some media and commentators have raised concerns about the independence of monetary policy, including allegations of it being used to facilitate SDM [Sovereign Debt Management] by deliberately inflating away the debt (both sovereign and private) and easing the path of financing for large fiscal deficits. That would not be consistent with the mandates of the central banks concerned and there is no evidence to support such allegations, but if they became popularly accepted credibility problems could result.[270]

Does the interaction between the Bank of England's purchase of gilts and the DMO's concomitant issuance of gilts matter? The DMO has made very few comments on Quantitative Easing, but it made one – in the *Debt and Reserves Management Report* 2009–10 (the 'Dreamer') – which spoke volumes. It may serve as an epitaph on Quantitative Easing and be weighed by future generations of economists reflecting on the Bank's greatest gamble:

> There are potential linkages between the implementation of monetary policy by the purchase of gilts financed by the provision of central bank money and debt management policy.[271]

THE NEW BOYS

'We must always remember, in discussing the constitution of the
Bank of England, its essentially anomolous character. It is at once
our ultimate treasury, and our last lending house.'
Walter Bagehot, The Economist, *October 1864*

The trio of young politicians, besuited and with an air of
purpose about them, slipped unrecognised into the Bank
of England and were ushered into the Governor's Office
by Andrew Hauser, King's private secretary. It was early in 2010
and David Cameron, George Osborne and Matthew Hancock,
Osborne's chief of staff, were anxious to agree the terms of a putative overhaul of the discredited Tripartite system, and to review
the Bank's own *modus operandi*. It was to be implemented in
short order if – still 'if' rather than 'when' – the Conservatives
were returned to power in the upcoming general election. As the
politicians took their seats, they kept to hand a somewhat incen-
diary document which all parties had studied closely – Sir James
Sassoon's *Tripartite Review*, a report commissioned by Osborne
which did not spare the Bank in its criticisms of what had occurred
in the preceding eighteen months.

Notwithstanding this, the atmosphere was cordial. Despite the differences in age – King was a good twenty years his visitors' senior – and background, King trusted Cameron and, in particular, Osborne. He had not forgotten the latter's staunch support for his touch-and-go reappointment as Governor two years previously. Moreover, they broadly agreed on the options before them, the most radical of which saw the FSA abolished and much of its regulatory powers subsumed into the Bank. As they talked, King must also have felt an overwhelming sense of *déjà vu*: thirteen years previously, he and Eddie George had hammered out their deal with Gordon Brown and Ed Balls, the coming men of an eager and expectant new administration. On the Governor's side, there was one noticeable difference, however. This time, King held court alone; Paul Tucker, his deputy, was not invited.

While Cameron and Osborne – largely the latter – negotiated with King, Hancock and Hauser quietly took notes for their respective masters. Hancock, still only thirty-one, was not yet an MP, although he was shortly to become the prospective parliamentary candidate for West Suffolk (a seat he would go on to win at the general election). But he was on familiar ground. He had spent five years, from 2000 to 2005, at the Bank of England, after graduating from Oxford University with a degree in PPE. He had first been private secretary to Ian Plenderleith, the Bank's veteran former head of market operations and member of the MPC, before spending two years in the Monetary Policy Division. Hancock had left a modest mark there with a self-assured paper on the arcane subject of Divisia money, a gauge of the money supply. In 2005, as he was considering a career outside the Bank, he received a call from George Osborne. Osborne offered Hancock a role in his shadow Treasury team, which swiftly propelled him to the centre of the Cameron camp. Hancock was rapidly elevated to the role of Osborne's chief of staff. Crucially, as well as a nascent political instinct, Hancock knew what made the Bank – and Mervyn King – tick. Above all, he understood the Governor's devotion to the Monetary Analysis Division. For Osborne, who had good City contacts but precious few within the Bank itself, this was invaluable. He gave Hancock a wide brief, which allowed him to map a brave new world of the post-financial crisis City and its various embattled watchdogs. It is Hancock who was widely credited with the initiative to scrap the FSA altogether and replace it with the new regulatory bodies. Despite his youth he seems destined to become Chancellor of Exchequer at some point, possibly even as Osborne's immediate successor.

In all, there were five meetings between the Conservative team and the Governor and, in deference to King, they were always held at the Bank. On several occasions, Osborne and Hancock also sought out executives from the FSA, although its principals had to wait on the Conservative team at its offices in Portcullis House, in Westminster (as one Conservative said coolly, 'they came to us'). Hector Sants and Adair Turner were left in no doubt that the FSA's days were numbered.

King had other visitors, too. The Governor also welcomed Vince Cable MP, then Liberal Democrat Treasury shadow, to the Bank on two occasions, once with Nick Clegg, the Lib Dem leader, in tow. Cable was making something of a splash at the time, claiming much credit for some prescient warnings about the credit crisis. He and King are of the same generation and talk the same language, although Cable is a big-picture economist and has none of King's technical precision. Despite the Lib Dems' new-found popularity, however, it was a stretch to imagine the Conservative/Lib Dem coalition which eventually transpired. Cable had sought out King to leave his card and better understand the Bank's view of the shifting economic landscape, not to start discussing what he might do at 11 Downing Street.

A Conservative victory, while far from certain, seemed a more likely scenario. As he formed a picture of the Cameron team's intentions, however, King's concerns grew. While the young politicians had energy and vision, their lack of experience in government was all too apparent and many of their self-confident assertions came across as glib. King felt they did not fully grasp the enormity of the task which lay before them, particularly in addressing the UK's burgeoning national debt and its budget deficit. On 16 February 2010, King expressed these concerns to Louis 'Lou' Susman, the newly-installed US Ambassador to London. Susman, a retired Chicago investment banker nicknamed 'The Vacuum Cleaner' for his tireless fundraising for Barack Obama, was all ears. He wasted little time in relaying his conversation with King back to Hillary Clinton, US Secretary of State, in Washington. The day after his meeting with King, in a cable headed NOFORN (Not for Release to Foreign Nationals), Susman reported:

> While neither party has adequately detailed plans to reduce the deficit, King expressed great concern about Conservative leaders' lack of experience and opined that Party leader David Cameron and Shadow Chancellor George Osborne have not fully grasped the pressures they will face from different groups when attempting to cut spending.[272]

Susman went on to elaborate King's concerns, under the blunt heading 'Conservatives – Not Prepared':

> Conservative leaders David Cameron and George Osborne do not fully grasp the pressures they will face when attempting to cut back on spending, when 'hundreds of government officials will

make pleas of why their budgets should not be reduced,' stated King. In recent meetings with them, he has pressed for details about how they plan to tackle the debt, but received only generalities in return. Both Cameron and Osborne have a tendency to think about issues only in terms of politics, and how they might affect Tory electorability [sic]. King also raised concerns that Osborne's dual roles as Shadow Chancellor of the Exchequer but also as the Party's general election coordinator could create potential problems in the approach on economic issues.[273]

King did not leave Susman in any doubt as to his view of the Cameron team's limitations:

King also expressed concern about the Tory party's lack of depth. Cameron and Osborne have only a few advisers, and seemed resistant to reaching out beyond their small inner circle. The Cameron/Osborne partnership was not unlike the Tony Blair/ Gordon Brown team of New Labour's early years, when both worked well together when part of the opposition party, but fissures developed – for many reasons – once Labour was in power. Similar tensions could arise if Cameron and Osborne disagreed on how to handle the deficit, and the lack of depth in their inner circle, would aggravate the situation.[274]

King's candour with Susman was noteworthy. Susman had been in post in London for only four months and, while he may have met King on the circuit in the past (Susman was at Citigroup for many years), he was certainly not a close friend or confidant. Nevertheless, he had Obama's ear and he was busy on the President's behalf, having had early meetings with the likes of Ben Bernanke and with Timothy Geithner. A consummate deal maker, arm twister and fixer, he was a perfect conduit for King, who would have been well aware that his comments about the aspiring Conservative government would have been immediately transmitted back to Washington. Was King meddling in politics? It was a charge which would be levelled at him with vehemence by the press when Susman's cable was disclosed during the Wikileaks debacle in the autumn of 2010. He was certainly treading a fine line.

£££

If King had his doubts about Cameron, Osborne and their young colleagues, so did they about him. There was one overriding impression: that under King, the Bank of England had become more of a 'monetary authority' than a central bank. One very senior former central banker, who met with the Conservative leadership in the weeks leading up to the general election, was left in no doubt as to their thoughts on the matter: the politicians had analysed their discussions with the Governor coolly and concluded that, despite all that had happened in the past three years, financial stability still played second fiddle to monetary policy at the Bank. They felt strongly that it should be the other way around. And, the argument went, if the Conservatives were to make sweeping changes to financial regulation and the banking industry, was King really the right man to have at the Bank? Two suggestions were made: one was to remove King altogether; the other was to ease him out of the chair of the new Financial Stability Committee, in favour of his deputy Paul Tucker.

There was speculation within the Bank, too, that King would be asked to step down and that he would be replaced either by Tucker or by Lord (Adair) Turner, former chairman of the FSA, who is regarded as exceptionally able but, as one former Bank official put it, 'has an ego as big as St Paul's Cathedral'. John

Varley, then the outgoing head of Barclays, was also mentioned as a possible contender, although as an outside candidate. Barclays had weathered the storms of the financial crisis remarkably well, largely thanks to its failure to secure the acquisition of the Dutch banking giant ABN Amro in 2007 (not for want of trying), but it would have been a braver Chancellor than Osborne who selected a banker as Governor of the Bank of England at that highly charged time.

As the election drew nearer, however, and there was the increasing likelihood of a hung Parliament, the plotting fell by the wayside. In the event, Bank insiders maintain, the government lacked 'the confidence', as one put it, to make a move which might have unsettled already jittery markets. If the Conservatives had been more certain of an outright majority, it might have been a different story.

£££

Despite King's misgivings about the 'lack of depth' in the Conservatives' aspiring Treasury team, there was plenty of activity at Portcullis House, where Osborne and Hancock were building their operation. Hancock brought in Rupert Harrison, a bright, young economist from the Institute for Fiscal Studies, and a clutch of more junior staff, many of whom were still in their twenties and thirties. Osborne recognised the need to add some Establishment gravitas to this troop of bright young things. This came in the sinuous form of Sir James Sassoon, an *eminence grise* of Whitehall and the City. Sassoon had spent his early career as an investment banker at SG Warburg (later UBS Warburg), before throwing in his lot with Labour and becoming the Treasury's eyes and ears in the Square Mile, with the cumbersome title of Special Representative for Promotion of the City. In September

2008, however, he abruptly left the Treasury and severed his ties with Gordon Brown's inner circle. While Sassoon insisted it was an amicable parting, others are not so sure. 'He fell out with Labour,' recalls one former colleague. 'He had been promised something. He was very bitter.' Sassoon transferred his allegiance to the Conservatives and, in particular, to Osborne, with whom he struck up a close friendship. In early 2009 Sassoon was asked to chair the Tories' new Economic Recovery Committee, which brought together business grandees such as Sir Christopher Gent, former chief executive of Vodafone, and Simon Wolfson, of Next, as well as Eric Schmidt, of Google (an odd choice, delivered by Steve Hilton, the Cameron team's strategy guru). Their brief was, essentially, to answer the question 'how do we get out of this mess?'

While this committee met every fortnight to schmooze ideas for Britain's economic recovery, Sassoon was also tasked by Osborne to write the report which would figure large in his discussions with the Governor of the Bank of England. Osborne wanted a detailed analysis of the Tripartite system and recommendations for its reform. Sassoon duly spent several months with a team from PricewaterhouseCoopers, the accountancy firm, conducting research and interviews. He delivered *The Tripartite Review* in March 2009. In his preface, Sassoon noted mournfully that while the Bank and the FSA were obliging in his inquiries of them, his former colleagues at the Treasury 'have not felt able to speak to me'.[275] Nevertheless, it was a comprehensive survey of a blasted and cratered landscape. It provided the blueprint for a prospective new Tory government's policy on financial regulation and, indeed, for a newly constituted Bank. It also had a bit of 'thud factor', which Osborne desperately needed, so that he could demonstrate that the Conservatives had done some hard thinking about policy.

Sassoon pulled no punches in his report. The thrust of it was that the Tripartite was a mess and all three parties had been incompetent, lacking the necessary skills to deal with a financial crisis, and had been entirely uncommunicative with one another. Sassoon noted icily that there had been just one meeting between the three principals – Governor, Chancellor and head of the FSA – in ten years (a conference call with the Fed in 2006). For its part, the Bank had failed to take seriously its financial stability role, had run its expertise down and narrowed its focus. Its proposed new Financial Stability Committee was, wrote Sassoon, 'flawed'. In addition, despite its manifest failings, the Bank had not felt it necessary to conduct an internal post-mortem of its handling of the financial crisis: 'It is striking that the Bank, unlike the FSA, has produced no public assessment of its own conduct in the period leading up to the collapse of Northern Rock. It should do so…'[276] And so on. Sassoon peppered his report with examples of better regimes in the Netherlands, Australia and elsewhere. One model deserving of praise was the use of 'dynamic provisioning' to mitigate bank capital risk, used in the Spanish banking system (the subject of the young Bank analyst's presentation so scorned by King all those years ago).

Sassoon made a battery of forty recommendations, which the Tories devoured. The report paved the way for the abolition of the Tripartite system and, specifically, of the FSA (an option Sassoon proposed), with many of its responsibilities devolving to the Bank of England. Above all, Sassoon suggested, the Bank should have 'the primary responsibility for evaluating systemic threats to financial stability'. This was the genesis of the Conservatives' plans for the Prudential Regulatory Authority (PRA) and the Financial Policy Committee (FPC). Sassoon's report was pored over in Threadneedle Street, in Whitehall and at the FSA's lonely outpost in Canary Wharf. Although it did not make comfortable reading, it did, at least, demonstrate that there was a way forward and that the Conservative team, wet behind the ears as it was, was engaged and serious about creating a new regime, in which the governance of fiscal, monetary and regulatory policy could co-exist.

£££

The May 2010 general election saw the three main political parties caught in a power struggle which left Britain's political future temporarily in limbo. The Conservative–Lib Dem coalition, finally announced on 11 May after much horse-trading between the parties, meant that the Tory Treasury team had to bring their new Liberal Democrat colleagues rapidly up to speed on their discussions with the Bank of England. According to David Laws, MP for Yeovil and one of the Liberal Democrats' negotiating team, Osborne said:

> If we can deliver the £6bn of cuts, that will send out a very power-
> ful message. I will get the figures to Vince [Cable] for him to look
> at and he will find that Mervyn [King] and Nick [Macpherson]
> are very supportive of what we want to do.[277]

This comment was widely interpreted as evidence that the Governor and the Permanent Secretary (Macpherson) had been in cahoots with the Conservative leadership all along and led to accusations that King, at least, had crossed a line between the Bank and the political arena again. It indicated, too, that King and Osborne had formed a consensus on how to tackle Britain's burgeoning budget deficit and, for the Bank, how to move back to a 'peacetime' footing.

The mood in both Whitehall and the City in those first days of government was a mixture of optimism and anxiety. The infamous note left by Liam Byrne, Labour's Chief Secretary to the Treasury, for his successor, David Laws, seemed to sum it up perfectly: 'Dear Chief Secretary, I'm afraid there is no money. Kind regards – and good luck! Liam.' The Bank was, of course, accustomed to watching politicians come and go and there was little sign of any change of tack in Threadneedle Street. There was the briefest nod to the age of austerity which the coalition ushered in when the Bank purchased a senior railcard for the Governor for £26, allowing him discounted rail travel.

Sitting in the Governor's Office, perhaps feeling his age a little, King cast a beady eye down the list of ministers in the new government. A slot had been found for Vince Cable, one of the Lib Dems' few big guns, who was appointed Business Secretary. King was perhaps more interested in the team immediately around Osborne, who at thirty-eight years old was the youngest Chancellor since Randolph Churchill assumed the role in 1886 at the age of thirty-seven. One of Osborne's first heavyweight appointments was that of Mark Hoban as Financial Secretary to the Treasury, a role he had performed in opposition since December 2005. Hoban chaired the nine-strong Advisory Implementation Team, which was formed to plan the structuring of the proposed new regulatory regime. It brought together a clutch of names from the City, two of which were very familiar to King: Michael Foot, last seen heading tearfully for the exit at the Bank in 1997 en route to the FSA; and Carol Sergeant, who joined the Bank in 1974 and spent fourteen years there before joining the FSA and, subsequently, Lloyds Banking Group as its chief risk officer.

Sir James Sassoon was not forgotten in the government's new line-up. Following the general election he was immediately ennobled as Lord Sassoon of Ashley Park and appointed the government's first ever Commercial Secretary. He was given a wide remit, in a role he described to the *Daily Telegraph* as 'half

... in financial services ... and the other half focusing on the wider economy and growth'.[278] Specifically, he was handed ministerial responsibility for the Debt Management Office, putting him at the centre of the government's prodigious gilts issuance programme (and making him the man to whom awkward questions about the unwind of Quantitative Easing will be put, if and when that occurs). One of his first actions in his new office was to lead an investor roadshow to the Middle East, parading the DMO's Robert Stheeman in front of gilts investors – principally sovereign wealth funds – in Saudi Arabia, Kuwait, Dubai and Abu Dhabi. Their appetite for UK government debt remained all-important. While there was no doubt gilts would still be available in superabundance, Sassoon wanted to reassure investors that they remained a rock-solid investment.

Further evidence of Osborne's commitment to fiscal prudence came in the reassuringly named Office for Budget Responsibility (OBR), which was established in May 2010 'to assess the state of public finances'[279] and to provide unbiased economic analysis and forecasting for the government. Accountable to Parliament, it was originally chaired by Sir Alan Budd, one of the founding members of the MPC back in 1997. In the event, Budd came and went quickly, spending little more than two months putting the OBR together. His replacement was Robert Chote, then director of the Institute for Fiscal Studies and a former journalist. Chote was joined by a clutch of non-executives, with some familiar names among them: Kate Barker, who had served three terms on the MPC (and had only left it in May 2010), and Lord (Terry) Burns, the former Treasury mandarin. The OBR was a puzzle for the Bank of England, which does a great deal of economic forecasting of its own, and for the Treasury Committee, which noted some parallels between the fledgling OBR and the august MPC:

The previous Government wished to improve monetary policy-making by giving control of interest rates, within a policy framework set by Government, to an independent Bank of England: the current Government aims to improve fiscal policy making by giving responsibility for forecasting to an independent body. It is a bold step. However the MPC has a clear task and controls the means to achieve it. The OBR has a more complex relationship with Government.[280]

As it turned out, the OBR has had complex relationships not only with the government, but also with the Bank. Some MPs have noted, for example, that there is the possibility of duplication and inconsistencies in their inflation forecasts; others are more sanguine, pointing out that in recent times the Bank's record at forecasting inflation has been little short of disastrous and that the OBR may make it up its game.

While this and other nascent relationships were worked out, the Bank braced itself for the annual Lord Mayor's dinner on 16 June, when Osborne gave his first major speech as Chancellor. True to tradition, there was a brief preamble by Nick Anstee, the then Lord Mayor, after which he asked the assembled guests, save the Chancellor, to stand, as he proposed the toast 'Prosperity to the Public Purse and the Health of the Chancellor of the Exchequer'. Flanked by King and with half an eye on his predecessor Alistair Darling, sitting among the groundlings, Osborne confirmed the sweeping changes to the Tripartite system he was intent upon. In its way, it was as significant a moment as when the Bank was granted its independence in 1997.

Reflecting on the fact that it was three years since the start of the financial crisis, Osborne struck a not altogether convincing statesmanlike tone, invoking the spirit of Winston Churchill, who had delivered one of his best lines (also at the Mansion House, in

1942): 'Now this is not the end. It is not even the beginning of the end. But it is, perhaps, the end of the beginning.'[281] With this hanging in the air, the Chancellor then gave his own succinct and tactful summary of the failures of the past three years:

> At the heart of the crisis was a rapid and unsustainable increase in debt that our macroeconomic and regulatory system utterly failed to identify, let alone prevent. Inflation-targeting succeeded in anchoring inflation expectations, but the very design of the policy framework meant that responding to an explosion in balance sheets, asset prices and macro imbalances was impossible.

Then came the rap on the knuckles, albeit with a judicious use of the passive tense:

> The Bank of England was mandated to focus on consumer price inflation to the exclusion of other things. The Treasury saw its financial policy division drift into a backwater. The FSA became a narrow regulator, almost entirely focused on rules-based regulation. No one was controlling levels of debt, and when the crunch came no one knew who was in charge.

He noted the 'uncertainty that hangs over the future of our domestic regulators' and swiftly put an end to it, confirming that 'the government will abolish the Tripartite regime, and the Financial Services Authority will cease to exist in its current form.' Osborne then outlined the Conservatives' thinking as to why the structure for a new regulatory regime would be parked firmly on the Bank's doorstep:

> Our thinking is informed by this insight: only independent central banks have the broad macroeconomic understanding,

the authority and the knowledge required to make the kind of macro-prudential judgements that are required now and in the future. And, because central banks are the lenders of last resort, the experience of the crisis has also shown that they need to be familiar with every aspect of the institutions that they may have to support. So they must also be responsible for day-to-day micro-prudential regulation as well. That case is particularly strong where the banking system is highly concentrated as it is in the UK, where the boundary between micro- and macro-prudential regulation is not easy to define.

Although there can have been few surprises in the speech for King, sitting alongside the Chancellor, it must have seemed like the tearing up of two decades of the Tripartite's work. On the other hand, it gave the Bank a hugely extended role and power base.

£££

The Conservatives' proposals for a new regulatory regime represented the dismantling of much of the edifice which the Labour administration had put together in 1997 and 1998. Where Brown and Balls had so diligently created the Tripartite, with the Financial Services Authority as its shiny new centrepiece, so Osborne and Hancock set about demolishing it with gusto. The bill for their new edifice will be a large one – the Treasury's best guess is £770m[282] – but is perhaps a small price to pay if it helps avoid a repetition of the catastrophes of the last few years.

The government's principal proposals were threefold. First, to create a new Financial Policy Committee – a mirror, in many ways, of the MPC – to provide 'macro-prudential' oversight of financial stability. Second, to replace the FSA with a new 'micro-prudential' banking supervisor called the Prudential Regulatory Authority (PRA) to oversee the regulatory detail in banks, building societies, insurers and large brokers. Finally, to translate the rump of the FSA into a new body called the Financial Conduct Authority (FCA), responsible for 'conduct of business' among financial companies, policing how they interact with customers, counterparties and competitors. In addition, the government established an independent commission on the banking industry, chaired by Sir John Vickers, a former chief economist at the Bank, to look at the structure of banking in the UK and the state of competition in the industry.

Having digested these lumpy proposals, the Bank requested that the legislation to give effect to the reforms be in the form of a new Act, which would provide a clean slate to work on. The government refused and chose to amend the existing Bank of England Act 1998, the Banking Act 2009 and the Financial Services and Markets Act 2000 (FSMA), rather than to repeal, redraft and re-enact them. In June 2011, it duly produced a voluminous White Paper, to be followed by a draft Financial Services Bill. Royal Assent is expected by the end of 2012 and this new, somewhat cobbled-together, regime will finally come into force in 2013.

Whether it liked the drafting of the legislation or not, the Bank was to play a large part in this Brave New World. For a start, the PRA would be parked firmly on the Bank's doorstep. King has made it clear that this was imposed on the Bank, rather than something it had looked for. Presented with this *fait accompli*, he was at pains to ensure, however, that the PRA was constituted as a subsidiary of the Bank, rather than being incorporated as a new division. As a subsidiary, there was an element of distance: it could not influence the Bank's core mandate to direct monetary policy and, more prosaically, it removed the enormous headache of trying to merge the pay scales and pensions of the 1,000-odd

FSA staff expected to arrive, refugee-like, from Canary Wharf, with those of the Bank's own staff. It was an uncomfortable fact that the FSA had paid its staff a great deal better than the Bank. Indeed, Hector Sants, the FSA's chief executive, receives an annual pay package of around £800,000 – two and a half times that of the Bank's Governor.

The question of the governance of the PRA exercised the Tories. While they were dubious about many of the FSA's top brass, they liked Sants and had observed his work with the Bank and the Treasury during the darkest days of the financial crisis. Sants had, however, had enough of the vagaries of the FSA and announced his intention to step down in early 2010. Osborne picked up the telephone and asked him to consider a new arrangement, whereby he would become not only the PRA's founding chief executive, but also a new deputy governor ('for prudential regulation') of the Bank. This ingenious offer was difficult to refuse. It opened the door for Sants to try his hand at central banking and, conceivably, to have a tilt at the Governor's job in 2018.

The introduction of the PRA was all news to the Bank and it ruffled feathers there. The prospect of Sants, who has lost none of his investment banking *savoir faire*, stalking the corridors of Threadneedle Street as an instantly created deputy governor did not play well with those who had spent decades slaving away in pursuit of high office. While Sants got on well with King and Tucker, he was an unknown quantity to many of the Bank's executive directors. To balance Sants's unexpected arrival, it was agreed that Andrew Bailey, who had been the Bank's point man during Northern Rock in 2007 and intimately involved in the banks bailout in 2008, would become Sants's deputy. Bailey will be joined by Sarah Breeden, who is leading the 'PRA Transition' programme at the Bank, which involves meetings with the 'old' FSA every six weeks.

The PRA promises to have more teeth than the old FSA. It is spoken of as a 'hands-on' regulator, with teams of staff having forensic knowledge of each of the large banks' and insurers' business models and balance sheets. Such financial institutions can expect annual risk assessments and stress tests. It will demonstrate the importance of having intimate knowledge of the 1,019 deposit takers in Britain which will come under its aegis – and, particularly, of the five institutions which account for more than 50 per cent of all deposits.

The PRA's presence at – or near – the Bank should, it is argued, mean that communication between the two bodies is greatly enhanced. But it will also shake up the Bank, according to Bailey, who told the *Daily Telegraph*:

> I would be very surprised if the culture of the Bank doesn't change as a result of this. For anybody now working in the Bank this will be the first time they have expanded in their working lives. This will be a big change for the Bank. It won't change the basic function of the central bank, which is very well established, but it will change the culture. It will infuse it with an organisation doing different things and that's bound to have an effect.[283]

Whether the existing staff at the Bank wished to 'expand' is another matter. The PRA's arrival gave Tucker, in particular, pause for thought. It would either augment or threaten the Bank's own financial stability function and there would have to be compromise to make it work. The imposition of a third deputy governor is hardly something Tucker – or Charlie Bean, for that matter – would have looked for. On the other hand, the abolition of the FSA and the fact that its replacement fell under the Bank's aegis not only drew a line under the failings of the old Tripartite, some of which lay squarely in Threadneedle Street, it also gave very considerable new powers to the Bank.

PART IV

AN OVERMIGHTY CITIZEN

'The Bank finds itself in a position rather like that of a church whose congregation attends weddings and burials but ignores the sermons in between.'
Mervyn King, Lord Mayor's Banquet, Mansion House, 17 June 2009

'The whole construction is misconceived.'
Alistair Darling MP, evidence to the Joint Committee on the Draft Financial Services Bill, October 2011

O nce a month, Mervyn King and George Osborne have an early morning meeting, fuelled by 'a good English breakfast',[284] either at the Bank of England or at 11 Downing Street. It is an opportunity for each to update the other, not only on the state of the economy and the way the political wind is blowing, but also on the shape of the Bank itself. These meetings are not minuted and therefore what passes between the Governor and the Chancellor remains secret. Oddly, we are back to where we were before the Bank's independence, when, as Philip Snowden, a long-forgotten Chancellor, once put it, 'the relations between the Chancellor and the Governor of the Bank are intimate and confidential. What takes place between us is inviolable as if under the seal of the confessional.'[285]

What does the Bank of England look like in 2012? After all the upheavals occasioned by the financial crisis and the proposals to dismember the Tripartite, the Bank remains battered, unbowed and noticeably unapologetic. Indeed, it has in many ways been a beneficiary of the crisis; in the immediate aftermath of the credit crunch, the Bank suddenly became wildly profitable. In mid-May 2009, it produced its Annual Report for the year ending 28 February 2009, which showed that pre-tax profits had quintupled, from £197m in the previous year to a thumping £995m. The increase was directly attributable to the penalties, fees and accrued interest the Bank had charged to the financial institutions it had bailed out and shored up. The £995m included a £4m fee from the Northern Rock bailout, £7m from Bradford & Bingley and no less than £664m from the Special Liquidity Scheme, which by May 2009 still held nearly £300bn of illiquid assets parked there by the banks and for which it had swapped Treasury bills. The Treasury took its pound of flesh from the Bank's £1bn pot, receiving its 50 per cent share of the post-tax profit, or £417m, in lieu of a dividend. A year later, the Bank showed pre-tax profits of £231 million. That was not all. The Bank of England Asset Purchase Facility Fund (BEAPFF), the vehicle for the Bank's QE purchases, also became a profit centre. The Bank of England's 2010 Annual Report noted that it remained a wholly owned subsidiary of the Bank and that purchases of assets by BEAPFF – those gilts – are financed by a loan from the Bank, which amounted to £199.9bn. Like any good lender, the Bank charged interest on the loan, which, the annual report noted, now amounted to a hefty £626m for the year ending 28 February 2010. Equally, BEAPFF also held a deposit at the Bank of a tidy £3.8bn, which was, in turn, busy receiving interest. In the year, this amounted to £8.1m. However, the accounts also note that BEAPFF had to pay a management fee to the Bank of £5m.

In rude financial health and with a raft of new powers heading its way, some believe that the Bank of England is in danger of becoming an 'overmighty citizen'; this was the phrase lobbed at Eddie George in the early 1990s, describing a danger which might result from the Bank being responsible for both monetary policy and banking supervision. Ironically, this has now come to pass.

The Bank is still 'uniquely influential'. Its Court of Directors – 'Court' – continues to preside over the entire edifice like a board of dusty school governors, while its Governor, his deputies and executive directors go about their business of running a central bank. The monthly deliberations of the Bank's Monetary Policy Committee still top the news agenda and the pronouncements of its senior figures – King and his praetorian guard of Tucker, Bean, Haldane, Dale and Fisher – move markets. Despite all the trials and tribulations of the previous four years, the Bank is still firmly in control of the levers of monetary policy and committed, limpet-like, to achieving the same inflation target of 2 per cent, no matter how remote that may seem (in late 2011, it was heading towards 5 per cent). It is also now much preoccupied with the new Financial Policy Committee, which will direct financial stability, gauging and testing the resilience of Britain's myriad financial institutions.

From this singular vantage point, the Bank reaches out, with varying degrees of enthusiasm, to the Treasury, its sole share-holder, to the Debt Management Office and to the condemned edifice of the FSA. It has to deal with the transient occupants of 10 and 11 Downing Street, Parliament, and with the petulant and occasionally dim-witted inquisitors on the Treasury Committee. (After twenty-odd years of appearing in front of the committee, King has the measure of it, reminding its members cn June 2011, for example, that if they did not like the way the MPC operates, they were quite at liberty to take back its responsibilities and set interest rates themselves). Outside this immediate family, it is also, of course, much involved with financial markets practitioners, the banks, brokers, bullion dealers and so on.

£££

King has referred to the Bank as a 'machine', but it rather resembles a large, hierarchical anthill. The seven storey above ground and three below, spread across a three-and-a-half-acre site, house its 1,857 current staff in a more or less self-contained environment, complete with library, gym, conference centre and multi-faith prayer room. Many staff come and go from Threadneedle Street on flexi-time, often working part time or from home, servicing the Bank's many administrative functions, analysing data and conducting economic and econometric research which ranges from the pure to the practical. There are strict ranks of seniority and associated pay grades, resembling those in the Civil Service or the BBC, running from Band 7 ('new entrants and junior clerical staff'), through Band 5 (Team Leader) and Band 3 (Senior Economist) right up to Band 1, which is reserved for Head of Division. Inevitably, these bands have become a shorthand for employees as they climb the Bank's career ladder – woe betide that a mere Band 6 should question the judgement of a Band 5. Most of the staff are well paid; eighty-two of them, at the last count, received salaries of more than £100,000 per annum and another 103 receive between £80,000 and £100,000. Although all employees are eligible for annual bonuses, most are relatively modest – the average in 2009–2010 was £3,000. A select few receive much more substantial sums of between £20,000 and £30,000. Governors do not receive bonuses, but are well paid for their work: in its most recent disclosures, the Bank showed that King was paid a salary and benefits of £308,252, making him one of the highest-paid officials who have their remuneration determined by the government (although the Bank's salaries do not come directly from public funds). His deputy governors, Paul Tucker and Charlie Bean, receive annual salaries of £263,063 and £260,988 respectively.

King, Bean and Tucker remain the triumvirate to which the entire Bank defers. Below them sits a tier of ten executive directors – or EDs – who range from seasoned Bank employees such as Paul Fisher and Andy Haldane to new boys such as Nils Blythe, recently arrived from the BBC as the Bank's communications chief. Many of the EDs are also on the Executive Team (ET), which is the Bank's most senior management committee (and whose members, incidentally, enjoy salaries of between £166,642 and £209,133). King's relationship with his Executive Team is mostly good, occasionally fraught, and most remain admirably diplomatic when questioned about it. Witness the following exchange at the Treasury Committee, in July 2008, between Charlie Bean and Philip Dunne MP:

Mr Dunne: 'Some have described the managerial style within the Bank of England as something akin to that of the monarchy. Do you agree with that assessment and, if so, does that make you the heir apparent?'

Professor Bean: 'It certainly does not make me heir apparent and I would not agree that it is a monarchy either. Mervyn is clearly a strong figure, he has a very good mind, but he is open to persuasion that different approaches are appropriate if you provide the arguments. From the inside it does not look as monarchical or autocratic as perhaps it is painted from the outside.'

Others go further. King, they say, has a quick temper but more frustratingly, an implacable resistance to changing his mind or revisiting a decision, even after the lapse of several years and a change in circumstances. Once a decision is made, there is no going back: 'Mervyn has stamped his foot' is the last word on many matters. In the Bank's many committees, King's word almost always goes, even if there is a vote and he is in the minority. The exception is the MPC and its collegiate nature remains more or less intact. But even though the great revolt of the 'externals' in 1999 has not been repeated, some former MPC members still hint at division. As recently as May 2011, Kate Barker, a highly regarded MPC member for nine years, told the Treasury Committee:

> I also think it is important to reflect that personalities change over time. This potentially is a role for Court ... I think Court should inquire into processes and should ensure that people are free to make comment. To be fair, during the time that I was on the Bank, I saw considerable improvements in this regard with the staff being explicitly encouraged to challenge current thinking. So I don't think we should be too depressed about that, but that's something the Court could specifically ask about, 'Do staff feel able to challenge?'[286]

The Governor's kingdom is split into five divisions, namely Monetary Analysis and Statistics, Markets, Financial Stability, Banking Services and the slightly sinister Central Services, which is responsible for the day-to-day running of the Bank, right down, to borrow King's phrase, to the paperclips.

Monetary Analysis and Statistics, known simply as MA (hence the fabled 'MA Way'), is still the most prestigious of the five divisions, attracting the brightest economists and directly informing the deliberations of the MPC. This is the Bank's 'brain', which pumps out the economic analysis and statistics to fuel the Bank's monetary policy, with its core focus on the inflation target and growth. Once data have been thoroughly chewed over, they are often summarised in the Bank's *Quarterly Bulletin* and the *Inflation Report*. At the head of MA is Spencer Dale, forty-four, who is also the Bank's chief economist. Given that MA was King's grand project, it is unsurprising that Dale was his *protégé*, acting as King's private secretary in 1997, that critical moment in the Bank's – and King's – history. Having worked with the Governor on the shaping of the 'new' Bank from those heady days, Dale is now the guardian of the MA flame. This has not stopped him breaking ranks in the MPC in recent years, repeatedly recommending Bank Rate rises in the face of King's stolid resistance. But, despite this and a little profile-building of his own (including a prominent interview in the *Financial Times* in May 2011 which may have given King pause while reaching for his breakfast marmalade), Dale remains a fiercely loyal lieutenant.

While MA continues to be the Bank's intellectual powerhouse, Markets, its second major division, is a much more up-and-at-'em operation, headed by the dogged, cerebral but perennially grey-suited Paul Fisher. His department is in charge of such heavy weaponry as Quantitative Easing, but on a day-to-day basis it plays in the sterling money markets and provides liquidity insurance to the banking system. It is the ultimate wholesaler. As it does this, Markets keeps a close eye on the Bank's own balance sheet, known as the Bank Return, which is published each Thursday morning and shows the position at the close of business the previous day.

In some respects, Markets has taken on characteristics of an investment bank, albeit with the uneasy ambiguity of whether it exists solely to manage money, or to manage it 'actively'. In other words, whether it can make money. One of its main roles, for example, is to act for the Treasury as agent in managing the UK's foreign exchange reserves. Among its several hundred employees is a select group called Reserves Management, which sits at the heart of the Bank's dealing room. They are highly qualified portfolio managers, who form what resembles nothing so much as a hedge fund, or what might be called a proprietary trading group at an investment bank. The team actively trades many hundreds of millions of the Treasury's funds every day. Five portfolio managers specialise in investing in bonds and in interest rate derivatives. The team is encouraged to generate 'alpha' – proprietary trading strategies to beat the market – and trades both 'long' and 'short', for the latter using repo (repurchase) markets to enhance leverage and cover short positions. Recently, the group went a step further, introducing futures-bond basis trading; in other words, it is trading contracts on the future prices of bonds for hedging – and, in all likelihood, speculative – purposes. Like any self-respecting hedge fund in Mayfair or Connecticut, this admirably sophisticated trading team has internal benchmarks for its returns and annual profit targets, although neither is disclosed; and, in common with the vast majority of Bank employees, the employees in Reserves Management receive annual bonuses. The issue of whether a central bank should make a profit from reserve holdings is a thorny one, but the Bank of England seems relaxed about it: '[The] Bank's portfolio managers are permitted, within limits, to take positions relative to the benchmarks in order to generate returns. This is described as "active management".'[287]

John Nugée, who was the highly regarded chief manager of the Bank's Reserves Management team before moving on to work in an investment bank, also addressed the issue in a publication for the Bank's Centre for Central Banking Studies: '[It] is generally accepted that central banks are fully entitled to so invest their reserves as to maximise the gain they can make on them. This is not to say that central banks have *carte blanche* to deal and seek profits without restraint.'[288]

Quite separately from managing the Treasury's foreign exchange reserves, the Markets division has the Bank's own foreign currency reserves to look after. This pool was initiated back in May 1997, when Gordon Brown first wrote to Eddie George to set out the new Monetary Policy Framework. While the government would still be responsible for determining the exchange rate regime, he wrote, 'the Bank will have its own separate pool of foreign exchange reserves which it may use at its discretion to intervene in support of its monetary policy objective.'[289] This was a fillip for the Bank, but there was a problem: where were these foreign reserves to come from? The answer lay in the capital markets. In 2006, the Bank embarked upon its own Debt Issuance Programme for the issuance of 'medium-term notes', which are essentially bonds, to sell them to the market, just as many commercial and investment banks do to raise capital. The Markets team, therefore, now finds itself squarely in the bond business, selling $2bn of debt, in the form of dollar-denominated Eurobonds, each year. In February 2011, for example, it announced its fifth such issue, in the form of a $2bn three-year Eurobond which pays a coupon of 1.375 per cent per annum and matures in March 2014. The Bank issued a prospectus for the bond, in which it named Bank of America Merrill Lynch, Deutsche Bank, HSBC and J. P. Morgan as joint lead managers and a host of other investment banks, including Goldman Sachs and Morgan Stanley, as co-lead managers. In return for their fee, the banks will sell the bond to their institutional clients around the world. Naturally, as the bonds of one of the world's leading central banks, with the British government standing behind it, they are rated 'AAA' – the highest possible rating; their gold-plated security therefore mitigates the rather meagre return.

The money raised by such bond issues may, as Gordon Brown intimated in his letter, be used to 'intervene' in the currency markets, in support of the Bank's monetary policy objective. Such an intervention would be extremely unusual. In a Treasury Committee session in April 2009, Paul Fisher was asked about the MPC's use of such a contingency:

> They have considered it in the past. There are four occasions in the MPC minutes which record them discussing whether foreign exchange intervention would be appropriate. They were all in the context of sterling being too strong and whether the MPC should intervene to put some sort of lid on sterling. Most of those discussions were short and the MPC fairly quickly came to the conclusion that they should not intervene. It is an instrument of policy which you cannot neglect and you cannot say never.[290]

The MPs questioning Fisher were intrigued at the possibility that the Bank – via the MPC – might possibly intervene in sterling independently of the government's own policy towards the exchange rate. Andrew Tyrie MP asked whether it was possible that the Bank might intervene in a way which even contradicts government policy. Fisher was diplomatic, but his answer highlights the uneasy relationship with government which lies at the heart of an independent central bank:

> The exchange rate policy is part of monetary policy. The monetary policy framework we have is an inflation target. We do not have an exchange rate target. The MPC can intervene in exchange markets if it thinks it is appropriate to help meet the inflation target. That is the situation at the moment and the government has a policy of not intervening in currency markets directly itself.[291]

Markets is followed by Financial Stability, the third of the Bank's big beasts. Overseen by Paul Tucker and Andy Haldane, the

division's remit is to 'detect risks to the structure and functioning of the UK financial system'. This runs the whole gamut of
macro-prudential strategy and is concerned with anything and
everything to do with 'risk'. As part of this, it is the division's role
to gather and process 'market intelligence', making it the most
outward-looking part of the Bank. Much of this is down to Tucker,
who is at ease in City circles and knows many leading bankers
and financiers personally. Haldane, meanwhile, is a hardworking
lieutenant, toiling away on the Bank's risk assessment committees,
monitoring the walking wounded financial institutions and overseeing the mighty payments systems which the Bank controls and
on which much depends. A youthful-looking 44-year-old with a
buzz cut, Haldane has been at the Bank since 1989 and may yet be
elevated to deputy governor in the shake-up which will accompany
King's departure in 2013. Haldane took a leading role for the Bank
during the long days and nights of October 2008, trying to win
the Governor's approval for the various plans to rescue Britain's
crippled banks. Away from the Bank, he devotes his energies to
Pro Bono Economics, a charity he co-founded in 2009 whose aim
is to 'broker economists into the charitable sector', parachuting
them into charities which might not otherwise be able to afford
professional advice.

While Charlie Bean and Spencer Dale's Monetary Analysis
Division has long had the MPC to answer to, until 2011 the
Financial Stability Division was, to some extent, a directorate
looking for a committee. It now has the new Financial Policy
Committee (FPC) to look after. Much of the division's time has
been taken up with planning for the integration of the FPC, which
in turn is tasked with 'identifying, monitoring, and taking action
to remove or reduce, systemic risks' in Britain's financial system
and, in particular, spotting asset price bubbles as they form. A
key plank of the government's replacement for the old Tripartite,

THE BANK

it sprang from a simple and undeniable truth, articulated in the Treasury's White Paper: 'The Government has identified the lack of a single, focused body with responsibility for protecting the stability of the financial system as a whole as one of the main shortcomings of the regulatory system before the financial crisis.'[292]

The FPC, it added firmly, will 'fill this gap'. The introduction of the FPC is, in its way, as significant a development as that of the MPC in 1997. Among other things, it will have responsibility for publishing the Bank's bi-annual *Financial Stability Report*, which is an important part of the Bank's output and which occasions a flurry of activity in the weeks before its publication.

As deputy governor with responsibility for financial stability, Tucker might have been forgiven for thinking he should have been offered the chairmanship of the FPC, particularly as King will not be around when it is formally inaugurated in 2013. But it was not to be. In June 2011, an interim FPC was formed and, at its first meeting, King was firmly in the chair. The interim committee got off to a rather lame start, two members short and plagued by criticism that it hands the Bank too much power and not enough accountability. It also promised fireworks. As well as King, the FPC brought together the Bank's big guns – Tucker, Bean, Fisher and Haldane – as well as Hector Sants, in his capacity as deputy governor and PRA boss-in-waiting, and Adair Turner, the last man standing at the FSA. The committee was also supposed to have four external members. One of them, Richard Lambert, a former journalist and director of the CBI, withdrew his candidacy. Another, Alastair Clark – a man of many reincarnations at Threadneedle Street – was appointed but judged by the Treasury Committee to be insufficiently independent to be an external member. It was, the committee said, 'difficult not to regard him as an "insider"'.[293] Clark will serve on the interim committee but not on the fully fledged FPC in 2013. Thankfully, Donald Kohn, the dependable man from the Fed who had authored the Kohn report on the MPC a decade ago, and Michael Cohrs, a Goldman Sachs alumnus and senior executive at Deutsche Bank, were both accepted as being suitably external. Finally, the Bank made room at the table for two non-voting members: Martin Wheatley, chief executive designate of the Financial Conduct Authority, and Jonathan Taylor, a senior Treasury official who will act as its eyes and ears at the committee, just as his colleague Dave Ramsden does at the MPC.

To all intents and purposes, the FPC has been conceived as the mirror of the MPC (although the FPC is technically a committee of the Bank's Court, whereas the MPC is independent of it), which begged the question whether it was a good idea for the Bank to have two committees, rather than one. Some thought not. Writing in the *Financial Times*, Sushil Wadhwani, a former MPC member, said it was 'a poor idea to have two one-club golfers; a single player with multiple clubs to choose from would be preferable'[294] and pointed to the dangers of 'coordination failure'. Given the dismal record of coordination of the old Tripartite in previous years, he may have a point, although this time, the protagonists will at least be in the same room four times a year.

In the FPC's remit, much was made of the macro-prudential 'toolkit' it would assemble to do its work under the bonnet of the UK's banking and financial services industry. At its inauguration, it was not clear what would be in that toolkit, although there were dark hints of such heavy lifting gear as Time-Varying Capital Requirements (TVCR). As Wadhwani pointed out, this particular tool is largely untried and its modelled effects on the wider economy 'differ by a factor of ten'. Just as Quantitative Easing was launched out of the literature of academic economics, so it seems will some of the new tools to patch up the battered banking sector.

King might not disagree that the FPC is imperfectly formed. For his part, he has complained, for example, that it lacks an 'information collection power', whereby it could request data from a particular financial institution it might have concerns about. Instead, it will have to transmit such requests via the Prudential Regulatory Authority (PRA). Again, while the FPC will issue directions to the PRA, the latter will dictate its own timetable to respond to such directions. While these may be seen as classic King niggles, they hint at the ill-disguised distaste he has for 'not-invented-here' initiatives. Although he has broadly welcomed the new powers the FPC brings to the Bank, its arrival represents, after all, a sharp about-turn. King was delighted to see the back of banking supervision in 1997 and for many years regarded the Bank's Financial Stability Division, according to insiders, as 'trying to do the FSA's work for it'. Indeed, before the financial crisis he was rarely seen anywhere near the division; one former employee recalled his presence no more than once every six months.

The FPC brings some baggage with it. The legislation which will bring the new regulatory regime to bear, albeit still in draft form, includes some rather pointed clauses which clean up the Bank's act. For example, it requires the Governor to have six-monthly update meetings with the Chancellor on financial stability matters and, crucially, requires the Bank and the Treasury to draw up a memorandum of understanding (echoes of the half-hearted MoU which formalised the relationship between the original Tripartite) on how they will 'coordinate and manage a crisis situation'.[295]

While MA, Markets and Financial Stability have become the Bank's three star departments, its Banking Services Division battles on in the background, managing the issuance of banknotes, grinding through millions of daily payments and settle-ments and generally doing the dogsbodying for the rest of the institution. Banking Services is run by Chris Salmon, another of King's trusted deputies, having been his private secretary during the financial crisis. Salmon is also Chief Cashier, responsible for the Bank's notes (never 'banknotes') and their circulation. Deep in the bowels of Banking Services are some of the functions which any account holder at a high street bank would recognise, except that the Bank's customers are, principally, some sixty banks and building societies who hold 'reserve' accounts there.

The Bank's relationships with private, as opposed to institutional, customers remain singularly opaque. One of the perks of working in Threadneedle Street is that full-time employees are entitled to a Bank of England bank account, albeit one with no overdraft facility. In the year to February 2010, 'Governors and Executive Directors' had deposits of £464,000 with the Bank and loans from it of £24,000.[296] Whether the Bank has other personal account holders remains something of a mystery. Its creation in 1977 of a company called Bank of England Nominees Limited (BOEN) has long been a preoccupation of inquisitive MPs, journalists and conspiracy theorists. They strongly suspect that this entity – and its sister company Houblon Nominees, named after Sir John Houblon, the Bank's first Governor – may act as the anonymous holding companies for investments made by heads of state, such as the Queen, or by sovereign governments. BOEN's secrecy is compounded by the fact that it enjoys an exemption from the Secretary of State (under Section 796 of the Companies Act 2006) which means it is not subject to 'notification provisions' – in other words, it is not obliged to disclose its activities, its long-form accounts or, crucially, its beneficiaries. The Bank is coy about BOEN. It admits that BOEN 'acts as a nominee company to hold securities on behalf of certain customers' and refers to 'persons on whose behalf securities are held by BOEN'[297] but declines to disclose the Bank's own records about its subsidiary's activities, citing a confidentiality clause relating to 'the provision of private banking services'. BOEN's scant official documents show that its two shareholders are the Bank itself and John Footman, who holds his share as nominee on behalf of the Bank. Footman also acts as a director of BOEN, along with the Bank's Andrew Bailey.

While Bailey, soon to be translated to the PRA, is highly regarded in the City for his work rearranging the banking landscape during the financial crisis, Footman is much less well known. His current billet is the fifth of the Bank's divisions, Central Services, which he has run since 2003, when Mervyn King cannily appointed him its executive director. King was well aware that Footman knew the inner workings of Threadneedle Street – and his colleagues' foibles – better than anyone. A Bank of England 'lifer', Footman has, according to a former colleague, 'unbelievable antennae for what goes on in Threadneedle Street'. He joined the Bank in 1969 and has worked in many of its departments, including the press office, the Governor's Office and its personnel and financial stability divisions. As well as being in charge of Central Services, Footman is also secretary of the Bank, a role which carries the responsibility for keeping the Bank's precious seal 'in a secure place under lock and key'.[298] Trusted with this and many other duties, Footman is the Bank's consummate fixer and the equivalent of its chief whip, keeping the Executive Team in line and making sure there is no dissent further down the ranks. He has described himself as its 'keeper of secrets'[299] – those of BOEN and much else besides.

Footman and his nine fellow executive directors may compose the Bank's inner circle, but there are others who also have the Governor's ear. One such is Graham Nicholson, the Bank's chief legal adviser and adviser to the Governor, the latter handle a sign of the increasing importance of his position. Nicholson took up his appointment on 1 January 2009, having joined from Freshfields

Bruckhaus Deringer, the magic circle City law firm, where he had spent his entire previous 37-year career. Nicholson now heads a ten-strong team, which advises both on internal Bank matters and on the more commercial matters which the Bank found itself embroiled in when it was untangling the mess of failing financial institutions in 2007 and 2008.

Nicholson's presence and his pedigree highlight the close relationship between the Bank and his old firm, which goes back some two hundred and fifty years to 1743, when Samuel Dodd, one of Freshfields' partners, was appointed solicitor to the Bank. The relationship has flourished, particularly since the 1990s, much to the envy of Freshfields' rivals. Nicholson's old colleague Michael Raffan, a senior Freshfields partner and head of its financial services group, has often been first port of call for the Bank. Raffan deals mostly with Nicholson, Andrew Bailey, and the legal team, which includes Geoff Davies, another of Freshfields' brightest stars, who was seconded to the Bank and stayed on.

Freshfields has long advised the Bank during many of its darker days, not least when it suffered the indignity of being sued for misfeasance by Deloitte & Touche during the BCCI debacle. As we have seen, Freshfields' final bill, settled in the summer of 2006, came to some £75m, dwarfing the £38m fees charged by Lovells, which represented the BCCI creditors. Two years later, in April 2008, Freshfields' Raffan led the team which advised the Bank on its £50bn Special Liquidity Scheme. The same week, Freshfields was also busy advising Royal Bank of Scotland on its £12bn rights issue. As the law firm proudly noted: 'Within the space of a week, Freshfields has played a major role in two very different but significant illustrations of the impact of the global credit crisis.' It was a busy time for the firm. In the financial year ending 30 April 2008, fees from the Bank helped the law firm to total revenues of £1.18bn, a rise of nearly 20 per cent on the previous year. By the last week of September of that same year, it had also stepped up to advise the Bank on the nationalisation of Bradford & Bingley. Raffan led Freshfields' team of an estimated forty lawyers for the Bank, with three other partners at his side – including Nicholson.

Evidently, the Bank soon decided it could not do without Nicholson and a matter of days later, his appointment as chief legal adviser was announced. For the Bank, it meant saying goodbye – somewhat abruptly – to Dame Juliet Wheldon, who had held the post for only two years. A consummate Whitehall insider, previously the Treasury solicitor and head of the Government Legal Service, Dame Juliet was essentially a civil servant, albeit a rather glamorous one who was fond of networking lunches and dinners. But for all her charms she was not, in the words of a former colleague, 'commercial'. As her replacement, Nicholson brought with him shrewdness honed by nearly four decades of City legal practice. (He was, incidentally, also following in the footsteps of a former Freshfields colleague, Peter Peddie, who had held the role at the Bank from 2002 to 2006.) It is a well-trodden, two-way street between the Bank and Freshfields. For example, when Len Berkowitz (who had trained at Linklaters) retired as the Bank's chief legal adviser in 2001, he immediately joined Freshfields as a senior consultant.

£££

As well as engaging with City institutions, the Bank's beefed-up legal department has also strengthened its links with its opposite numbers at the Treasury. During the financial crisis it became painfully obvious that the Treasury lacked the expertise necessary to navigate the web of credit exposures held by banks such as RBS and Lloyds. It has had to up its game. At the same time, its relationship with the Bank has remained a difficult one.

The presence of the Treasury representative at meetings of the MPC and FPC – usually Dave Ramsden at the MPC and, so far, Jonathan Taylor at the FPC – serves as a slightly sinister reminder that the Bank's ultimate paymaster is never far away. For all its independence, the Treasury remains the Bank's watchful pater-familias – it does, after all, retain a reserve power (in Section 819 of the Bank of England Act 1998) to give the Bank 'directions' in relation to monetary policy in an emergency. In non-emergency times, the Treasury exerts its authority not through the public deliberations of the Treasury Committee, chaired by the donnish and sardonic Andrew Tyrie and assorted other MPs, but in more subtle ways. It is an uneasy relationship and one which Sir Howard Davies, the Bank's former deputy governor, has described as 'the science of inter-institutional dynamics'. More prosaically, he has written that 'Treasuries and central banks, like cats and dogs, are put on earth to bark and hiss at each other.'[300]

In theory, the old Tripartite system meant the Bank, the Treasury and the FSA working in tandem; in practice, the Bank and the Treasury jockeyed relentlessly to be first among equals, while the FSA was relegated to the role of back office. The Treasury has always been first among equals in the roster of government departments. It resides in the heart of Westminster, on a corner site overlooking Horse Guards Road and Great George Street, in offices known as GOGGS (Government Offices Great George Street). Famously described by Norman Lamont as resembling 'a Russian psychiatric hospital'[301] in the mid-1990s, during the Labour administrations it had a thorough makeover and now looks more like a hotel, albeit retaining a Kafkaesque atmosphere. The Treasury and the Bank are, therefore, a couple of miles apart, but umbilically attached. Technically, the Treasury funds the Bank – and that funding can be altered as the Treasury sees fit – although in recent years, the Bank has paid its own way. The Bank's profits and the concomitant dividend which flows to the Treasury are, it is generally accepted, 'agreed' between the two parties before the Bank's accounts are finalised. In recent years, the dividend, as we have seen, has been particularly healthy.

But there is little love lost between the two institutions. The gentlemanly collaboration between what were known as 'the authorities' in Keynes's day, based on the idea of public service for the common good, has dissipated. One former Bank executive recalls the period before the Bank's independence as being clearer cut: the Treasury was accepted as the 'senior partner' in the relationship. In those days, it was unthinkable that Treasury warhorses such as the great Sir Nigel Wicks, let alone his minions, would go to the Bank for meetings – the Bank came to the Treasury. Since 1997, the balance of power, or at least of deference, has shifted. Today, the Treasury is often seen as the 'enemy' or, at the very least, an eavesdropper on important discussions within the Bank. The most important of these are the MPC's monthly meetings, at which a Treasury 'observer' – in recent times almost always Dave Ramsden – attends. Ramsden has a good relationship with the committee members but on other occasions, when Treasury teams arrive at the Bank, there is often frostiness in the air. 'The machismo of the Treasury is palpable,' says one Bank insider. 'They positively strut.'

Although of roughly similar size – the Treasury has some 1,400 staff to the Bank's 1,850 – the two institutions have very different characters and hierarchies. While Mervyn King has his cabal of academic economists and Paul Tucker his own corps, the Treasury's top team comprises a group of career civil servants who have witnessed and participated in the cut and thrust of the political fray. There, power ebbs and flows around three departments – PERM, IF and MPF. It is concentrated principally in PERM, the domain of Sir Nick Macpherson, Permanent Secretary. IF is the International and Finance Division, overseen by Tom Scholar as second permanent secretary, while MFP is the Macroeconomic and Fiscal Policy Division, headed by Dave Ramsden, chief economic adviser and joint head of the Government Economic Service. While Macpherson and Scholar have achieved some celebrity for their heroism during the credit crisis, Ramsden has gone largely unrecognised. He continues on his rounds, plodding dutifully from the Treasury to the Debt Management Office and on to the Bank, attending meetings, observing committees and signing off accounts.

Macpherson is the Treasury's star turn. An Etonian and Oxford economics graduate, he has spent twenty-five years at the Treasury, becoming the quintessential mandarin, seeing all, hearing all, but saying very little, as least not publicly. He has been described by Alistair Darling as 'engaging, and somewhat idiosyncratic'.[302] Since 2007, Macpherson's working life has become dominated by the department's nexus with the Bank and, to a lesser extent, the FSA. He has had a particular involvement with the aftermath of the credit crisis and the government's voluminous financing requirements which have sent the DMO into overdrive. As Permanent Secretary, his influence extends to all of the Treasury's demesnes. He was responsible for hiring Robert Stheeman as chief executive of the DMO and for grilling Paul Tucker on his appointment as deputy governor in late 2008. Equally, it was he to whom Sir Alan Budd tendered his resignation as interim head of the Office for Budget Responsibility in July 2010, and he who wrote back.

In 2009, the New Year's Honours List saw Macpherson admitted into knighthood 'to recognise his extraordinary work in response to the crisis in the financial services industry'. Efficient, diplomatic but steely, he is not normally given to public statements. Nevertheless, perhaps in deference to the fact that his family own Attadale, a 30,000-acre estate in Wester Ross, in Scotland, Macpherson succumbed to an interview with a local West Highland newspaper in 2008. He was asked about the perspective the mountains and bogs of the remote Scottish countryside gives him: 'There is a tendency to think that, if you are working in Whitehall, you can pull levers and the effects will be the same across the whole country. It's very useful to have a corrective to that and to ask: "How will it affect Lochcarron and Attadale?"'[303]

Perhaps more convincing are Macpherson's subsequent comments about the role of the Treasury. He is in no doubt that it is there that power resides:

> The big issues that have affected Britain have played themselves out in the Treasury over the past twenty-five years, whether it was Nigel Lawson's Budget, the ERM decision, the transition in 1997 or today's challenges. The action is always in the Treasury. This is where the big trade-offs happen.[304]

There, perhaps, is the most concise description of the Treasury's role, as the place where 'the big trade-offs happen'. Certainly, it is still the power broker and kingmaker, not least where the Bank of England is concerned. For all the Bank's independence, it came with strings attached and Macpherson and his colleagues have a firm grasp on them.

Equally, the financial crisis gave Macpherson's team a shock. In a rare semi-public pronouncement, in the form of a lecture delivered at All Souls College, Oxford, in December 2009, Macpherson acknowledged that in the space of eighteen months the Treasury had transformed from being a 'small, influential policy department' to one with 'very significant delivery responsibilities and a huge and complex balance sheet':

The department has had to fire on all cylinders. Multi-tasking has become the order of the day: at periods in the last year, every directorate in the Treasury was working flat out ... The Treasury has had to adapt quickly to changing circumstances. At times it has had to act with extraordinary speed. The department has had to learn along the way.[305]

Thus, the Treasury, as with the Bank, occasionally lifts its veil to reveal its inner workings, its foibles and its human frailties. Ultimately, the relationship between the two institutions is a working one, based on the transmission of power and policy, and the constant flow of data, memoranda and briefing papers which passes back and forth. The Bank's independence remains all but sacrosanct, and is generally still regarded as 'A Good Thing' in Whitehall, although there has clearly been the occasional temptation for the Treasury – and the Chancellor – to tweak the silken thread which joins the two institutions as a gentle reminder of their watchful eye.

THE LAST GOVERNOR

'Most Governors of the Bank of England are cautious merchants, not profoundly skilled in banking, but most anxious that their period of office should be prosperous and that they should themselves escape censure.'
Walter Bagehot, Lombard Street, *1873*

'Whenever a central banker is tempted to think he knows enough about the economy to fine tune it with monetary policy, the right response is to go and listen to Mozart.'
Mervyn King, ECB Colloquium in Honour of Otmar Issing, March 2006

On Tuesday 15 November 2011, Mervyn King, accompanied by his wife Barbara, had an important appointment to keep, at Buckingham Palace. On this occasion, the Governor's presence was not required to explain the dire state of Britain's economy or its fractured banking system to the Queen, but to be admitted into knighthood. At 11 a.m. precisely, dressed in a slightly oversized grey morning suit, King found himself in the Palace's ballroom standing among ninety-four other recipients of the Queen's Birthday Honours as the National Anthem was

played. Alongside him were military personnel, senior civil servants and a sprinkling of celebrities including Henry Cecil, the
racehorse trainer, and Emma Freud, the television personality and
leading light of Comic Relief. The Governor, who had requested
to be on the 'No Filming List' to avoid the cameras' attentions,
was the first to be called up to the dais. In time-honoured fashion,
he knelt on an Investiture stool as the Queen dubbed him with
the sword which once belonged to her father, George VI.

King's honour was a suitably grand one: he became a Knight
Grand Cross of the Order of the British Empire, the same honour
bestowed on Eddie George in 2000, three years before his retirement. It allows Sir Mervyn, should he wish, to wear a ceremo-
nial uniform of mantle, hat, gold collar and assorted badges
and ribbons. Like all such honours, it has little bearing on his
day-to-day work and at the Bank, Professor Sir Mervyn King
GBE remained firmly 'Mr Governor'. Rather, when it was first
announced in June 2011, the honour marked the beginning of
the end, the start of the last two-year stretch before the Governor
finally takes his leave of the Bank, in June 2013.

It looked like a long haul. Apart from the knighthood, there
were precious few plaudits for King in 2011. The Bank's fortunes
were dogged by particularly bleak economic news in the United
Kingdom and even worse news from the Eurozone, its largest
trading partner. Throughout the year there was exceptionally weak
growth in the British economy and steadily increasing inflation,
which peaked in October at 5.2 per cent, a whopping 3.2 per cent
higher than the 2 per cent target. The pile of envelopes and stamps
which King had once joked to the Treasury Committee were
ready in case he had to write the required letters to the Chancellor
must have been all but used up. As it was, the Governor's letter
to George Osborne of 6 October reiterated that inflation was
high because of the one-off increase in VAT and elevated energy

prices, both of which would soon fall away. In order, therefore, to avoid undershooting the inflation target, the Monetary Policy Committee had decided to keep Bank Rate at 0.5 per cent and inject another £75bn slug of Quantitative Easing:

> In the light of that shift in the balance of risks, and in order to keep inflation on track to meet the target over the medium term, the Committee judged that it was necessary to inject further monetary stimulus into the economy.[306]

While the authorities, the media and the public pondered that 'shift in the balance of risks' – the phrase that signalled things were really dire – the Bank had other battles to fight, particularly in Westminster.

The issue of the Bank's 'accountability', or lack of it, which rumbled on in the background throughout 2011, was bound up not only with its Court – its historic governing body – but also with its Governor's singular personality. Politicians and others had become exercised by the fact that, since 2003, King had built something of an empire, whose powers now extended beyond Threadneedle Street and seemed to override those in Westminster and Whitehall.

Moreover, the Governor seemed to make light of the criticism that the Bank was becoming an 'overmighty citizen'; in his Mansion House speech, in June, he compared himself to a former Governor, John Saunders Gilliat, who, faced with the Metropolitan Railway's demand for some of the land on his Chorleywood estate to extend their railway in the 1880s, insisted that the company build him his own station, to ease his journey to Threadneedle Street. 'I regret to say', King told his audience, 'that the present Governor neither has the power to command a private railway station nor would he know where to put it if he did.'[307]

Exactly a week before his trip to Buckingham Palace, on 8 November, the House of Commons Treasury Committee published its report *Accountability of the Bank of England*. Overshadowed by the sovereign debt crisis engulfing the Eurozone, it made remarkably few headlines, despite calling for a 'radical overhaul'[308] of the Bank's governance, highlighting what it perceived as a woeful lack of accountability. In one of the sharpest barbs to emanate from Portcullis House in recent years, the committee pointedly recommended that a Governor's term be limited to eight years 'so that there is less risk of a Governor remaining in office past the point when his or her effectiveness is diminishing'.[309] One can only imagine King's reaction to reading this poison-tipped phrase when the report thudded onto his desk.

Having taken a swipe at the Governor – or at least at 'a' Governor – the committee went on to recommend that the Bank's historic 'Court' should be abolished, both in name and body, and swiftly replaced with a 'Supervisory Board of the Bank of England'. This new board should, it suggested, comprise only eight members (the chair, the Governor, his two deputies and four externals) rather than the current twelve, whom even the loyal Professor Charles Goodhart had damned with faint praise as 'a fine collection of eminent people'.[310] Ultimately, however, the Bank accepted the suggestion of eight-year terms.

The committee's work had been nothing if not thorough. The report was a distillation of six lengthy evidence sessions which stretched from March to July. The inquiry was led by Andrew Tyrie MP, the committee's chairman, whose early deference to King and his colleagues at the Bank steadily dissipated. Tyrie and his fellow MPs grilled the great and the good of the Bank's Court, including its chairman, Sir David Lees, as well as former members of the MPC (Goodhart, Buiter, Barker and Wadhwani) and a clutch of academics and experts in corporate governance. The Governor himself, accompanied by his lieutenants Bean, Tucker, Haldane and Bailey, gave evidence in June; George Osborne and his Treasury henchman Sir Nick Macpherson provided the finale in July.

As the committee gathered its evidence from its witnesses, it could not help but notice that Alistair Darling, now consigned to the back benches, also had some strong opinions about the Bank's accountability. His memoirs, published in September 2011 amid a blizzard of publicity, had vividly described his frustrations at dealing with the Governor and the Bank in general during his years as Chancellor. Darling was called before the separate Joint Committee on the Financial Services Bill, which was considering the proposed changes to financial regulation legislation, to give his views. He did not mince his words:

> It is terribly important that Parliament, perhaps even on a non-partisan basis, can take a view as to the governance of the Bank and get it right. Basically, what we have just now goes back to 1946, with the odd tweak along the way. We need to get this right because I think the governance arrangements are antiquated, frankly. It is all to do with the Governor being some sort of sun king around which the Court revolves.[311]

In Darling's forthright view, it seemed that the Bank was an edifice which was now barely fit for purpose: 'The whole construction', he told the Committee bluntly, 'is misconceived.'[312]

Back at the Treasury Committee, MPs found it difficult to disagree with Darling's analysis. The Bank's cause was not helped by the fact that it had proved supremely obstinate in not carrying out an inquiry into its conduct during the early days of the financial crisis, not least at the height of the cricket season in August 2007. It rankled with the MPs that no such inquiry had been carried out, particularly since the FSA carried out an 'internal audit review', published in March 2008, in which it admitted its failings to monitor adequately the deteriorating situation at Northern Rock, and published a further weighty account of the collapse of Royal Bank of Scotland.

The Bank, on the other hand, had remained entirely silent on its own shortcomings. It became clear to the committee that the Bank's own post-mortem over Northern Rock had been little more than a quiet chat between the members of the Court and the Governor one afternoon in the Court Room:

> Sir Roger Carr [a member of Court] told us that 'it was not necessary to call for a review. A review was done as part of normal Court business'. However, he went on to tell us that this was not a formal review but merely a discussion with the Governor: 'It was not done on a question and answer basis; it was a question of reviewing the strengths and weaknesses of the system we had.' When we asked the Court why no record of this review had been made public he told us that the minutes of the Court's meetings are limited to summaries of broad discussions.[313]

The committee's witnesses lined up to agree that it was extraordinary that no proper review had taken place. Professor Bob Garratt, of Cass Business School, for one, expressed his incredulity:

> I am amazed – and a lot of my work is international and overseas folk I know are just astonished – that we have never had a proper investigation as to what went wrong.[314]

The committee's annoyance at the lack of internal Bank inquiry was, however, nothing compared to its irritation that the Bank's Court had refused point blank to share with the committee minutes taken during the financial crisis:

Despite the exceptional nature of the crisis period, the Court has been unwilling to make available to us the minutes of its meetings. It has, despite our suggestion that it provide us with a redacted version, said that giving us copies of its minutes would provide the Court with no private space for deliberation.[315]

And the final indignity, as far as the MPs were concerned:

[The Court] has also relied on the provisions of the Freedom of Information (FoI) Act as a basis for denying the Committee access to the information.[316]

None of this did the Bank's senior management any favours. The picture drawn by the Treasury Committee was one of arrogance and a disregard for process. King looked increasingly beleaguered, a lame-duck Governor in charge of a Bank which had all but lost the confidence of a highly influential part of the Parliamentary machine. No one mentioned the possibility of resignation or early retirement – it would be unprecedented that a Governor of the Bank of England should not see out his full term. Instead, the Governor and the Bank withdrew into the remoteness afforded by the great, blind curtain wall which snakes around its perimeter. Its only public comment on the Treasury Committee's report was: 'The Bank has always made clear that with the expansion of its responsibilities … new arrangements for the governance and accountability of the Bank would be necessary.'[317]

£££

Amid all the brickbats of the autumn of 2011, there was, however, a bouquet for the Governor and it came just as the Chancellor, the Treasury and the Office for Budget Responsibility were laying out their grim prognosis for Britain's economy in the form of the Chancellor's Autumn Statement. The Bank made no comment on the extended austerity drive and hugely increased government borrowing laid out by George Osborne in the House of Commons. In fact, it was greatly preoccupied with events in the Eurozone, where the sovereign debt crisis continued to play out like a slow-motion car crash.

Throughout the autumn, European leaders had dithered and liquidity had seeped away from the credit markets. From mid-November, the cost of converting unloved euros into dollars crept up to its highest since October 2008 as investors reined in their euro exposure. At the Bank, alarm bells began ringing. It was King, to his credit, who picked up the telephone to his counterparts on the Economic Consultative Committee, a group formerly known as the G10 Governors. King, who is chairman of the ECC, alerted his fellow central bank governors in the United States, Canada, Switzerland and Japan to a situation which, as it steadily deteriorated, bore of all the hallmarks of another credit crunch.

On Wednesday 30 November, the Federal Reserve announced that it would drastically reduce the rate it charged the European Central Bank for short-term dollar loans from 1.1 per cent to 0.6 per cent, essentially providing dollar liquidity to cash-strapped European banks at a highly preferential rate. The other banks put in place what King described as a similar 'network of swap agreements across all the currencies'.[318]

The markets welcomed the central banks' move – a symbolic rather than systemic one – as a sign that they would not leave the Eurozone to die a slow death. King reiterated, in statesmanlike tones, that if similar stressed situations emerged in other, non-dollar currencies 'then the solution was there to be found'. Briefly, at least, he was the hero of the hour.

£££

King's valiant actions to make available dollar liquidity for Eurozone banks gave the Governor a fillip at the end of 2011. Nevertheless, as 2012 began, there were already stirrings in the undergrowth about his succession. The first official shortlist will be put together by the Treasury in the autumn of 2012 and will doubtless involve a great deal of back-room negotiation with the Conservative–Lib Dem coalition. There is a balance to be struck between continuity and modernisation, particularly as the Bank will still be assimilating the Prudential Regulatory Authority, whose executives have made no secret of the fact that they do not intend to play second fiddle to the Bank.

Partly by virtue of his good relations with Osborne and Cameron, King will undoubtedly have a say in who will be his successor. His preference will almost certainly be for Charlie Bean, deputy governor since 2008 and a rock-solid disciple of the 'MA Way'. Bean would continue King's economics-led legacy and preserve the status quo. But whether his appointment would play well in Whitehall and the City is less certain. He has had a couple of stabs at building a profile in the media in recent years, including a rather lacklustre interview on Channel 4 television, but he is not a natural performer and retains the air of an amiable academic thrust reluctantly into the limelight.

Paul Tucker, the Bank's other deputy governor who will have been at Threadneedle Street for thirty-three years by 2013, is an entirely different matter. It is widely assumed within the Bank that he will be the next Governor unless, that is, his bid is scuppered by the powers that be. Tucker has made little secret of his ambition for the top job and, in many ways, would be eminently suited to it. He knows the Bank intimately and he is well connected in the City. If he does not become Governor, it is said, he will be off to Goldman Sachs (just as Kit McMahon, deputy governor in the early 1980s, left Threadneedle Street for Midland Bank in 1985 after Margaret Thatcher declined to sanction his candidacy for the Governorship).

Tucker is not an economist *per se*, although he has a voracious appetite for the subject and is admired for his 'breadth and depth' of knowledge. One senior colleague describes him as a 'polymath'. But he is also, in the words of another, 'one of the Bank's most complex characters'. He is not always easy to work with and is a demanding boss. Above all, he is regarded as a 'political animal', who has built both a following and a power base at the Bank as well as in the City, Whitehall and at Westminster. Alistair Darling was among those who found him a straightforward man to deal with, in stark contrast to the Governor. In Tucker's favour is his energy, intellect and his grasp of the inner workings of the institutions which interact daily with the Bank and, to some extent, influence its fortunes. Former colleagues note that he has often been 'the smartest guy in the room'. His power base resides firmly in the Financial Stability Division, but his long career in Threadneedle Street has ensured there are loyal colleagues dotted around other parts of the Bank whom he has cultivated over the years.

It is perhaps not surprising if an air of Machiavellianism hangs around Tucker. After all, says one senior former colleague, 'he has spent thirty-odd years biting his lip.' Many say that Tucker's relationship with the Governor has deteriorated significantly over the past few years, while others recall spats between them as far back as 2003. But whereas senior figures such as Sir John Gieve would sometimes disagree openly with King, Tucker has avoided outright confrontation. On occasion, however, colleagues say Tucker expresses exasperation at the Governor, and something akin to disbelief at some of the edicts which flow from his office. Outside the Bank, too, senior figures in the banking industry acknowledge that the relationship between King and Tucker has 'changed' in recent years; among the elite corps of bank chief executives and chairmen who are occasionally admitted to the Bank's Parlours it is an open secret that the Governor and his deputy do not see eye to eye. Whether this will have any bearing on Tucker's candidacy for the top job is a moot point.

While Bean and Tucker prepare to make their pitches, in the ranks, or at least among the Bank's ten executive directors, there are those who must bide their time. Spencer Dale is an obvious candidate for some future Governorship but the chief economist, at forty-four, is probably still too young. His hour may come in 2018, 2023 (or, if the Treasury Committee's recommendation of a single, eight-year term is adopted, in 2021). Dale will also have Andrew Bailey and Hector Sants, who by that time will have had several years' experience as a deputy governor himself, to contend with. There will also doubtless be places at the top table for Andy Haldane and Sarah Breeden, who is now working with Bailey and Sants on the PRA 'transition'. Some of her colleagues believe that Breeden could become a deputy governor and eventually the first female Governor in the Bank's long history.

Besides the Bank's own, there will be external candidates for King's job and this may well be an attractive option for the Treasury and for the coalition government. Lord Sassoon's name crops up with regularity, particularly among Bank insiders. He is close to the Prime Minister, the Chancellor and to Matthew Hancock MP, the Chancellor's right-hand man. Another obvious contender for the Governor's Office is John Varley, the feisty former head of Barclays, who left the bank in March 2011. The passage of time until 2013 may make the appointment of a former banker more palatable to politicians and to the public. Varley, who has the distinction of once beating King at tennis, had a 'good war' in the financial crisis, thanks to a narrow escape from

Barclays' putative acquisition of ABN Amro in 2007. He would bring vim and vigour, as well as his trademark braces and natty suits, to the role of Governor.

Another likely candidate is Sir John Vickers, who serves as chair of the Independent Banking Commission, the body charged by George Osborne with examining the future structure of retail and investment banks with a view to reducing systemic risk. This could not be more apropos. The commission's weighty final report, delivered in September 2011, marked the end of a long process of investigation and analysis of banking models, which gave Vickers a unique insight into the industry and which would make him eminently qualified to oversee them from a perch at Threadneedle Street. Vickers has previous form at the Bank. He succeeded Mervyn King as its chief economist in 1998 and also served his time on the Monetary Policy Committee. Although he abandoned the Bank for a stint at the Office of Fair Trading in 2000, he has continued to move in weighty economists' circles, becoming president of the Institute for Fiscal Studies and the Royal Economic Society and, latterly, Warden of All Souls College, Oxford, one of the last bastions of the British Establishment.

The other likely external candidate is Lord (Adair) Turner, who has been the dapper chairman of the FSA since September 2008, when he found himself closeted with King and Darling in the first wave of the financial crises of that autumn. With the demise of the FSA in 2013 Turner will be without a job and many favour him as the compromise candidate for Governor. His background as a McKinsey consultant, investment banker and former director general of the CBI has given him a suitably glossy curriculum vitae. Turner's former colleague Sir Callum McCarthy, chairman of the FSA during some of its least distinguished days from 2003 to 2008 and a regular sparring partner of the Governor, has more or less ruled himself out of the competition by taking up a role with

JC Flowers, the enigmatic private equity firm with a penchant for investments in the banking sector.

Whoever takes up King's mantle will face the challenge of fully assimilating the Bank's new-found responsibilities for prudential regulation, as well as regilding the Monetary Policy Committee, which will have seen sixteen years' service itself by 2013 and is looking a little worn around the edges. The changeover will also represent an opportunity to mould a more modern central bank out of the current Bank of England, which, for all its diversity and inclusion policies and gay and lesbian networks, retains its superannuated Court, a hidebound hierarchy and centralised bureaucracy.

£££

By the time Sir Mervyn King comes to the end of his second five-year term, in June 2013, he will have been at the Bank of England, in a full-time capacity, for twenty-two years. Not a bad innings, although little more than half of his predecessor Eddie George's 41-year score. While not one of its 'lifers', King will have served as the Bank's chief economist, its deputy governor and, for ten years, its Governor. He has gained the measure of this singular, enigmatic and proverbial institution, and, to a large extent, he has made it his own.

Some of King's harshest critics believe that he has 'trashed' George's paternalistic Bank of England and go so far as to question whether King should have given the eulogy at George's memorial service at St Paul's Cathedral in July 2009 (it was, as it turned out, a very fine tribute). But others applaud King for making the Bank a leaner, more single-minded operation. One thing they agree on is that, apart from its great, unchanging physical presence, the Bank is almost unrecognisable as the institution which King first encountered in 1990. He has witnessed, and engineered, more upheavals than at almost any time in the Bank's 317-year history. He was, in part, the architect of its independence in 1997 and, to a far greater degree, instrumental in its reshaping in the subsequent decade as a formidable powerhouse of monetary analysis. His timing has been remarkable, his career bookended by two of the great turning points in the Bank's recent history: independence and the dispersal of its regulatory powers in 1997 and the restoration of them in 2013.

But while there have been successes, there have also been failures on King's watch, particularly during the financial crisis of 2007–2009. He has expressed his regrets, chiefly at not having spoken out more forcefully about the build-up of leverage in the financial system, but to many this is mealy mouthed. One of the harshest critics of the system King instigated has been Willem Buiter, a founding member of the MPC and now senior economist at Citi, the investment bank:

> There was a belief, I think, [at] the Bank that inflation targeting and independence had solved the central banking problem for all time and we didn't realise – and I was very much part of that same mindset – that we were incredibly lucky, or maybe unlucky, that we had the world's gentlest economic environment ever within which to build up the illusion that inflation targeting was enough. The Bank was completely unprepared, in terms of the prisms in which it looked at the economy, to respond when the crisis happened and to develop an approach to illiquidity, when to intervene, how to go at [it] with the Treasury, who to bail out. So it was a night at the improv for about three years.[319]

Throughout those three years the Governor stuck stubbornly to his dictum of 'moral hazard', first learned in the playground at Old Town Primary School. He piloted a grievously underprepared institution through a severe financial crisis, indeed, a series of crises. Latterly, he has introduced a daring scheme of fiscal stimulus on a scale unimaginable to his contemporaries, let alone his predecessors, the mechanics of which have been handled clumsily at best. (As it is, Quantitative Easing remains an enormous, enigmatic elephant in the room awaiting the judgement of history. The fact remains that Britain's central bank, in the words of one of the most senior officials in the Treasury, 'should not really be buying all this government debt'.)

For the rest, neither King nor the Bank has ever been officially censured for their failings; and, unlike the legendary Governor Montagu Norman, King has never had to travel incognito (Norman occasionally assumed the *nom de guerre* Professor Clarence Skinner) when the Bank has been in particularly bad odour. King has brazened it out, ultimately falling back on his position as a humble public servant at a government-owned institution: his pugnacious refrain to the MPs on the Treasury Committee hearings has been, in not so many words, 'back me or sack me; if you don't like the way we do things, you are perfectly at liberty to change the rules.' This has usually shut them up. King is a good deal cleverer than his inquisitors on the Treasury Committee. The Governor's detailed expositions of the Bank's money market operations or of its Quantitative Easing programme have left them consummately outfoxed, their questions hanging in the air. Occasionally, MPs have challenged the Governor on particularly sensitive matters (George Mudie MP's recent question about the Bank's reluctance to utilise the Asset Purchase Facility to buy more corporate bonds springs to mind). But the Governor, invariably choosing his words with infinite care and offering exquisitely nuanced answers, has always managed to stay one step ahead of them.

MPs come and go, but the markets, like the poor, are always

with us. It remains a puzzle to the handful of officials among the 'authorities' and members of the MPC who have experience in the capital markers that the governor of Britain's central bank should regard those markets with such disdain. King, the purist economist to his core, leaves the impression of *de haut en bas* whenever they intrude on the Bank's policy-making. Sushil Wadhwani, the former member of the MPC, articulated some of this in a recent submission to the Treasury Committee:

> Over the last decade, many of the mistakes made by the BoE stemmed from the prevailing doctrine that financial markets were efficient. In my experience at the Bank, any attempt to question the 'efficient markets' theory was strongly resisted. It is very important that we avoid further policy mistakes arising from too much weight being placed by the Bank on some particular theory of how the world is supposed to work.[320]

Many of those theories will doubtless be reconsidered in June 2013. One thing all can agree on is that the Governor's departure will herald an entirely new era at the Bank. While some will miss what Lionel Barber, editor of the *Financial Times*, has called King's 'trademark twinkle',[321] others will be relieved to see the end of what has become something of an *ancien régime*. Among 'the authorities' – the Bank, the Treasury and the FSA – and in the Houses of Parliament, there will also be mixed feelings about King's departure. But one very senior figure in their uppermost echelons, who has worked with the King for many years, offers a carefully considered verdict on his Governorship which many may agree with: it is that Professor Sir Mervyn King is a brilliant economist, but he is not a central banker.

£££

How might King reflect on his career at the Bank of England? In 2008, on his appointment for a second term, King was asked by John McFall MP how he would wish his performance to be judged for that coming term:

> I think in two main ways. First, I would like people to recognise, as I hope will be the case, that we have got pretty close to meeting the inflation target and done all we can reasonably in the circumstances to have set interest rates to meet the target, that the regime remained credible ... secondly, I think that I have left behind a framework for the [Monetary Policy] Committee, for the Bank as a whole and particularly the younger people in the Bank coming through, to take over and that people would feel that the change was seamless and that they would not notice any difference at all when I left.[322]

As this response indicates, King, like Eddie George before him, is pragmatic enough to know that the Bank's work is a continuum. His own major contribution has certainly been to the framework of monetary, or price, stability. It has been at the heart of his career at the Bank and a guiding principle. In his October 1996 speech 'Monetary Stability: Rhyme or Reason?' he noted:

> In an era when, to paraphrase Andy Warhol, policies are famous for fifteen minutes, a central bank must not be afraid to eschew distractions and focus on the single objective of price stability.[323]

It is a concept to which King has given his unswerving attention. In that same speech he was moved to quote lines from *The Rock*, the play by T. S. Eliot (a former banker himself), to make his point about the sanctity of monetary stability:

> The endless cycle of idea and action,
> Endless invention, endless experiment,
> Brings knowledge of motion, but not of stillness;
> Knowledge of speech, but not of silence;
> ...
> Where is the wisdom we have lost in knowledge?
> Where is the knowledge we have lost in information?[324]

The relentless pursuit of price stability can also be what King has described as 'an endless marathon'.[325] As Alan Greenspan has famously said: 'You never reach the point where you shut up shop and break out the champagne. Nor should you.'[326]

What of the man himself – the bookish intellectual thrust into the role of the Governor of the Bank of England? Very occasionally, King has disclosed something of what lurks under the carapace of the spectacles and the dark business suit. In June 2004, he revealed his musical tastes to Gilbert Kaplan, the founder of *Institutional Investor* magazine and amateur conductor. King chose pieces by Beethoven, Bruckner, Verdi (*La Traviata*) and Mozart and – a nod to his impecunious Cambridge youth – Edith Piaf's 'Non, je ne regrette rien'. Kaplan asked King whether he wished he could have been a musician instead of an economist.

> In some ways, I think I do. I think I would like to have started as a violinist and then become a conductor. I think I would really have enjoyed that. I think the role of conductor combines the ability to be a free spirit, to use imagination, as well as to be an intellectual study, which is what I did for most of my life. I've only been at the Bank of England for the last thirteen years. The ability to do that, and also to lead a team, just to get a team of people playing for you. That's what I've tried to do at the Bank of England and what I think I would have much enjoyed doing as a

conductor. And of course, the great virtue of being a conductor is that you can go on forever.[327]

Like conductors, Governors of the Bank of England are expected to leave the stage quietly and without a lot of fuss. Occasionally, they are invited back – King hosted a well-timed dinner at the Bank for Lord George and Lord Kingsdown at the height of the financial crisis in September 2008 – but mostly they leave their successors in peace. For King, retirement will definitely not be spent pottering around his garden in Kent or on short breaks to the Scilly Isles. When he steps down as Governor, he will only be sixty-five years old. Having received his knighthood on schedule, he may also reasonably expect a life peerage, just as his predecessors Eddie George, Robin Leigh-Pemberton, Gordon Richardson and Leslie O'Brien did when they retired. Sitting in the House of Lords as Lord King – of Calderdale or of Wolverhampton, perhaps – he would provide a unique perspective on the UK's economic policy of the previous few decades. He may well return to academe, perhaps at one of the Ivy League universities in the United States, or be invited to take up the role of Master at St John's College, Cambridge, or that of Provost at King's College, his *alma mater*. (King is, after all, the first Kingsman to become Governor of the Bank of England and complete his degree; neither Montagu Norman nor Cameron Cobbold, both Governors in their time, actually graduated). He will doubtless want to publish, although he will probably confine his thoughts to monetary policy, taxation and econometrics, as it is a long-held principle that the Bank's Governors and deputy governors keep their vow of *omerta* and do not write autobiographies. In retirement there will also be time for gentler pursuits – his beloved Worcestershire County Cricket Club and Aston Villa Football Club and the consolations of Wisden and Bagehot.

Always something of an outsider, King nevertheless has a strong sense of his own place in the Bank's history and he has referred to the years he has witnessed at the Bank as 'a period of immense historical significance'.[328] He has also been at pains to have the Bank's story recorded, at least with its own imprimatur, and in 2004 he invited Forrest Capie, Professor of Economic History at Cass Business School, to write the official history from the 1950s to 1979. King contributed a foreword to this dense and scholarly work, in which he noted that the period had been characterised by 'policy failure', out of which 'the seeds of the modern Bank became discernible'. This 'modern Bank' is, of course, partly King's and there is perhaps a hint of self-congratulation in his choice of words:

> While the Bank struggled, with exasperated loyalty, to hold a fractured system together, there were those who fixed their gaze on a more rational and stable system, in which the objectives of monetary policy were clear, and the central bank had the authority to deliver them.[329]

While King, writing this in July 2009, was referring to the period from the late 1950s to the late 1970s, he might just as well have been writing about the previous couple of years – 2007 and 2008 – when the Bank found itself in the eye of a storm which on several occasions threatened to engulf the 'rational and stable system' he had attempted to impose since June 2003. He himself was to survive, but it was a close and brutal call.

The legislation proposed to overhaul the financial services industry and redefine the limits of its appetite for risk will not come into effect until 2013, too late for King to test it. He will have to watch the next chapter of the Bank's long history unfold from the sidelines. There will be the last Mansion House banquet in mid-June, at which the Chancellor will doubtless thank the Governor for his dedication and hard work. Then there will be a few days to attend to unfinished business at the Bank and, no doubt, an opportunity for one or two last speeches. Perhaps, in valediction, he will remind his audience once more of those elegant and carefully weighed words of Robert Rubin:

> First, the only certainty is that there is no certainty. Second, every decision is a matter of weighing probabilities, or the balance of risks, as we say. Third, despite uncertainty we have to decide and act. Fourth, decisions should be judged not only on the results but also on how they were made.[330]

Finally, on the evening of Friday 28 June, 2013, as Sir Mervyn King closes the doors of the Governor's Office for the last time, he may reflect that, as he has said before, 'institutions outlast us all'[331] and few with more resilience than the Bank of England. And then the Governor, in very many ways the last Governor of his ilk, will bid farewell to his 'Company', perhaps shake the hands of the 'pinks' in the lobby, climb into the waiting Daimler and take his last leave of the Old Lady of Threadneedle Street. She is a little older, and perhaps a little less ladylike, than when they first met in 1990, but, to borrow a line from Ian Fleming, she still has some teeth left in her head.

NOTES

1   Bank of England, *Working at the Bank: An Introduction.*
2   Bank of England, *A Guide to Your Employment* staff handbook.
3   Evidence to the Treasury Committee, 15 March 2011.
4   Mervyn King, IFS Annual Lecture, Chartered Accountants' Hall, London, 1 June 1994.
5   Mervyn King, speech at Newcastle Civic Centre, 25 January 2011, quoting Ken Dodd's 1964 song 'Happiness'.
6   Willem Buiter, uncorrected oral evidence to the Treasury Select Committee, 23 May 2011.
7   Sir John Gieve interview, *Sunday Times*, 1 March 2009.
8   Ibid.
9   Professor Bob Garratt, evidence to the Treasury Committee, Ev w115, w133, 2011.
10   Mervyn King interview, *Daily Telegraph*, 4 March 2011.
11   Mervyn King, Foreword to *The Bank of England: 1950s to 1979*, Cambridge University Press, 2010.
12   Labour Party Manifesto, 1997.
13   Kenneth Clarke, 'The Quest for the Holy Grail' in *The Chancellors' Tales*, Polity Press 2006.
14   Ibid.
15   John Major, *John Major: The Autobiography*, HarperCollins 1999.
16   Ibid.
17   *Accountancy Age*, 15 November 2007.
18   Paul Tucker, speech on central banking and the political economy, University of Cambridge, 15 June 2007.
19   Ibid. Footnote 20.
20   Quoted in address by Mervyn King, memorial service for Lord George, London, 27 July 2009.
21   Peter Hain MP, Early Day Motion, 25 January 1993.
22   Howard Davies, ed., *The Chancellors' Tales*, Polity Press 2006.
23   Paul Tucker, *Secondment to Baring Brothers* report, 30 January 1987.
24   Ibid.

25   Ibid.
26   Paul Tucker, speech on central banking and the political economy, 15 June 2007.
27   Quoted in Mervyn King interview, *Daily Telegraph*, 4 March 2011.
28   Mervyn King, 'The MPC Ten Years On', lecture to the Society of Business Economists, London, 2 May 2007.
29   Ibid.
30   Gordon Brown, statement, 6 May 1997.
31   Sir Samuel Brittan, evidence to the Economic Affairs Committee, 23 March 2004.
32   Ibid.
33   Anthony Hotson, *British Monetary Targets, 1976 to 1987: A View from the Fourth Floor of the Bank of England*, Special Paper 190, LSE Financial Markets Group Paper Series, April 2010.
34   Willem Buiter, 'Maverecon', *Financial Times*, 19 April 2009.
35   Mervyn King, 'The MPC Ten Years On'.
36   Ibid.
37   Mervyn King, interview with the *Financial Times*, 1 May 2007.
38   Ibid.
39   Peter Mandelson, *The Third Man*, HarperPress 2010.
40   Ibid.
41   Howard Davies, *The Financial Crisis*, Polity 2010.
42   Farrer & Co. George Walker, Centre for Commercial Law Studies, London.
43   Peter Viggers, evidence to the Treasury Select Committee, 1 February 2007.
44   Sir Nicholas Macpherson, ESRC seminar, All Souls College, Oxford, 9 December 2009.
45   Robert Chote, Business Standard, August 1997.
46   Ed Balls, 'Open Macroeconomics in an Open Economy', lecture to the Scottish Economic Society, Edinburgh, October 1997.
47   Sushil Wadhwani, *The Future of Finance*, LSE Report, 2010.
48   Willem Buiter, *Financial Times*, 19 April 2009.
49   Michael Fallon MP, Treasury Select Committee, 23 May 2011.
50   Mervyn King, 'The MPC Two Years On', lecture to the Queen's University, Belfast, May 1999.
51   Cited in Mervyn King, Adam Smith Lecture, Kirkcaldy, 2006.
52   Arthur H. Beavan, *Imperial London*, J. M. Dent & Co., 1901.
53   Quoted in *PR Week*, 3 May 1996, from the AGM of IRPN, April 1996.
54   Kenneth Clarke, 'The Quest for the Holy Grail' in *The Chancellors' Tales*, Polity Press 2006.
55   Hansard, 7 May 1999.
56   Ibid.
57   David Clementi, speech at the FT World Gold Conference, London, 14 June 1999.
58   European Central Bank, Bank of England and thirteen other central banks, *Joint Statement on Gold*, 26 September 1999.
59   Ibid.
60   Stephen Nickell, 'Life on the Monetary Policy Committee', *CentrePiece*, Autumn 2007.
61   Ibid.
62   Ibid.

63 Ibid.

64 Ibid.

65 Donald Kohn, 'Report to the Non-Executive Directors of the Court of the Bank of England on Monetary Policy Processes and the Work of Monetary Analysis', 18 October 2000.

66 Ibid.

67 Ibid.

68 Ibid.

69 Lord Peston, House of Lords Economic Affairs Committee, 20 April 2004.

70 Mervyn King, 'The Monetary Policy Committee: Five Years On', speech to Society of Business Economists, 22 May 2002.

71 'Bank Appointments', memo to Chancellor of the Exchequer, HM Treasury, 22 November 2002.

72 HM Treasury briefing note, November 2002.

73 Reported in the *Hebden Bridge Times*, 25 July 2006.

74 Mervyn King, interview with Gilbert Kaplan for 'Mad About Music', broadcast, 109.5 FM WQXR, June 2004.

75 Mervyn King, interview on 'A View from the Boundary', *Test Match Special*, BBC Radio 4, 16 August 2003.

76 Mervyn King, speech at the Best of the Black Country Awards, Wolverhampton, 16 November 2006.

77 Tony Judt, 'Meritocrats', *New York Review of Books*, August 2010.

78 Mervyn King, speech at the Economic and Social Research Council Seventh Annual Lecture, 17 October 1996.

79 Quoted by Angus Deaton, *Cambridge Economics Alumni Newsletter*, Autumn 2011.

80 Martin Weale, obituary of Professor Brian Reddaway, *The Independent*, 31 July 2002.

81 Ibid.

82 Angus Deaton, *Cambridge Economics Alumni Newsletter*, Autumn 2011.

83 Jean-Claude Trichet, letter to the author, 19 December 2011.

84 Mervyn King, Ely Lecture, 2004.

85 Mervyn King, interview with Gilbert Kaplan for 'Mad About Music', broadcast, 109.5 FM WQXR, June 2004.

86 Dick Taverne, *The Launch of IFS* (1970 to 1979).

87 Ibid.

88 Ibid.

89 Dick Taverne, Foreword to *The Structure and Reform of Direct Taxation: Report of a Committee Chaired by J. E. Meade*, George Allen & Unwin Ltd, 1978.

90 Mervyn King, IFS Annual Lecture, Chartered Accountants' Hall, London, 1 June 1994.

91 Anthony Hotson, *British Monetary Targets, 1976 to 1987: A View from the Fourth Floor of the Bank of England*, Special Paper 190, LSE Financial Markets Group Paper Series, April 2010.

92 Andrew Logan, 'The Early 1990s Small Banks Crisis: Leading Indicators', Financial Industry and Regulation Division, Bank of England.

93 HM Treasury/Bank of England, 'ERM Project: The UK's Membership of the ERM', 21 December 1993.

94 Ibid.
95 Ibid.
96 Ibid.
97 Ibid.
98 Mervyn King, ECB Colloquium in Honour of Otmar Issing, March 2006.
99 Quoted in *The Independent*, 2 October 1992.
100 HM Treasury/Bank of England paper, 'The Cost of Intervention', 25 August 1993.
101 Ibid.
102 Ibid.
103 Opening remarks by Mervyn King, *Inflation Report* press conference, 12 February 2003.
104 Bank of England, *A Guide to Your Employment*.
105 Mervyn King, 'Monetary Stability: Rhyme or Reason?' Economic and Social Research Council Seventh Annual Lecture, 17 October 1996.
106 David Clementi, Annual Leonard Sainer Lecture, 14 November 2000.
107 Ibid.
108 Eddie George interview, *The Observer*, 8 June 2003.
109 Ibid.
110 Gordon Brown, speech at Lord Mayor's Banquet, 18 June 2003.
111 Sir Edward George, speech at Lord Mayor's Banquet, 18 June 2003.
112 Anthony Hotson, *British Monetary Targets, 1976 to 1987: A View from the Fourth Floor of the Bank of England*, Special Paper 190, LSE Financial Markets Group Paper Series, April 2010.
113 Mervyn King, speech at the Best of the Black Country Awards, Wolverhampton, November 2006.
114 Mervyn King, *Test Match Special*, BBC Radio 4, August 2003.
115 *Sunday Times*, 16 April 2006.
116 David Cooksey, Foreword to Bank of England Annual Report 2004.
117 Ibid.
118 Ibid.
119 Mervyn King, Governor's Foreword to Bank of England Annual Report 2004.
120 David Clementi, Annual Leonard Sainer Lecture, 14 November 2000.
121 Mervyn King, evidence to the Treasury Select Committee, 28 June 2007.
122 Gordon Brown, evidence to the House of Lords' Economic Affairs Committee, 19 May 2004.
123 Mervyn King, Bank of England press conference, 13 August 2003.
124 Mervyn King, interview with the *Financial Times*, 1 May 2007.
125 Mervyn King, speech at EMDA/BoE dinner, Leicester, October 2003.
126 David Blanchflower, Bloomberg, 13 July 2010.
127 Mervyn King, letter to Gordon Brown, 4 October 2005.
128 Ibid.
129 Ian Bond, 'Managing a Bank-Specific Crisis: A UK Perspective', BBA workshop, 26 October 2006.
130 Ibid.
131 Ibid.
132 Ibid.

133 Mervyn King, speech to the Society of Business Economists, 2 May 2007.
134 Ibid.
135 Mervyn King, speech at the Eden Project, Cornwall, 12 October 2004.
136 Mervyn King, speech at the Lord Mayor's Banquet, 20 June 2007.
137 Ibid.
138 Ibid.
139 Ibid.
140 Ibid.
141 Sir David Lees, director of Court, evidence to the Treasury Select Committee, 15 March 2011.
142 Paul Tucker, evidence to the Treasury Select Committee, 20 September 2007.
143 Sir John Gieve, 'Uncertainty, Policy and Financial Markets', speech at the Barbican Centre, 24 July 2007.
144 Gilles Glicenstein, November 2008.
145 BNPP IP.
146 Mervyn King, *Inflation Report* press conference, 8 August 2007.
147 Paul Tucker, *Inflation Report* press conference, 8 August 2007.
148 Mervyn King, evidence to the Treasury Select Committee, 20 September 2007.
149 Mervyn King, interview with Robert Peston, *File on Four*, BBC Radio 4, 6 November 2007.
150 Alistair Darling, *Back from the Brink: 1,000 Days at Number 11*, Atlantic Books, 2011.
151 Ibid.
152 Mervyn King, submission to the Treasury Select Committee, 12 September 2007.
153 Conference Paper A08577770, Financial Markets Law Committee, undated.
154 Ibid.
155 *The Resolution of International Financial Crises: Private Finance and Public Funds*. Bank of England and the Bank of Canada, November 2001.
156 Adam Applegarth, uncorrected evidence to the Treasury Select Committee, 16 October 2007.
157 Matt Ridley, uncorrected evidence to the Treasury Select Committee, 16 October 2007.
158 Ibid.
159 Adam Applegarth, uncorrected evidence to the Treasury Select Committee, 16 October 2007.
160 Mervyn King, evidence to the Treasury Select Committee, 18 December 2007.
161 Ibid.
162 Alistair Darling, *Back from the Brink: 1,000 Days at Number 11*, Atlantic Books, 2011.
163 Ibid.
164 Adam Applegarth, uncorrected evidence to the Treasury Select Committee, 16 October 2007.
165 Mervyn King, letter to John McFall MP, 12 September 2007.
166 'Turmoil in Financial Markets: What Can Central Banks Do?', paper submitted to the Treasury Select Committee by Mervyn King, 12 September 2007.
167 Ibid.
168 Michael Fallon MP, uncorrected evidence to the Treasury Select Committee, 20 September 2007.

169 Mervyn King, evidence to the Treasury Select Committee, 18 December 2007.
170 Ibid.
171 Ibid.
172 Tripartite statement by HM Treasury, Bank of England and Financial Services Authority, 14 September 2007.
173 Informal Ecofin meeting, statement by ministers and governors, Oporto, 14 September 2007.
174 Alistair Darling, *Back from the Brink: 1,000 Days at Number 11*, Atlantic Books, 2011.
175 Mervyn King, interview with Robert Peston, *File on Four*, BBC Radio 4, 6 November 2007.
176 Ibid.
177 Mervyn King, uncorrected evidence to the Treasury Select Committee, 20 September 2007.
178 Alistair Darling, *Back from the Brink: 1,000 Days at Number 11*, Atlantic Books, 2011.
179 Ibid.
180 Alistair Darling, statement on Northern Rock, 17 September 2007.
181 Press release, HM Treasury, 20 September 2007.
182 Mervyn King, evidence to the Treasury Select Committee, 18 December 2007.
183 Bank of England announcement, 19 September 2007.
184 Mervyn King, evidence to the Treasury Select Committee, 18 December 2007.
185 Mervyn King, evidence to the Treasury Select Committee, 20 September 2007.
186 Ibid.
187 Uncorrected evidence to the Treasury Select Committee, 20 September 2007.
188 *The Economist*, 22 September 2007.
189 Transcript of *Inflation Report* press conference, 14 November 2007.
190 Alistair Darling, *Back from the Brink: 1,000 Days at Number 11*, Atlantic Books, 2011.
191 Evidence to the Treasury Select Committee, 18 December 2007.
192 Alistair Darling, *Back from the Brink: 1,000 Days at Number 11*, Atlantic Books, 2011.
193 Ibid.
194 Mervyn King, speech at IoD South West/CBI dinner, Bristol, 22 January 2008.
195 Ibid.
196 Ibid.
197 Martin Kellaway, *Public Sector Interventions in the Financial Crisis: Statistical Classification Decisions*, Office for National Statistics, 2009.
198 US Embassy London cable to Secretary of State, Washington, and others, 19 June 2008.
199 *Financial Times*, 22 April 2008.
200 Alistair Darling, *Back from the Brink: 1,000 Days at Number 11*, Atlantic Books, 2011.
201 Oral evidence, Treasury Select Committee, 2 July 2008.
202 The Bradford & Bingley plc Transfer of Securities and Property etc. Order 2008.
203 Bank of England announcement, 17 September 2008.

NOTES

204 'Additional Information…', Bank of England announcement, 24 November 2009.

205 Ibid.

206 Mervyn King, evidence to the Treasury Select Committee, 24 November 2009.

207 Paul Tucker, evidence to the Treasury Select Committee, 24 November 2009.

208 Reproduced here by kind permission of Freshfields Bruckhaus Deringer LLP.

209 Sir Nicholas Macpherson, evidence to the Treasury Select Committee, 5 July 2011.

210 Nikhil Rathi, uncorrected evidence to the Treasury Select Committee, 17 March 2009.

211 Mervyn King, Bank of England Annual Report, 2009.

212 *Agents' Summary of Business Conditions*, Bank of England, December 2008.

213 Mervyn King interview, *Daily Telegraph*, 4 March 2011.

214 Dave Ramsden, uncorrected evidence to the Treasury Select Committee, 28 April 2009.

215 Paul Tucker, 'Managing the Central Bank's Balance Sheet: Where Monetary Policy Meets Financial Stability', speech to mark the fifteenth anniversary of Lombard Street Research, 28 July 2004.

216 David Miles, 'Monetary Policy and Financial Dislocation', speech to the Royal Economic Society, 10 October 2011.

217 Mervyn King, uncorrected evidence to the Treasury Select Committee, 24 March 2009.

218 George Osborne, quoted in the *Daily Telegraph*, 7 January 2009.

219 Bank of England, 'The Bank's Current Operations in the Sterling Money Markets', The Red Book, December 2011.

220 Bank of England Asset Purchase Facility Fund Limited, Annual Report 2009/10.

221 Minutes of the Monetary Policy Committee, Bank of England, 4 and 5 March 2009.

222 Mervyn King, letter to Alistair Darling, 17 February 2009.

223 Ibid.

224 Minutes of the Monetary Policy Committee, Bank of England, 4 and 5 March 2009.

225 Bank of England, Market Notice, 5 March 2009.

226 Bank of England, 'The Bank's Current Operations in the Sterling Money Markets', The Red Book, December 2011.

227 Paul Fisher, 'An Unconventional Journey: The Bank of England's Asset Purchase Programme', speech at Stonehouse Court, Gloucestershire, 11 October 2010.

228 Ibid.

229 Ibid.

230 Ibid.

231 Ibid.

232 Ibid.

233 UK Debt Management Office, Gilt Market Operational Notice.

234 Bank of England, Financial Markets Law Committee, Issue 56, Emergency Powers Legislation, November 2003.

235 Joint Bank–DMO Statement on Gilt Lending, 6 August 2009.

236 Ibid.

237 Mervyn King interview, *Daily Telegraph*, 4 March 2011.

238 Letter to HM Queen from Peter Hennessy and Tim Besley, British Academy, 22 July 2009.

239 Ibid.
240 *Financial Times*, 23 April 2009.
241 Reuters report, 23 April 2009.
242 Willem Buiter, *Financial Times*, 23 April 2009.
243 Ibid.
244 Alistair Darling, *Back from the Brink: 1,000 Days at Number 11*, Atlantic Books, 2011.
245 Mervyn King, speech at the Lord Mayor's Banquet, Mansion House, 17 June 2009.
246 Ibid.
247 Alistair Darling, *Back from the Brink: 1,000 Days at Number 11*, Atlantic Books, 2011.
248 Mervyn King, evidence to the Treasury Select Committee, 24 June 2009.
249 Michael Joyce, Ana Lasaosa, Ibrahim Stevens and Matthew Tong, 'The Financial Market Impact of Quantitative Easing', Working Paper 393, July 2010.
250 Spencer Dale, 'QE: One Year On', remarks at the CIMF and MMF Conference, Cambridge, 12 March 2010.
251 Ibid.
252 Charles Bean, 'Quantitative Easing: An Interim Report', speech to the London Society of Chartered Accountants, 13 October 2009.
253 Mervyn King, speech to the Institute of Directors, Liverpool, 11 October 2011.
254 Michael Joyce, Matthew Tong and Robert Woods, 'The United Kingdom's Quantitative Easing Policy', *Bank of England Quarterly Bulletin*, 2011 Q3.
255 Ibid.
256 Ibid.
257 Ibid.
258 Ibid.
259 Ibid.
260 Ibid.
261 Mervyn King, letter to George Osborne, 6 October 2011.
262 Mervyn King, ITN interview with Laura Kuenssberg, 6 October 2011.
263 Bank of England statement, quoted by Bloomberg, 10 October 2011.
264 Bloomberg report, 10 October 2011.
265 Article 123 (ex Article 101 TEC), The Treaty on the Functioning of the European Union, 2008.
266 Charles Bean, 'Your Questions Answered on Quantitative Easing', Bank of England website.
267 Ibid.
268 Charles Bean, 'Quantitative Easing: An Interim Report', speech to the London Society of Chartered Accountants, 13 October 2009.
269 BIS Committee on the Global Financial System, *Interactions of Sovereign Debt Management with Monetary Conditions and Financial Stability*, CGFS Papers No. 42, May 2011.
270 Ibid.
271 *Debt and Reserves Management Report* 2009–10, Debt Management Office.
272 US Embassy London cable to RUEHC/SECSTATE, Washington DC, 17 February 2010.
273 Ibid.

NOTES

274 Ibid.

275 Sir James Sassoon, *The Tripartite Review*, March 2009.

276 Ibid.

277 David Laws, *22 Days in May*, Biteback Publishing, 2010.

278 *Daily Telegraph*, 4 June 2010.

279 HM Treasury Press Notice, 17 May 2010.

280 House of Commons Treasury Select Committee, 4th Report of Session 2010–11: *Office for Budget Responsibility*.

281 Winston Churchill, The Lord Mayor's Luncheon, Mansion House, 10 November 1942.

282 'A New Approach to Financial Regulation: Impact Assessment for Two Regulator Model', HM Treasury, June 2011.

283 *Daily Telegraph*, 31 May 2011.

284 Mervyn King, interview on 'A View from the Boundary', *Test Match Special*, BBC Radio 4, 16 August 2003.

285 Philip Snowden, *The Spectator*, October 1932.

286 Kate Barker, uncorrected evidence to the Treasury Select Committee, 23 May 2011.

287 *The United Kingdom's Official Reserves of Foreign Currency and Gold*, Bank of England, June 2008.

288 John Nugée, *Foreign Exchange Reserves Management*, Handbooks in Central Banking no. 19, Centre for Central Banking Studies, Bank of England.

289 Letter from the Chancellor to the Governor of the Bank of England, 6 May 1997.

290 Paul Fisher, uncorrected evidence to the Treasury Select Committee, 21 April 2009.

291 Ibid.

292 *A New Approach to Financial Regulation: The Blueprint for Reform*, HM Treasury, June 2011.

293 Treasury Committee, 7 June 2011.

294 Sushil Wadhwani, *Financial Times*, 14 June 2011.

295 *A New Approach to Financial Regulation: The Blueprint for Reform*, HM Treasury, June 2011.

296 Bank of England Annual Report 2010.

297 Letter from Ben Norman, deputy secretary of the Bank, to E. Danielyan, 5 March 2010, following Danielyan's request for information under the Freedom of Information Act 2000.

298 Bank of England, *Governance of the Bank Including Matters Reserved to Court*, November 2009.

299 Quoted in *PR Week*, 3 May 1996, from AGM of IRPN in April 1996.

300 Howard Davies, review of Forrest Capie, *The Bank of England: 1950s to 1979*, Cambridge University Press, 2010.

301 Norman Lamont, 'Out of the Ashes' in *The Chancellors' Tales*, Polity Press 2006.

302 Alistair Darling, *Back from the Brink: 1,000 Days at Number 11*, Atlantic Books, 2011.

303 Interview with Sir Nicholas Macpherson, *West Highland Free Press*, 2008.

304 Ibid.

305 Sir Nicholas Macpherson, ESRC Seminar, All Souls College, Oxford, 9 December 2009.

306 Mervyn King, letter to the Chancellor of the Exchequer, 6 October 2011.

307 Ibid.
308 Treasury Select Committee, *Accountability of the Bank of England,* 8 November 2011.
309 Ibid.
310 Professor Charles Goodhart, uncorrected oral evidence to Treasury Select Committee, 23 May 2011.
311 Alistair Darling, uncorrected evidence to the Joint Committee on the Draft Financial Services Bill, 11 October 2011.
312 Ibid.
313 Treasury Select Committee, *Accountability of the Bank of England,* 8 November 2011.
314 Ibid.
315 Ibid.
316 Ibid.
317 Reported in the *Financial Times,* 8 November 2011.
318 Mervyn King, Q&A, *Financial Stability Report,* 1 December 2011.
319 Willem Buiter, uncorrected oral evidence to Treasury Select Committee, 23 May 2011.
320 Sushil Wadhwani, written evidence to the Treasury Select Committee, 2011.
321 Lionel Barber, 'The World in 2011', *The Economist.*
322 Mervyn King, evidence to the Treasury Select Committee, 29 April 2008.
323 Mervyn King, speech at the Economic and Social Research Council Seventh Annual Lecture, 17 October 1996.
324 T. S. Eliot, *The Rock,* quoted by Mervyn King in a speech at the Economic and Social Research Council Seventh Annual Lecture, 17 October 1996.
325 Mervyn King, IFS Annual Lecture, Chartered Accountants' Hall, London, 1 June 1994.
326 Quoted by Mervyn King, IFS Annual Lecture, Chartered Accountants' Hall, London, 1 June 1994.
327 Mervyn King interview with Gilbert Kaplan for 'Mad About Music', broadcast, 109.5 FM WQXR, June 2004.
328 Mervyn King interview, *Daily Telegraph,* 4 March 2011.
329 Mervyn King, Foreword to *The Bank of England: 1950s to 1979,* Cambridge University Press, 2010.
330 Robert Rubin, quoted by Mervyn King, the Queen's University, Belfast, May 1999.
331 Mervyn King, speech at the Lord Mayor's Banquet, Mansion House, 20 June 2007.

INDEX

INDEX